Gold Tested in Fire

Gold Tested in Fire

A New Pentecost for the Catholic Priesthood

Ronald D. Witherup, SS

LITURGICAL PRESS
Collegeville, Minnesota

www.litpress.org

Imprimatur: ✠ Most Rev. Edwin F. O'Brien, DD, Archbishop of Baltimore, Baltimore, Maryland. November 15, 2011.

Cover design by David Manahan, OSB. Illustration courtesy of Thinkstock iStockphoto Collection.

1 2 3 4 5 6 7 8 9

Library of Congress Cataloging-in-Publication Data

Witherup, Ronald D., 1950–
Gold tested in fire : a new Pentecost for the Catholic priesthood / Ronald D. Witherup.
p. cm.
Includes bibliographical references (p.) and index.
ISBN 978-0-8146-3382-3
1. Priesthood—Catholic Church. 2. Catholic Church—Clergy. I. Title.

BX1912.W58 2012
262'.142—dc23

2011044684

Dedicated to my brother priests of
the Society of the Priests of St. Sulpice
1642–2012
who for 370 years have faithfully
served the ministry of
initial and ongoing formation of priests
around the world.

Ad multos annos!

Contents

Preface

A flood of publications on the priesthood accompanied the Year for Priests (June 2009–June 2010), promulgated by Pope Benedict XVI to celebrate the 150th anniversary of the death of St. Jean Vianney, the Curé of Ars, and to bolster the image of the priesthood in the twenty-first century. Thus, it may seem surprising to be offering yet another book on the same topic. Yet it is warranted for three reasons.

First, the topic of priesthood is a perennial one. Interest in the priesthood has not been in any way diminished by the controversies that have surrounded it, especially with regard to various scandals that have been in the limelight in the last decade. Indeed, one might say that interest in the priesthood has been piqued by the controversy. I believe modern Western culture is still fascinated by the priesthood. Media images of priests, not always unflattering, continue to appear, most recently with regard to the priestly role in combating evil through exorcisms. In other words, the priesthood is still a mysterious and intriguing profession.

Second, many publications that appeared for the Year for Priests went over familiar church teaching on the topic or offered timely personal and spiritual reflections on priestly ministry. Many of these are inspiring, and some are attempts to synthesize church teaching on the topic of the priesthood. I have wanted to offer my own voice to this conversation, based upon reflections on selected biblical, theological, and pastoral perspectives that I have thought to be important. My own approach comes from the experience of thirty-five years of priesthood, many of them spent in initial and ongoing formation of priests. It does not attempt to offer a "theology" of the priesthood or a comprehensive model for priestly ministry. Instead, it offers some diverse but key insights on the challenges of contemporary priestly ministry. One characteristic of these essays that will be noticeable, however, is that they are all *biblically* based. That is, they take their orientation from insights based on the Bible. Many of the chapters of this book began as presentations at priest retreat conferences or were published as essays in magazines intended specifically for priests. Previously published essays have been revised, updated, or expanded to some degree, as seemed suitable.

Finally, while this book is not intended as an *apologia* for the priesthood, it is borne of a love of the priesthood and the firm conviction that the priesthood is an essential, God-given ministry in the church. I believe the entire church benefits from wrestling with the challenges that have emerged in the priesthood since the Second Vatican Council (1962–65). As the fiftieth anniversaries of the opening and closing of the council approach, I believe we have an excellent opportunity to deepen our understanding of the council's teaching and its aftermath. In this spirit, anything that helps promote deeper reflection on the priesthood can be profitable. The struggles experienced in the priesthood in recent decades are not a sign of disintegration but a call to renewal and a return to the authentic roots of priestly ministry. My earnest desire is to reinstill confidence in the priesthood through a careful reading of some of its essential foundations and in the context of all ministry exercised in the life of the church.

My gratitude extends to many different individuals who have encouraged me in this project, particularly Peter Dwyer and Hans Christoffersen of Liturgical Press, and their excellent staff. I also thank my fellow Sulpicians, Fathers Thomas R. Hurst, SS, Thomas R. Ulshafer, SS, Lawrence B. Terrien, SS, Melvin C. Blanchette, SS, and Frederick J. Cwiekowski, SS; as well as Abbot Jerome Kodell, OSB, and Msgr. Paul Langsfield, who read parts of the manuscript or assisted me with other details. Although I alone bear responsibility for any errors in this book, their keen advice has been much appreciated. Father Hurst, president-rector of St. Mary's Seminary and University in Baltimore, deserves my special gratitude for having read the full manuscript with care and for having offered some helpful corrections. I also thank the many seminarians and priests with whom I have been privileged to work in ministry over the years. Their questions, observations, and feedback have given me encouragement and often made me seek a more profound understanding of the priesthood that is such a precious gift to the church.

As indicated by the dedication, I am particularly grateful to my brother Sulpicians around the world for their selfless service to the church and for their personal support of my own ministry as the twenty-sixth superior general of La Compagnie des Prêtres de Saint-Sulpice.

R.D.W.

Feast of the Presentation of Mary in the Temple, 2011

Acknowledgments

Photo on page 3 by Saydou - Bernard Tall 2011 © Society of Saint Sulpice. Used by permission.

Chapters 2, 3, 6, and 9, as well as the preface, introduction, and epilogue, appear here for the first time in print. I wish to thank the following for granting permission to use in this book previously published material, often in considerably revised and updated format.

Our Sunday Visitor Publishing, for an earlier version of chapter 7, "Priest and Poet," *The Priest* 52:9 (1996): 12–18.

Our Sunday Visitor Publishing and the *Bulletin de Saint-Sulpice*, for earlier versions of chapter 10, published as "The 'Intellectual' Formation of Priests," *The Priest* 49:6 (1993): 46–52; and "The Role of Scripture Studies in the Intellectual Formation of Future Priests," *Bulletin de Saint-Sulpice* 18 (1992): 240–54.

The Seminary Department of the National Catholic Educational Association, for an earlier version of chapter 5, "A Biblical Spirituality of Celibacy," *Seminary Journal* 9:2 (2003): 43–49.

Liturgical Press, for an earlier version of chapter 4, "The Biblical Foundations of the Priesthood: The Contribution of Hebrews," in *Ministerial Priesthood in the Third Millennium* (Collegeville, MN: Liturgical Press, 2009), 1–23.

St. Anthony Messenger Press, for extensive revisions of chapters 4 and 12. "What the Bible Says About Growing Old," reprinted with permission of St. Anthony Messenger Press. www.AmericanCatholic.org. © 2007. All rights reserved. "The Emerging Priesthood: Letter to the Hebrews," reprinted with permission of St. Anthony Messenger Press. www.AmericanCatholic.org. © 2010. All rights reserved.

The Pastoral Review, for an earlier version of chapter 11, "Ongoing Priestly Formation: Option or Necessity?" *The Pastoral Review* 6:2 (2010): 33–39; and for parts of chapter 1 containing excerpts from "The Year for Priests: Shepherds and

Sheep," *The Pastoral Review* 6:1 (2010): 4–10, republished with the permission of the editor.

For an earlier version of chapter 8, see "Wisdom & Ministry: The Search for Sages," *Church* 11:4 (1995): 15–18.

Abbreviations

Basic Plan	The Basic Plan for the Ongoing Formation of Priests
CCC	*Catechism of the Catholic Church*
DMLP	Directory on the Ministry and Life of Priests
NABRE	New American Bible, Revised Edition
NRSV	New Revised Standard Version of the Bible
NT	New Testament
OT	Old Testament
PDV	*Pastores Dabo Vobis*
PO	*Presbyterorum Ordinis*, Decree on the Ministry and Life of Priests
PTCM	The Priest and the Third Christian Millenium

Charles Le Brun, *Pentecost*, 1665–68. Oil on wood, 395 x 275 cm. Paris, Séminaire Saint Sulpice.

Introduction

> Accept whatever befalls you, and in times of humiliation be patient. For gold is tested in the fire, and those found acceptable, in the furnace of humiliation.
>
> —Sirach 2:4-5

> In this you rejoice, even if now for a little while you have had to suffer various trials, so that the genuineness of your faith—being more precious than gold that, though perishable, is tested by fire—may be found to result in praise and glory and honor when Jesus Christ is revealed.
>
> —1 Peter 1:6-7

The chapel of my current residence in Paris contains a large, famous painting of Pentecost, the dramatic scene in the Acts of the Apostles that describes the coming of the Holy Spirit in tongues of fire upon the apostles and their companions (Acts 2:1-4). This particular painting by Charles Le Brun (1619–90), the favorite artist of King Louis XIV, was commissioned by Father Jean-Jacques Olier (1608–57), founder of the Society of the Priests of St. Sulpice, of which I am a member. He commissioned this painting as a reminder of the guiding image for his community of diocesan priests founded specifically for priestly formation. The church was in need of a new Pentecost. He set about responding to that need through the renewal of the clergy.

A little history helps put Father Olier's vision of priestly formation in perspective. In the early seventeenth century, the priesthood was in disarray. This state of affairs had existed, in fact, for some time. The lack of training for priests, their lack of knowledge of the Bible, and their occasional immoral behavior were all factors that led Martin Luther and others to the Protestant Reformation in the sixteenth century. Until the Counter-Reformation and the call of the Council of Trent (1545–63) to establish "seminaries" (metaphorically, "seedbeds" for vocations), places where priests could be professionally trained for their ministry, the church had done very little to formally educate priests and to give them a solid spiritual, intellectual, and moral formation. As a result of the council's call for more direct priestly formation, numerous bishops founded seminaries as an attempt to provide formal training for priests and to assure the presence of faithful and morally upright servants in ordained ministry. Most famous among these bishops is St. Charles Borromeo (1538–84), who set about priestly formation in his diocese of Milan.

In France, however, it was not until the time of Father Olier that attempts at reforming and educating the clergy were able to establish a strong foothold. Along with many other members of what became known as the French school of spirituality, Olier could see that the church needed reform. But he believed such reform could best be accomplished if the clergy themselves were first reformed. Cleanse the shepherds, and the sheep will follow. Thus he invited a group of young men to join him in the parish of St. Sulpice, of which he was the pastor. He believed that the best priestly formation came from modeling priesthood. His efforts met with almost immediate success and, before long, a separate center or seminary was needed to form the young men who arrived to answer the vocational call to be priests. Over time the Sulpician model of priestly formation took hold throughout France and spread further abroad, including to Canada (1657) and the United States (1791).

In this context the reason for Father Olier's demand for a painting of Pentecost becomes clearer. Theologically, Pentecost represented a true rebirth for the community of disciples. Initially, after the crucifixion and resurrection of Jesus, the apostles and their companions had hidden in terror. Fearful that their fate would be the same as that of Jesus, they hid themselves, ignoring their call to an apostolic worldwide mission to which Jesus had summoned them. Pentecost changed all that. God sent the Holy Spirit upon the apostles, fired them up, so to speak. They regained their courage and, guided by the Holy Spirit and filled with God's grace, they went forth courageously to spread the Good News that Jesus Christ was the true Savior of the world.

Olier, who was familiar with and devoted to the Bible as the Word of God, believed the church in his day was in need of a new Pentecost. As one gazes upon Le Brun's unique rendering of the scene, two things are striking. One is that the apostles are also surrounded by other figures, many of them women. In fact, in the center of the painting is Mary, the mother of Jesus, whose presence stands out. Olier, as with many other members of "the French school," had an intense Marian devotion, which has historically been a feature of Sulpician spirituality. Subtly Le Brun's picture communicates a basic truth that the inspiration of the Holy Spirit does not just come to the apostles but is a gift to the entire church. Even more important is the understanding that Mary herself, especially in her portrayal in Luke-Acts, is preeminently a model disciple of Jesus, her own Son. She is the one who embodies discipleship because she both "hears" and "accomplishes" the Word of God (Luke 8:21; also 1:38). And Acts places her in the midst of the disciples on the day of Pentecost (Acts 1:14).

A second striking feature is the literal but discrete depiction of the tongues of fire settling on those assembled in the Upper Room. Symbolic of inspiration, being filled with fervor and renewed with strength, the fire represents a new birth, an empowerment, a bestowing of grace-filled courage to embark on the worldwide mission to which Jesus called the apostles. Pentecost is thus always a new birth, a new start.

Yet this portrait at Pentecost hides an even more subtle truth known by the ancients—the strengthening power of fire.[1] The two biblical citations (one OT, one NT) at the head of this introduction express this insight. Fire was known to purify and strengthen metals. Fire is able to temper metals in such a way that they can endure enormous amounts of stress and fulfill their purpose better. Metals are made more durable through fire. Fire thus became a prominent image for strengthening the faith through severe testing. For the early Christians, persecution, suffering, rejection, ridicule—all these were like being molded by fire. Their faith led them to an acknowledgment that fire does not always destroy. Sometimes it makes one stronger.

Although one cannot naively compare the priesthood in the seventeenth century to that of the twenty-first in all its details, I believe there is a similarity that cannot be ignored. As in the seventeenth century, we currently live in a time when the priesthood has suffered a serious image problem. Although the causes and circumstances are not the same, the priesthood has undergone an incredible testing in both eras.

When it comes to the priesthood in the second decade of the twenty-first century, the most obvious challenge has come from the sexual abuse scandal and other serious moral lapses among the clergy. The priesthood has been sorely tested in ways unimagined in the immediate wake of Vatican II. The scandal that emerged in 2002, and that has continued on various continents, has put the priesthood under intense scrutiny. There is no need to deny this reality or try to hide it. Some priests have failed miserably in their duties as shepherds, faithful servants of God and God's people. In fact, Pope Benedict XVI has purposefully drawn attention to it in numerous talks he has given during his pontificate. One recent intervention was rather lengthy and explicit, and it deserves citation here.

In his customary Christmas greeting to the members of the Roman Curia on December 20, 2010, the pope referred to a vision of one of his favorite mystics, St. Hildegard of Bingen (1098–1179).[2] In a mystical vision recounted in AD 1170, Hildegard described the image of a beautiful woman, ornately dressed, who appeared to her. The woman's attire, however, was torn and stained. Hildegard explains that the words of the woman came to her thus:

> "I lay hidden in the heart of the Father until the Son of Man, who was conceived and born in virginity, poured out his blood. With that same blood as his dowry, he made me his betrothed. For my Bridegroom's wounds remain fresh and open as long as the wounds of men's sins continue to gape. And Christ's wounds remain open because of the sins of priests. They tear my robe, since they are violators of the Law, the Gospel and their own priesthood; they darken my cloak by neglecting, in every way, the precepts which they are meant to uphold; my shoes too are blackened, since priests do not keep to the straight paths of justice, which are hard and rugged, or set good examples to those beneath them. Nevertheless, in some of them I find the splendour of truth."

A voice from heaven then explains to Hildegard the meaning of the image of the woman:

> "This image represents the Church. For this reason, O you who see all this and who listen to the word of lament, proclaim it to the priests who are destined to offer guidance and instruction to God's people and to whom, as to the apostles, it was said: go into all the world and preach the Gospel to the whole creation" (Mk 16:15).

This is undoubtedly a powerful vision. The image of priests is both disparaged and praised. The pope insightfully saw in this mystical vision a parallel with our own day. He expressed it in these words:

> In the vision of Saint Hildegard, the face of the Church is stained with dust, and this is how we have seen it. Her garment is torn—by the sins of priests. The way she saw and expressed it is the way we have experi-

> enced it this year. We must accept this humiliation as an exhortation to truth and a call to renewal. Only the truth saves. We must ask ourselves what we can do to repair as much as possible the injustice that has occurred. We must ask ourselves what was wrong in our proclamation, in our whole way of living the Christian life, to allow such a thing to happen. We must discover a new resoluteness in faith and in doing good. We must be capable of doing penance. We must be determined to make every possible effort in priestly formation to prevent anything of the kind from happening again.

I find both the vision of Hildegard and the words of the Holy Father encouraging. They explicitly and humbly admit the harm done by the sins of some priests, but they do not wallow in hopelessness. At numerous times in its history, the church has been seriously tarnished by the horrendous actions of some of its leaders. Yet all is not lost, though the church must do absolutely everything to ensure that such evil is excised from the priesthood. In particular, any abuse of the flock, especially the "little ones" entrusted to our care, can never be tolerated. We must ensure that it never happens again.[3]

The image of the priesthood in our day is stained as much as, if not worse than, ever before. It is in need of serious repair. Some priests and some bishops have done irreparable harm to victims of abuse. Furthermore, there have been various revelations of financial impropriety and dereliction of duty among some clerics. But this need not be seen as the death knell of an antiquated institution. On the contrary, as Pope Benedict clearly indicates, it is a clarion call to renewal. It is also a summons to complete purification. It is a time of intense testing. We are being tested in fire. We are also being called to be remade, precisely so that we can become better shepherds of the sheep entrusted to our care. It is an opportunity for the priesthood to be cleansed, to be remade and to become stronger. For people of faith, the sentiment of Ben Sirach and First Peter is as sound as it ever was in their day. Like gold tested in fire, the priesthood can emerge stronger, more faithful, and wholly renewed because of this challenging period of severe testing.

As a Sulpician and a diocesan priest, my faith in the priesthood has not been shattered by the events of the last twenty years and beyond. Interestingly enough, neither has the attraction to the priesthood dimmed inordinately (at least in the United States) in the wake of the recent scandals. Although I too have been angered, embarrassed, and shocked at the widespread kinds of criminal and immoral behavior of a small percentage of priests[4] (and even some bishops), I also know how frail and human we priests really are. The fact is that we suffer from virtually every kind of human aberration possible. This does not excuse the behaviors or mitigate their consequences. Even less does it excuse the cover-ups by church authorities that are more scandalous and disheartening. But all of this points to the need for renewal and the grace of conversion in the lives of priests and seminarians.

And so we return to Pentecost. We need to open ourselves up again to the Holy Spirit and the fire of renewal. Pentecost is not a one-time-only event, just as conversion cannot be limited to a once-and-forever happening.[5] My hope is that these essays can contribute to the renewal of the priesthood in our day to support the ongoing process of proving the strength of the priesthood by the "firing" process. We pray for the gift of the Holy Spirit once more to come upon all priests (and seminarians) to strengthen and guide us once more on paths that are straight and true. Being tested by fire is not easy. We will indeed be sorely tested and perhaps even humiliated. But the results can lead to a rebirth. Just as happened at the first Pentecost or at the time of the Protestant Reformation, the trials led to renewal and transformation, so now I believe we can anticipate a renewal as effective and refreshing as has ever occurred in the church's history.

Chapter One

The Priest as Shepherd

Many priests and most laypeople have probably never read the late Pope John Paul II's 1992 apostolic exhortation on priestly formation or *Pastores Dabo Vobis* (*PDV*), which grew out of the 1990 bishops' synod on the same topic.[1] The reasons are doubtless rather simple. First, most think it is only about priestly formation and therefore is exclusively directed to those who work in the highly rarified atmosphere of priestly formation. Second, it is rather long and does contain some ecclesiastical jargon, which tends to be daunting for laity and busy priests alike. Yet it would be a real mistake to overlook this document, for its influence has been widespread since it was promulgated. Moreover, I suggest its impact goes far beyond initial priestly formation (the seminary context). Rather, *PDV* puts real flesh on the theological bones of the priesthood that emerged in the wake of the Second Vatican Council (1962–65).

Given its seminal character and the fact that I often refer to this document throughout this book, this chapter will present several aspects of *PDV* that continue to shape the priesthood. Most especially through its pastoral orientation and its insistence that there are four main pillars for priestly formation (human, spiritual, intellectual, and pastoral), and consequently for priestly life, *PDV* offers a good starting point for contemporary reflections on the priesthood.

Three Key Elements of *Pastores Dabo Vobis*

Scriptural Basis

The first observation about this remarkable document, which is the most important teaching on priestly formation since Vatican Council II, is that it is rooted in Scripture. The title itself comes from the Latin version of a passage in Jeremiah, "I will give you shepherds after my own heart" (Jer 3:15). This promise of God to provide shepherds to care for the people is enhanced in *PDV* by two prominent NT passages. One is from John's gospel, in which Jesus speaks of himself as "the Good Shepherd" (John 10:11), and the other is the Letter to the Hebrews' mention of Jesus Christ as "the great shepherd of the sheep" (Heb 13:20). These passages, along with related complementary ones, give the pastoral exhortation its scriptural foundation in the desire of God to provide pastoral caretakers for the "flock." Priests are called to be true shepherds to their people, and *PDV* attempts to provide guidance at every level of formation, both initial and ongoing, to achieve this goal.

Pastoral Orientation

This scriptural orientation is, of course, consistent with Vatican II's own teaching about the priesthood, most notably in *Presbyterorum Ordinis* (*PO*), the Decree on the Ministry and Life of Priests (1965). Although *PDV* quotes from this document frequently, one notes a more pastoral orientation in *PDV* than in the council's decree. This is a second key element.

The pastoral style and goal of *PDV* is quite evident and implies that the goal of all ministry in the church is ultimately pastoral in nature. Ordained ministry does not exist for its own sake but for service to God's people. In fact, *PDV* explicitly uses *PO* in pointing out the close bond between a priest's own spiritual life and the ministry that he gives to his people.

> Therefore, an intimate bond exists between the priest's spiritual life and the exercise of his ministry, a bond which the Council expresses in this fashion: "And so it is that they are grounded in the life of the Spirit while they exercise the ministry of the Spirit. . . . For by their everyday sacred actions, as by the entire ministry which they exercise in union with the bishop and their fellow priests, they are being directed toward perfection of life." (*PDV*, 24)[2]

This profound bond between a priest's spiritual life and the service of his people is one of the most comforting assurances to come from the church's understanding of the priesthood. It points to a paradox in ministry. Though we are ordained to serve others and are thus called to personal holiness to do so, we paradoxically find our own spiritual lives enriched by those whom we serve. Our people often bring out the best in us. They can also challenge us to deepen our spirituality, even as they seek to receive from us the very best ministerial services we have to offer.

I might note here that this is one aspect of ministry that distinguishes diocesan priestly spirituality from that of religious priests. Diocesan priests are ordained specifically for parochial ministry in the midst of a presbyterate and in cooperation with, and under the authority of, a diocesan bishop. Whereas religious priests derive their spiritual identity from the religious community to which they belong, diocesan priests are by definition bound to a diocese, a geographic region erected for the service of the local people of God.[3] Religious priests who serve in parishes, of course, also share in this priestly ministry and identity. But I believe their spirituality is rooted in the community to which they are bound by solemn vows, whereas diocesan priests are intimately bound to the communities of laity they serve. The closeness to our people is an aid to our own spiritual identity as shepherds.

Shift in Language

A third key element of *PDV* is the subtle shift in language that has taken place to describe the threefold ministry of priests. For ages the church has traditionally used the language of the threefold ministry of Christ the High Priest (who is the only priest of the new dispensation mentioned in the NT): priest, prophet, and king. These images come from the structure of leadership in the OT. God used such individuals to shepherd the people, each of whom contributed to the life of Israel, whether through cult (priest), the Word of God (prophet), or governance (king).

The church quickly adopted this three-tiered perspective for its ordained ministries. Bishops embody the fullness of the priesthood, but ordained priests[4] share in their ministry of shepherding the people. We still speak of priests being configured, by ordination and the laying on of hands and gift of the Holy Spirit, to Christ—priest, prophet, and king. This configuration gives us a share in the threefold ministry of Christ the shepherd and king of his people: sacrifice, proclamation of the Word, and ruling. These constitute the threefold "powers" (Latin, *munera*) of the priesthood.

PDV also makes use of this traditional model. Various observations about these three foundational aspects of priestly ministry are scattered throughout the document. But there is also an important shift in emphasis, evident from the language used. Referring to the threefold configuration, *PDV* speaks rather of the ministry of priests as Word, sacrament, and pastoral charity (26). Both the order and the wording are important, so we need to look at these three priestly "powers" more closely.

Ministry of Word

In line with Vatican II's reemphasis on the ministry of Word and sacrament in the lives of priests, *PDV* gives precedence to the Word of God. *PDV* states explicitly:

> The priest is first of all a minister of the word of God. He is consecrated and sent forth to proclaim the good news of the kingdom to all. (26)

This primacy of the Word of God leads us in two directions at the same time. Being ministers of the Word does not mean we priests merely give a message to others. We must also receive it ourselves. In the same section *PDV* reminds priests that we are not the "master" of the Word but its "servant":

> [The priest] is not the sole possessor of the word; in its regard he is in debt to the People of God. Precisely because he can and does evangelize, the priest—like every other member of the Church—ought to grow in awareness that he himself is continually in need of being evangelized. He proclaims the word in his capacity as "minister," as a sharer in the prophetic authority of Christ and the Church. As a result, in order that he himself may possess and give to the faithful the guarantee that he is transmitting the Gospel in its fullness, the priest is called to develop a special sensitivity, love and docility to the living tradition of the Church and to her magisterium. These are not foreign to the word, but serve its proper interpretation and preserve its authentic meaning. (26)

This dual dimension of the ministry of the Word, both outwardly and inwardly directed, is a novel emphasis that places a higher expectation on the ability of priests to effectively communicate God's Word today. It is also a reminder that we do not proclaim our own word when we are ministers of *the* Word. We remain servants of the church. In practical terms, it raises the anticipation about our ability to comprehend, to incarnate, and to preach and teach the Scriptures effectively.

Ministry of Sacrament

The priest as minister of Word and sacrament is a familiar designation from Vatican II (e.g., *PO*, 2), which helped the church restore a balance in ministry that had been distorted from the time of the Reformation. Without wishing to oversimplify the matter, one can say that the Reformation essentially led Protestants to emphasize the Word of God over the sacraments, and Catholics, in turn, did the opposite. Vatican II clearly brought the two, Word and sacrament, back together. In fact, in the reform of the liturgical rites of the church, Vatican II emphasized that the sacraments should never be celebrated apart from the Word of God. Word and sacrament are intimately bound together, and exercised together in the ministry of priests.

For its part, *PDV* calls priests to celebrate the sacraments, especially the Eucharist, because of its preeminence, with full dignity and heartfelt effort. The document also calls special attention to the sacrament of reconciliation, which is as important for ourselves as for our people (26). In summarizing the ministry of sacrament, *PDV* says the following:

> It is above all in the celebration of the sacraments and in the celebration of the Liturgy of the Hours that the priest is called to live and witness to the deep unity between the exercise of his ministry and his spiritual life. The gift of grace offered to the Church becomes the principle of holiness and a call to sanctification. For the priest as well, the truly central place, both in his ministry and spiritual life, belongs to the Eucharist, since in it is contained "the whole spiritual good of the Church, namely Christ himself our pasch and the living bread which gives life to men through his flesh—that flesh which is given life and gives life through the Holy Spirit. Thus people are invited and led to offer themselves, their works and all creation with Christ." (26)[5]

In short, the cultic ministry, traditionally identified with the "priestly" function of Christ, leads us to exercise our role as mediators between God and humanity in a most incarnational way. By means of the sacraments, we bring God closer to the people and vice versa.

Ministry of Pastoral Charity

The third pastoral role priests play is perhaps the most dramatically reoriented in *PDV*. Although the traditional Latin expression is invoked (*munus regendi*, "power of governance"; *PDV*, 26), it is described as "pastoral charity." The document calls it "a very delicate and complex duty" that should be exercised by priests in the manner of true elders (presbyters, from the Greek *presbyteroi*) in the community.[6] This is striking precisely because it does not evoke the image of the king, the ruler, the legislator, or the law-enforcer. Indeed, the text goes on to list essential pastoral qualities for priests with these words:

> This ministry demands of the priest an intense spiritual life, filled with those qualities and virtues which are typical of a person who "presides over" and "leads" a community, of an "elder" in the noblest and richest sense of the word: qualities and virtues such as faithfulness, integrity, consistency, wisdom, a welcoming spirit, friendliness, goodness of heart, decisive firmness in essentials, freedom from overly subjective viewpoints, personal disinterestedness, patience, an enthusiasm for daily tasks, confidence in the value of the hidden workings of grace as manifested in the simple and the poor (cf. Ti. 1:7-8). (*PDV*, 26)

To say the least, the list is daunting. Who of us really embodies all of these qualities? Nonetheless, in providing an ideal to strive after, *PDV* has given a rich interpretation to the traditional "ruling" ministry of priests in service to the people of God. The priority is exercising pastoral charity and not "lording" over people, which is exactly what Jesus asked his disciples to avoid (Matt 20:25-26; Mark 10:42-44; Luke 22:25-26).

Finally, *PDV* notes the complexity of this third *munus*:

> This *munus regendi* represents a very delicate and complex duty which, in addition to the attention which must be given to a variety of persons and their vocations, also involves the ability to coordinate all the gifts and charisms which the Spirit inspires in the community, to discern them and to put them to good use for the upbuilding of the Church in constant union with the bishops. (26)

This third power, then, is truly an exercise in pastoral charity in the sense of trying to bring all the people of God together for the good of the community.

The Four Pillars of Formation

Having examined three key elements of *PDV*, along with the three *munera*, we now turn to its most prominent teaching, namely, the four pillars of priestly formation: human, spiritual, intellectual, and pastoral. It has become so commonplace to speak of these four pillars that we may not be conscious of just how novel this structure is, for two reasons.[7] First, to the best of my knowledge, this is the first time in an official church document that human formation has been formally acknowledged as foundational. We shall comment on this in a moment. Second, acknowledging that there are four pillars of formation, covering four essential aspects of contemporary priestly ministry, means that they cannot be reduced to one. All four are important to achieve balance, unity, and perspective in priestly formation.

Human Formation: The Basis of All Priestly Formation

Previous church documents speak frequently of spiritual formation of priests. That was clearly also on the mind of Pope Benedict XVI when he proposed an *annus sacerdotalis*, a "Year for Priests." He wanted to bolster the priesthood and lend support to priests while also calling us to a deeply spiritual renewal.

In light of this, what are we to make of *PDV*'s bold statement that human formation is "the basis of all priestly formation" (43)? If we pause to reflect carefully, we find a profound wisdom in this document's perspective. It is deeply incarnational. It takes seriously God's work through human instruments. Without the proper human qualities *PDV* calls for—integrity, affective maturity, knowledge of the human soul, capacity to relate to others—priests can become mere automatons, mechanically performing rites for people but not really communicating the love of Christ in any meaningful way. More important, without good human formation the other three pillars cannot root themselves adequately or bear proper fruit.

In my years as a formator in seminaries, I found concrete evidence of this assertion among seminarians whom I taught and for whom I was either a formation advisor or spiritual director. If a seminarian has many or deep human deficits, such as an insecure identity or a lack of psychosexual maturity, he cannot take full advantage of spiritual growth, intellectual stimulation, or pastoral training. Virtually all one's energy goes into trying to address the basic human issues that sometimes are overwhelming. Unfortunately, such deficiencies, if left unaddressed, will manifest themselves in later ministry. In light of the sexual abuse scandal, we now can also see the wisdom of serious scrutiny in the admissions process for seminarians. The proper use of psychological testing, personal interviews, and teams of admissions personnel help to foster the proper discernment of a candidate's readiness for priestly formation.[8] All this is an aspect of the first pillar, human formation, but it is also a demand for the mature integration of all aspects of human growth, which begin with basic human qualities. This is precisely why the 1990 synod fathers insisted, "The whole work of priestly formation would be deprived of its necessary foundation if it lacked a suitable human formation" (*PDV*, 43).

The first pillar of human formation, then, provides a solid foundation, but it is not the only one. Three others remain to ensure a well-rounded priestly formation and identity. The remaining three pillars of priestly formation—spiritual, intellectual, and pastoral—are treated in *PDV* in ways that are fairly consistent with many prior church documents on priestly formation. Yet we can take a brief look at each of these pillars to see how they are intended to form a unified approach to priestly ministry and life.

Spiritual Formation

Without a healthy personal spiritual life and an intense life of prayer, priests obviously lose their way. One of the common denominators in the lives of priests who have wandered from their promises of celibacy, obedience, and simplicity of life is the lack of a deep life of prayer. Fostering a personal relationship with Christ is absolutely essential. *PDV* calls it "living intimately united" with Jesus Christ (46), and speaks of developing "a deep intimacy with God" (47). Using an image from John's gospel, *PDV* explains this intimacy in these words:

> Our union with the Lord Jesus, which has its roots in baptism and is nourished with the Eucharist, has to express itself and be radically renewed each day. Intimate communion with the Blessed Trinity, that is, the new life of grace which makes us children of God, constitutes the "novelty" of the believer, a novelty which involves both his being and his acting. It constitutes the "mystery" of Christian existence which is under the influence of the Spirit: it should, as a result, constitute the ethos of Christian living. Jesus has taught us this marvelous reality of Christian living, which is also the heart of spiritual life, with his allegory of the vine and the branches: "I am the true vine, and my Father is the vinedresser. . . . Abide in me, and I in you. As the branch cannot bear fruit by itself, unless it abides in the vine, neither can you, unless you abide in me. I am the vine, you are the branches. He who abides in me, and I in him, he it is that bears much fruit, for apart from me you can do nothing" (Jn. 15:1, 4-5). (46)

Without this profound spiritual relationship with Christ, which finds its concrete expression in periodic silence, *lectio divina*, daily Eucharist, the Liturgy of the Hours, days of recollection, meditation and contemplation, and a variety of spiritual exercises, priests can quickly become burnt out. At the same time, *PDV* notes that this intense personal spiritual life rightly leads us into the pastoral arena:

> Spiritual formation also involves seeking Christ in people. The spiritual life is, indeed, an interior life, a life of intimacy with God, a life of prayer and contemplation. But this very meeting with God and with his fatherly love for everyone brings us face to face with the need to meet our neighbor, to give ourselves to others, to serve in a humble and disinterested fashion, following the example which Jesus has proposed to everyone as a program of life when he washed the feet of the apostles: "I have given you an example, that you also should do as I have done to you" (Jn. 13:15). (49)

Intellectual Formation

PDV also notes the important role of intellectual formation. Faith is not merely a matter of prayerful, mystical, or cultic experience. Faith also demands the exercise of our minds to comprehend the mystery of God. The ancient dictum of *fides quaerens intellectum* ("faith seeking knowledge") applies especially to us priests. Essentially, *PDV* calls priests to become "pastoral theologians." We cannot nourish our people with pious platitudes, especially in our time when so many laity are well read and educated. They also seek guidance to serious theological, ethical, and pastoral questions that require some intellectual rigor. *PDV* describes this type of priestly theologian:

> The theologian is therefore, first and foremost, a believer, a person of faith. But the theologian is a believer who asks himself questions about his own faith (*fides quaerens intellectum*), with the aim of reaching a deeper understanding of the faith itself. (58)

The text goes on to warn of the danger of ignoring the importance of intellectual formation, something that at times is a temptation for seminarians and priests alike.

> It is necessary to oppose firmly the tendency to play down the seriousness of studies and the commitment to them. This tendency is showing

> itself in certain spheres of the Church, also as a consequence of the insufficient and defective basic education of students beginning the philosophical and theological curriculum. The very situation of the Church today demands increasingly that teachers be truly able to face the complexity of the times and that they be in a position to face competently, with clarity and deep reasoning, the questions about meaning which are put by the people of today, questions which can only receive full and definitive reply in the gospel of Jesus Christ. (56)

This is essentially a call to academic rigor in relation to a spiritual depth essential to live the celibate life of a priest.[9] The blend of the man of prayer, a believer, as well as one who struggles to understand the truths of the faith in all their complexity, in order to communicate them faithfully, is exactly the kind of priest needed today, especially in the context of the pluralism that characterizes modern society. It is easy to think that, from the viewpoint of overwhelming pastoral needs, priests don't have time to attend to ongoing intellectual formation, but not addressing this urgent need impoverishes priestly ministry and ultimately leads to an empty arsenal of pastoral insight to sustain ministry.

Pastoral Formation

The fourth and final pillar is, in a sense, where all four get integrated, namely, pastoral formation. This is one area that seminary teachers generally find easy to promote among seminarians. Indeed, one of the more successful elements of priestly formation since Vatican II has been the introduction in many seminary programs of the "pastoral year," a year of formation taken in a pastoral assignment apart from the seminary and under the supervision of trained guides and local mentors. This is one way in which seminarians can experience firsthand pastoral ministry. This year can also help a diocese and a seminary faculty determine the readiness and capacity for priestly ministry of an individual candidate. Seminarians usually revel in their pastoral placements, enjoying the concrete experience of ministry; and they are rewarded often with the support of people who affirm them and encourage their vocation. This is the arena where the future priests' human identity, experience in prayer and liturgy, intellectual acumen in philosophy and theology and the Word of God, and pastoral skills should all intertwine. I dare say also that this is the most fulfilling arena for priests personally. After all, the primary reason most of us accept this special vocational call is to serve God by serving God's people.

PDV, however, also emphasizes an interesting aspect of pastoral formation that should not be passed over lightly. In pastoral ministry seminarians learn to become "men of communion." Priests are by nature men of communion, men of the church. The message we proclaim is not our own, and the ministry in which we engage is shared with others. It is a free gift of God, not something we alone choose. We join a presbyterate, a group of priests working together in ministry and united with our bishop, and we exercise a collegial ministry with other ministers in the church, especially with deacons and lay ministers. All are part of the priestly people of God, and our priestly ministry is a sharing in this identity. Priesthood is not a license for personal employment. It is a vocation, a call issued by God, discerned by the church, and exercised for the good of God's people.

The task of integrating all four pillars of priestly formation is not easy. *PDV* offers no magical formula for integration and success. We priests know well our shortcomings and our failures. Experientially, many dioceses and seminaries have found that mentoring is one way to promote an effective and healthy integration of all the elements of priestly formation.[10] Pairing experienced pastors with newly ordained (regardless of their ages) can be an effective means of promoting integration while simultaneously fostering group identity. This is one way in which the ministry of presbyters, true "elders" in the community, can pass on their wisdom to succeeding generations.

Ongoing Applicability of *Pastores Dabo Vobis*

This analysis is not intended to be comprehensive but to provide an orientation or general overview of some key aspects of priestly ministry today that will be treated in this book. *PDV*'s relevance not only to priestly formation but also to priestly ministry and life should not be underestimated. *PDV* is a novel and important document. It is not merely a guide for priestly formation. It is virtually a treatise on the mystery of priestly identity. As such, I regularly recommend it to priests as a text to read during their retreats.

As Pope Benedict himself has acknowledged, the priesthood has gone through some rough times of late. Some of our brother priests (and bishops) have let the church down. They have seriously strayed from their priestly promises. As in the time of Jeremiah, some, who were supposed to be shepherds taking care of the flock, have been fleecing them instead. I once heard a layperson comment on a priest who had sexually abused: "This was no wolf in sheep's clothing; this was a wolf disguised as a shepherd!" No judgment could be more devastating or more revealing of the need for a true renewal in the priesthood to reestablish priests as faithful shepherds, modeled after the Good Shepherd himself.

Most priests and bishops have, thank God, been faithful to their calling. The Year for Priests in 2009–2010 was a great opportunity to rejoice in this fidelity. It also offered us priests a chance to deepen our reflection on the priesthood. And it gave the people of God a chance to honor those priests who have been faithful to their ordination promises and who have so faithfully served over the years in pastoral ministry. But that year was only a beginning. There remains much more to be done. Ultimately, the priesthood is a *lived* ministry, day in and day out on the "front lines" of the church's pastoral vocation to serve others as Christ has served all. We are called to follow Jesus Christ, the Good Shepherd, and to mold our lives according to his life. Shepherding God's people is both a privilege and an enormous responsibility. In *PDV* we have a sophisticated analysis of the challenges in priestly formation and ministry today that tries to flesh out the multiple dimensions of this call. In short, I suggest that this profound document invites us to incarnate in an ever-deepening way the identity of the one and only true priest, the great shepherd of the sheep, Jesus Christ.

Chapter Two

Priestly Ministry in Light of the Letters of St. Paul

Saint Paul's influence looms large in so many theological and spiritual areas, but it could seem somewhat unusual to apply the vocabulary of "priesthood" to Paul and his colleagues.[1] It is well known that the only NT writing to speak of "priesthood" in a Christian perspective is the Letter to the Hebrews.[2] This document alone speaks of Jesus Christ the High Priest according to the order of Melchizedek. Nowhere else in the NT is the vocabulary of priesthood applied to the ministerial priesthood as we have come to know it. Although some interpreters in the early church grouped this intriguing letter with those that more obviously bore the apostle's name, some church fathers noted that Paul was almost certainly not the author of Hebrews. Origen's famous dictum is often quoted: "Who wrote the epistle, God truly knows."[3] It is now taken for granted among scholars that Hebrews is not part of the Pauline corpus.

How, then, are we to look to Paul's letters to speak about the ministerial priesthood? Quite simply, we do so by analogy. Just as the early church soon began to apply sacerdotal language linked to Jesus Christ to priestly ministry in the Christian tradition, so the church began to interpret most of the Bible from the perspective of insights rooted in practices recounted in the NT.

Thus one can legitimately, from a theological perspective, speak about the roots of priestly ministry found in the letters of Paul.[4] In fact, I think that there are many aspects of Paul's ministry to his communities that can properly be described as "priestly," even though he was not, formally speaking, ever "ordained" a priest, although some would see the "being set apart" and the "laying on of hands" in Acts 13:3 as evidence of his ordination.[5] In addition, in one passage Paul calls himself "a minister of Christ Jesus" and mentions his "priestly service of the gospel of God" (Rom 15:16), which are probable allusions to a priestly kind of identity. Yet were Paul with us today, he would be wondering what on earth we are talking about, if we were to query him about his *priestly* ministry in the sense we mean it.[6] We cannot even be certain that Paul was familiar with the notion of Jesus as the High Priest according to the order of Melchizedek, since nowhere is this theme evident in any of the thirteen letters that bear Paul's name.[7]

I propose to proceed in four stages.[8] First, we will speak about the foundations of Paul's "priestly" ministry as they can be known from biblical studies. Second, we will focus on two key aspects of that ministry in the Pauline churches, namely, Word and sacrament. Third, we will examine five aspects of Paul's pastoral ministry as exercised in his churches. Finally, we will point out some implications for contemporary priestly ministry. I will conclude with a few general comments.

The Foundations of Paul's "Priestly" Ministry

To begin, I wish to examine some practical issues that bear on Paul's identity as a "priest," despite the absence of any such language in his letters. In what way can Paul be said to have a priestly identity?

The starting point for our reflections on the topic, it seems to me, has to be Paul's mysterious call to be an apostle. We all know that Paul was not one of the twelve apostles. He acknowledges that he did not know Jesus of Nazareth but was called by the risen Lord (Gal 1:1, 12; 1 Cor 15:5-10). Thus his call was experienced after Jesus' death and resurrection (Acts 9:4-6; Gal 1:12). Moreover, this call so changed Paul's life that he maintained thereafter an intense relationship with Christ that he expresses in intimate terms; Christ now lives in him:

> For through the law I died to the law, so that I might live to God. I have been crucified with Christ; and it is no longer I who live, but it is Christ who lives in me. And the life I now live in the flesh I live by faith in the Son of God, who loved me and gave himself for me. (Gal 2:19-20)

There are two types of accounts in the NT about Paul's call, the narrative versions in Acts and Paul's own references to the event. The Acts of the Apostles describes the extensive narrative version of this dramatic "call" that is so familiar and that has virtually become the archetypal "conversion" story.[9] Scholars today recognize that a more appropriate label for this event is "commission" or "call," precisely because this "conversion" is not a change of religion. Paul remained a Jew, albeit one who believed that Jesus was the Messiah.

Yet we cannot deny that this event was a dramatic turnabout in Paul's life. I believe, nonetheless, that "call" is a more accurate word to describe what Paul himself characterizes as something quite revelatory from the risen Lord. He never avers to the details of this thrice-told story found in Acts and immortalized in numerous artistic representations. Rather, in Galatians he uses language characteristic of a prophetic call, along the lines of the great classical prophets like Jeremiah or Isaiah (Gal 1:12-16; cf. Jer 1:4; Isa 49:1).[10] I believe we can appropriate the word "vocation" for this event, for it bestowed upon Paul a new identity as an apostle, one sent by the risen Lord for a specific ministry or mission.

The essentials of this vocation are consistent in Paul's letters and in Acts. Paul, a persecutor of the church, receives a mysterious invitation from the risen Lord and is told he will be the "apostle to the Gentiles" (Acts 22:21; Rom 11:13; Gal 2:8). He is to be an instrument of evangelization, and he is also warned that he will suffer "for the name" of Jesus (Acts 9:15). His call is accompanied by the laying on of hands (to heal him from his blindness) and baptism, after which he immediately begins a mission of preaching the gospel of Jesus Christ (Acts 9:17, 18, 20). When Paul, writing to the Galatians, describes his vocational call in more mystical terms ("through a revelation of Jesus Christ" [Gal 1:12]), it is in the context of defending his proclamation of the gospel message, which he considers unique and essential to his apostolic call.

Lest we think that Paul's vocation is simply a charismatic event outside any institutional bounds, we should note that Paul himself recognized that this vocational call was to be exercised within the very church he had once vehemently persecuted. In Galatians Paul says,

> But when God, who had set me apart before I was born and called me through his grace, was pleased to reveal his Son to me, so that I might proclaim him among the Gentiles, I did not confer with any human being, nor did I go up to Jerusalem to those who were already apostles before me, but I went away at once into Arabia, and afterwards I returned

> to Damascus. Then after three years I did go up to Jerusalem to visit Cephas and stayed with him fifteen days; but I did not see any other apostle except James the Lord's brother. (1:15-19)

Two things are striking about Paul's words. First, he insists that his call is from God, by means of his risen Son, and that he did not need to consult any human authority (Greek, lit., "flesh and blood," a Semitic expression for human beings) to confirm it. Second, however, Paul's eventual actions of going to Jerusalem to meet with acknowledged authorities in the church who were called before him (cf. 1 Cor 15:8-9) show that he recognized the need to exercise his apostolic vocation within the context of the church's official, established ministry. Both Acts and Paul's letters confirm that he desired, and received, permission to focus his mission on the Gentiles, as envisioned by his vocational call (Gal 2:9; Acts 15:13-22). There was, then, an institutional character to his vocation.

I believe these are the foundations of Paul's vocation and his "priestly" ministry. If, for Paul, "apostle" is his primary identity, we can nonetheless understand this call by our standards as a priestly identity. He received his call from the risen Lord, to be an apostle, to preach the gospel, and he did so in the context of the church's already established ministry going back to Jesus of Nazareth.

Word and Sacrament in Paul's Ministry

Having established a foundation for Paul's ministry in his (priestly) call, we now examine briefly some of its key elements. In particular, I focus on Word and sacrament in the Pauline churches, because of their prominence in the spiritual life of the church and their obvious connection to contemporary priestly ministry.

Ministry of Word

We must, of course, remember that for Paul the notion of "Scripture" (the Word of God) was limited to what we call "the Old Testament." Paul almost certainly knew the Word of God in the Hebrew Bible, but, as a diaspora Jew, he was accustomed to its Greek translation, called the Septuagint (LXX). His letters are full of quotations, allusions, and interpretations of God's Word, much of which he may have known by heart.[11] Paul is thus enormously steeped in the Word of God. He knows its power and he sees in it God's message, not only for his Jewish ancestors in faith, but also for him and his contemporaries. In fact, Paul shows an ability to creatively apply the Scriptures to his own day, in typically rabbinic fashion.[12] For example, Paul uses the OT image of "the rock," which was descriptive of God, as now applicable to Christ (1 Cor 10:4; cf. Exod 17:1-7). We might well consider this an example of "actualization" called for in contemporary interpretation of Sacred Scripture.[13]

Even more important than Paul's use of the OT, however, is his insistence that Christ had commissioned him to proclaim a new Word, namely, the gospel of Jesus Christ. For Paul, of course, the "gospel" does not refer to one of the four canonical gospels, which came later, but to the salvific message of Jesus Christ, as Redeemer and Savior of the world. It is, in short, the entire "Christ event." In numerous passages, Paul describes in explicit terms the importance of preaching the gospel in accordance with his apostolic ministry. Just a few examples will have to suffice.

- In the context of defending his apostleship and calling the Galatians back to faithful observance of the gospel, Paul writes, "I am astonished that you are so quickly deserting the one who called you in the grace of Christ and are turning to a different gospel—not that there is another gospel, but there are some who are confusing you and want to pervert the gospel of Christ" (Gal 1:6-7).

- In the context of defending the priority of proclaiming the gospel over and above any other duty, Paul says, "For Christ did not send me to baptize but to proclaim the gospel, and not with eloquent wisdom, so that the cross of Christ might not be emptied of its power" (1 Cor 1:17).

- Again in the context of explaining his duties as an apostle, Paul emphasizes the burden that has been placed upon him (by God) to proclaim the gospel message: "If I proclaim the gospel, this gives me no ground for boasting, for an obligation is laid on me, and woe to me if I do not proclaim the gospel!" (1 Cor 9:16).

- In the context of explaining to the Romans his apostleship, Paul says, "Nevertheless on some points I have written to you rather boldly by way of reminder, because of the grace given me by God to be a minister of Christ Jesus to the Gentiles in the priestly service of the gospel of God, so that the offering of the Gentiles may be acceptable, sanctified by the Holy Spirit" (Rom 15:15-16).[14]

These are just a few of many examples of how strongly Paul's ministry was focused on proclaiming the gospel forthrightly, consistently, and without hesitation. This is his "ministry of the Word," we might say, in season and out of season.

Moreover, we do not have to look far to explain Paul's insistence on this ministry of the Word. For Paul, the "gospel" is nothing less than the Good News that in Jesus Christ a new creation has come upon humanity (2 Cor 5:17; Gal 6:16). God has given the final gift of his own Son for the salvation of the whole world, and Paul's special ministry is to evangelize, to carry forth the gospel to the ends of the earth. Nothing can compromise this ministry. Nor can anything take its place. As an apostle, this is his priority.

But Paul's ministry was not just limited to evangelization in word.[15] It was also sacramental.

Ministry of Sacrament

That the Pauline churches had an active and extensive sacramental life is quite apparent from Paul's letters and from Acts. They contain hints of various liturgical influences and several explicit references.[16] The principal sacraments evident are baptism, Eucharist, reconciliation, and sacred orders. Keeping in mind that the Pauline understanding of these sacraments is not the same as later theological teachings of the church, we can nonetheless legitimately speak of the sacramental life of the community.

Baptism, which had prior Jewish and pagan roots in ritual baths associated with spiritual "cleansing," is evident in the Pauline churches. After his conversion, Paul himself was baptized (Acts 9:18), and baptism clearly was part of the early church's evangelization efforts, though the practice was not always uniform (see Acts 8:13, 38; 10:47-48). In Corinth, Paul had to directly address the issue of baptism when it became associated with supporting one or another faction in the community. Paul sternly warned the Corinthians to cease their factionalism, and he was insistent that baptism was never his *primary* mission as an apostle: "For Christ did not send me to baptize but to proclaim the gospel, and not with eloquent wisdom, so that the cross of Christ might not be emptied of its power" (1 Cor 1:17). Yet even he admitted to having baptized some in the community (1 Cor 1:16). His understanding of baptism, while not described in detail, was profound. Baptism is nothing less than putting on Christ, being baptized into his death, so that we can experience also the resurrection (Rom 6:3; Gal 3:27; cf. Col 2:12). It is part of becoming a "new creation" (2 Cor 5:17; Gal 6:15). Yet when we ask specifically who administered baptism and how, the information is less clear.[17] The practice had obviously not yet solidified into a uniform ritual. Most important, however, is to recognize that Paul engaged in baptizing and acknowledged its theological importance in his ministry.

As regards the Eucharist, we also lack specific details about who presided at these rituals. Although it is quite clear that the Pauline churches celebrated eucharistic meals in memory of Jesus (1 Cor 11:23-26), nevertheless we cannot always know who presided. In Acts, the language of "the breaking of the bread" (Acts 2:42; Luke 24:30, 35) is used, and Paul is said to have "broken bread" for a group of believers (Acts 20:11; 27:35[?]). This is clearly NT language for the Eucharist, but it does not provide the kind of details evident in later Christian documents (e.g., the *Didache*, 9–10; 14 [ca. AD 100]). Most important, rather, is to note that Paul considered the celebration of the Eucharist crucial for the spiritual life of his communities—so essential, in fact, that he did not tolerate abuses of what he calls "supper of the Lord" (1 Cor 11:17-22, esp. v. 20).

Reconciliation was obviously another important sacrament in Paul's communities. The most relevant text is the famous passage from Second Corinthians, in which Paul speaks of "ambassadors for Christ" who reconcile and are reconciled to God in Christ (2 Cor 5:17-20; cf. Rom 5:10-11; Col 1:20).[18] There was no question of "confession" per se, which developed much later in the practice of the church. Rather, this ministry of reconciliation involved repentance and forgiveness as proclaimed by Jesus and exercised by his apostolic ministers.[19]

Finally, although the authority structure of the Pauline churches ("house churches") is not entirely clear to scholars, later developments show a tendency to appoint leaders and give them authority through "the laying on of hands," language that became associated with the sacrament of orders. Only one undisputed Pauline letter mentions such figures ("the bishops and deacons" [Phil 1:1]), but the Pastoral Epistles demonstrate the growth of the ministry in a more institutionalized fashion (1 Tim 3:1-2; 5:17; Titus 1:7).[20] In other words, Paul's churches saw the need for formal leadership positions in the community that eventually evolved into the threefold "ordered" ministry of bishop, priest, and deacon that we know so well. Only once does Paul give a specific cultic meaning to his ministry in the context of his apostleship to the Gentiles. Near the end of Romans, Paul writes, "of the grace given me by God to be a minister of Christ Jesus to the Gentiles in the priestly service of the gospel of God, so that the offering of the Gentiles may be acceptable, sanctified by the Holy Spirit" (15:15-16).[21] Here Paul makes explicit his "priestly function" in service to his churches. He offers himself for their sake and in the name of the gospel of Jesus Christ.

The upshot of this brief review of the ministry of Word and sacrament is that it clearly demonstrates that Paul exercised an apostolic ministry that, later in the church's history, became identified with the ministerial priesthood. Thus far, I have proposed that Paul's "priestly" identity is found in these three characteristics: a unique vocational call, a charge to proclaim the gospel of Jesus Christ, and a mission to celebrate the sacraments in the life of the church.

Paul's Pastoral Ministry

Paul's vocational ministry of the Word and sacrament, as an apostle of Christ, is impressive enough. But there is much more that can be said about this implicitly "priestly" ministry. I will focus on five aspects: presence, prayer, community, parenthood, and collaboration.

Presence

A remarkable aspect of Paul's ministry is the quality of his "presence" to his communities. This applies to the communities he personally founded (like Thessalonica, Philippi, and Corinth) and to ones founded by others but which he visited (like Rome) and with whom he shared his own vision of Christian faith. By presence is meant the quality of Paul's attention given to them and the closeness with which he related to them. We can say without hesitation that Paul was intimately present to his communities. He loved them. He desired the best for them, and he remained constantly concerned about them, even when he was away on other missions. He admits, at times, to being overly concerned about them, as when he adds his communities to the list of his sufferings as an apostle: "And, besides other things, I am under daily pressure because of my anxiety for all the churches" (2 Cor 11:28).

Even the practice of letter writing is an example of the closeness to his faith communities. In his physical absence, Paul remains concerned about their well-being, as seen in all of his letters. Through colleagues, who served as couriers for his letters and conduits of information, he learned about the state of affairs in his communities, and through his letters he tried to respond forthrightly to developments. In the understanding of his day, a letter was not just a casual act but a sign of vicarious presence to loved ones or business associates. Paul goes so far as to call his communities a "letter": "You yourselves are our letter, written on our hearts, to be known and read by all" (2 Cor 3:2). He can also be challenging to them, giving them rather strong advice: "We have spoken frankly to you Corinthians; our heart is wide open to you. There is no restriction in our affections, but only in yours. In return—I speak as to children—open wide your hearts also" (2 Cor 6:11-13).

In short, Paul functions like any good pastor, being as present to them as humanly possible, and filled with concern for his flock.

Prayer

Also like a good pastor, Paul was a man of prayer who leads his communities in prayer, prays for them, and is not shy about asking for their own prayers.[22] His advice to "pray always" (1 Thess 5:17) and his example of regular prayer for the ones he served (1 Thess 1:2) are a model of spiritual leadership in ministry. One finds in Paul many examples of prayers, whether thanksgiving, praise, or petition (e.g., 2 Cor 9:14; Phil 1:3-5; Eph 3:14-21; Rom 11:33-36).

Paul may also have been susceptible to mystical experiences, for he claims he can speak in tongues (1 Cor 14:18-19; better than anyone!) and has been taken up "to the third heaven" (2 Cor 12:2-5), but such exceptional mystical experiences were not the most essential aspects of prayer.[23] More important was the acknowledgment that the Holy Spirit ultimately guides our prayer, even when we cannot find the words ourselves (Rom 8:26).

Community

Another feature of Paul's priestly ministry is his promotion of community life. Paul's letters, especially the Corinthian correspondence, testify to the value of community (Greek, *koinōnia*) for Paul. Community involves establishing and maintaining mutual relationships.[24] He is not naive in his perspective. Living in community is not easy. Being called by faith to live in the church (Greek, *ekklēsia*, "assembly of the called") requires flexibility. It also requires proper ethical conduct governed by the one Christian virtue that dominates all virtues—love (*agapē* and related words).[25] Implementing Jesus' own command to love, Paul insists to his communities that love trumps all the other virtues and is to be the measure of the quality of the community's life together (Rom 12:10; 13:8; 1 Thess 3:12; 4:9; 1 Cor 13:1-13; cf. Matt 5:44; 22:39-40).

Paul takes into account that community life involves both a recognition of the individual gifts bestowed by the Holy Spirit on each member of the community, and the need to use those gifts unselfishly to build up the community (1 Cor 14:12; cf. 1 Cor 8:1; 10:23; 14:2, 26; 2 Cor 12:19). Paul emphasizes the mutual nature of community life and reciprocal love, in which everyone in community is related by faith and everyone is charged with the "building up" of community. This is most evident in his use of the expression "body of Christ" for the community, extensively developed in 1 Corinthians 12. So influential is this spiritual relationship established in Christ that Paul can affirm, "If one member suffers, all suffer together with it; if one member is honored, all rejoice together with it" (1 Cor 12:26).

Paul shows further ministerial wisdom in an even more practical way. Recall that when Paul sought the approval of the "pillars" of the church for his mission to the Gentiles, the one thing they requested was that he be attentive to the needs of the poor in Jerusalem (Gal 2:10; Acts 11:29-30). To that end, his letters show a constant preoccupation with the collection (e.g., 1 Cor 16:1-4; Rom 15:25-28).[26] No good pastor can avoid the financial challenges of ministry! Paul was not afraid to beg for financial assistance. And he also took great pains to ensure that the collection was safely delivered (Rom 15:28).

While we might be tempted to suggest that Paul did this out of duress, in order to conform to the authorities' request, and that it was limited only to the poor of Jerusalem, I think this too narrowly interprets the data. Paul admits he was "eager" to cooperate with the request (Gal 2:10), and his letters also exhibit concern for those who lack economic resources in his own communities as well (as in the case of some Corinthians, 1 Cor 11:18-22; cf. 2 Cor 8:8 on concern for others). Indeed, perhaps his encouragement of local leaders who clearly had access to some wealth (such as Lydia of Philippi, Acts 16:14-15) is, in part, explained by the recognition that even (or especially!) missionaries need financial assistance to sustain their ministry.[27] In any case, Paul urged generosity in his communities, and he was not ashamed to invite wealthier members to share with those less fortunate.

For Paul as a "pastor," then, we can say that promoting community life in both a spiritual and physical manner was a priority, something that provides good modeling for priests today.

Parenthood

A surprising feature of Paul's priestly ministry is his relationship with his communities as a parental figure.[28] Throughout Paul's letters, in fact, we find various family metaphors used to describe pastoral ministry in its various facets. Members of Paul's communities considered themselves "brothers and sisters" (Greek, *adelphoi*), and Paul was not shy about stating his role as a "spiritual" parent to his communities, especially those he had personally founded.

For example, he tells the Corinthians they are his children, and he holds himself up as their (spiritual) father (1 Cor 4:15).[29] Sometimes, Paul also recognized that his young communities could be like infants who could only be fed milk (not substantive teachings) before they grew to the point of eating solid food (more mature faith, 1 Cor 3:8). That might at first seem to be insulting, but Paul is simply acknowledging that growth in faith, like growth as a human being, takes time, effort, and discipline. One does not become an adult overnight.

Perhaps one could understand Paul's use of "father" as a pastoral image, especially in his highly patriarchal society. But even more surprising is that he sometimes compares himself, with regard to his communities, to a nursing mother.[30] In one extended passage, Paul uses both the father and mother images together to emphasize that his pastoral embrace of them encompasses the obligations of both parents:

> But we were gentle among you, like a nurse tenderly caring for her own children. So deeply do we care for you that we are determined to share with you not only the gospel of God but also our own selves, because you have become very dear to us. . . . As you know, we dealt with each one of you like a father with his children, urging and encouraging you and pleading that you lead a life worthy of God, who calls you into his own kingdom and glory. (1 Thess 2:7b-8, 11-12)[31]

This passage shows a delicate balance in parental duties. Paul compares himself to both mother and father in relation to the Thessalonians. On the one hand, parents love their children and accept them for who they are. On the other hand, they discipline them and call them to accountability. This is part of the process of spiritual maturation (1 Cor 14:20).

One should also notice that Paul's use of this metaphorical language is genuinely based on his affection, or rather, his love for these communities. He functions like any good pastor. At times, people need to be disciplined, corrected, or called to better behavior. At other times, people need to be comforted, strengthened, and supported. Paul accomplished both in his "priestly" ministry. Paul exhorts and encourages at the same time.[32]

Collaboration

Yet a fifth aspect of Paul's pastoral practice is his promotion of collaborative ministry. He did not see himself as the sole minister, even in the communities he founded. Although he clearly ranks the designation "apostle" as the most important call one can receive from the Lord (1 Cor 12:28-30), he recognizes the diversity of ministerial charisms that exist, all for building up the body of Christ, the church (1 Cor 12:1-26; 14:12, 26). He also welcomes many collaborators in ministry: men, women, married couples, and widows.

If one examines the breadth of terminology for ministry used in Paul's churches, there is an incredible abundance of terms Paul applies to his colleagues. They are, for example, brothers and sisters, coworkers, fellow apostles, fellow soldiers, fellow slaves, and workers in the Lord. One of the married couples with whom Paul shared both pastoral ministry and the task of working for a living (by tent making) was Prisca and Aquila, former residents of Rome who met Paul in Corinth and collaborated with him extensively (1 Cor 11:5; 16:19; Rom 16:1, 3, 7; Phil 4:2-3; Acts 18:1-3, 18).[33] It is also likely that Junia and Andronicus (Rom 16:7) constituted another married couple tied to Paul's ministry.[34]

Even more striking is the number of names of female colleagues of Paul: Chloe (1 Cor 1:11), Julia (Rom 16:15), Euodia and Syntyche (Phil 4:2-3), Apphia (Phlm 2), Nympha (Col 4:15), and others. Women featured significantly in ministry in the Pauline churches, and Paul seemed to have no difficulty working with them and affirming them in major roles of leadership in the church. Thus, for example, Phoebe is called a deacon (masculine, *diakonos*; Rom 16:1) of the church of Cenchreae. And Lydia, Paul's first convert on the European continent, appears to have been the head of a house church (Acts 16:13-15, 40). To these names, to be sure, must be added the names of Paul's more famous male colleagues, Silvanus (Silas), Timothy, and Titus.[35]

The point is that Paul did not engage in his ministry alone. Although his call by the risen was personal and apostolic, he exercised that ministry in collaborative fashion, even to the point of designating colleagues to keep in touch with his communities once he moved on to further evangelical pastures. In the context of our post–Vatican II ministry, where lay ministry has grown exponentially, Paul's example of collegiality is quite relevant.

Summary

These five aspects of Paul's pastoral "priestly" ministry, then, give us an implicit witness to the way Paul lived out his vocation as an apostle and proclaimer of the gospel. Coupled with his ministry of Word and sacrament, we get a well-developed sense of priestly ministry from the viewpoint of a major figure in the early church. Indeed, so significant did Paul become in the history of Christianity that he received the honored title of "the Apostle" (capital *A*). It is paradoxical that one who was not a member of the original Twelve chosen by Jesus but one called by the risen Lord "out of the normal course" (1 Cor 15:8) became the apostle par excellence. As Paul himself says,

> Last of all, as to one untimely born, he appeared also to me. For I am the least of the apostles, unfit to be called an apostle, because I persecuted the church of God. But by the grace of God I am what I am, and his grace toward me has not been in vain. On the contrary, I worked harder than any of them—though it was not I, but the grace of God that is with me. (1 Cor 15:8-10)

Now the time has come to pull these various strands of Paul's ministry together into a more comprehensive picture of how he serves so well as a model for priestly ministry today.

Implications for Contemporary Priestly Ministry

Obviously, my presentation of the material thus far has given some reasonably self-evident parallels to contemporary priestly ministry. Let me quickly review *ad seriatim* some of my affirmations.

- Paul was called by the risen Lord; he had a mysterious vocation to which he positively responded. This call dramatically changed the direction of his life.

- Paul subsequently maintained a deep personal relationship with Christ, who had called him.

- Paul cooperated with the "pillars of the church" who had been called before him and he sought their approval for his mission to the Gentiles.

- Paul was an apostle, sent on mission; he became the foremost Christian evangelist, traveling around the Mediterranean world proclaiming the gospel of Jesus Christ and establishing communities of faith.
- Paul's communities thrived on his ministry of Word and sacrament.
- Paul exercised an intense presence with his communities, even when at a geographic distance from them, and he promoted an intense life of prayer in his communities.
- Paul promoted a strong community life, recognizing a diversity of gifts as well as the one source of them all, the Holy Spirit; he urged all to use their charisms to build up the community.
- Paul related to his communities like a good parent (mother and father), instructing, exhorting, comforting, strengthening, correcting, and disciplining them as needed.
- Paul never ceased to call his communities to greater accountability, even when he affirmed their very natures; he urged them to put love into practice.
- Paul worked collaboratively with others—women and men—in ministry, and he took care to designate or affirm natural leaders in the community to continue his labors.

In my judgment, these ten points are remarkably applicable to contemporary ministry, even though they constitute just a brief overview of Paul's ministry in the first century, prior to the existence of a Christian "priesthood" per se.

I should also immediately note that there are some dissimilarities between Paul and ourselves. For example, priests today are not generally founders of communities. Nor are we equally as "charismatic" as Paul must have been or as loosely organized as his communities likely were. Even less are we literally missionaries or evangelizers in the same way as Paul and his colleagues. Yet, the priestly character of what he did, and what we priests are called to do, is valid.

If one thinks of some of the most pressing challenges of contemporary priestly ministry, I believe we would find many of them similar to what Paul faced. Our vocation is also rooted in a divine call, one we received and responded to but that also had to be discerned and evaluated by proper authorities. After ordination, most of us priests serve in parochial settings, establishing relationships with our congregations and having to function at times like parents with unruly children. As ministers of the Word, we, like Paul, have to proclaim a gospel that is not our own.

It is a precious message we have received and that impels us to proclaim with conviction, in power (1 Thess 1:5). Like Paul, we also have to be ministers of the sacraments, calling people to fidelity to the Eucharist, baptizing them and urging them to be faithful, and forging paths for reconciliation. We have to pray constantly and not be afraid to solicit prayers for our support, just as Paul did. Also like Paul the pastor, contemporary priestly ministry is confronted by multiple challenges. We must at times call people to greater accountability and at other times offer comforting words of strength. The multiple roles we must play, knowing when to push hard or to ease up the pressure on a community, is not easy. Yet our very closeness to our people, our ability to see them as "brothers and sisters" in the Lord, helps us in the fulfillment of this priestly duty.

We also have to recognize that priests are not the only ministers in the church. Like Paul, we need to be collaborative (a hallmark of Vatican II) and to recognize "the priesthood of the faithful."[36] We need to involve others in our ministry, invite women and men of talent and dedication for the building up of the body of Christ. Some priests, unfortunately, are threatened by such an inclusive vision, but I see no evidence of threat in Paul. When he defends his apostleship, his ministry, it is not out of jealousy or fear but because some have questioned the validity of his gospel or his authority. It is a righteous apology for his ministry rooted in his faith and a strong relationship with Christ. But it never compromised his commitment to collaborative ministry.

Like Paul, priests today have to minister in a changing world. We confront the multicultural, multilingual world of our day, much as Paul, as a diaspora Jew, had to manage a complex world in his own day. He had to adapt and remain open, all the while remaining faithful to the gospel of Jesus Christ with which he had been entrusted.[37]

In sum, we need not look much further than Paul the apostle for a model for contemporary priestly ministry.

Conclusion

As I bring this chapter to a close, I reiterate the purpose of my approach. My task has not been to propose a theology of the priesthood based upon St. Paul. Rather it has been to read the apostle's letters and understand his pastoral ministry with new eyes so that we can see ourselves in the process. Some of the very ideals seen in Paul's priestly ministry are enshrined in the most important teaching of the church on the priesthood since Vatican Council II, *Pastores Dabo Vobis*, of which we spoke above.[38] Some examples will suffice.

On the question of vocation, the apostolic exhortation evokes the image of Paul, in line with the prophetic call of others before him, like Jeremiah:

> The same truth is presented by the apostle Paul, who roots every vocation in the eternal election in Christ, made "before the foundation of the world" and "according to the purpose of his will" (Eph. 1:4-5). The absolute primacy of grace in vocation is most perfectly proclaimed in the words of Jesus: "You did not choose me, but I chose you and appointed you that you should go and bear fruit and that your fruit should abide" (Jn. 15:16). (*PDV*, 36)

Our priestly vocation is pure gift of God. It is neither a divine right nor fully our own choice. It is God's call to which we respond but which also has to be confirmed by the church through its system of priestly formation. Just as Paul had to work with the authorities of his day, so we too cooperate with contemporary church authorities to discern the authenticity of this call.

On the question of priests as ministers of Word and sacrament, the teaching of Vatican II itself is the proper starting point (*Lumen Gentium*, 4–6). *PDV* summarizes it well with the following words:

> Thanks to the insightful teaching of the Second Vatican Council, we can grasp the conditions and demands, the manifestations and fruits of the intimate bond between the priest's spiritual life and the exercise of his threefold ministry of word, sacrament and pastoral charity. The priest is first of all a minister of the word of God. . . . He is not the master of the word, but its servant. (26)

I could quote even further, but it will suffice to point out that the church's teaching on this threefold ministry rooted in Christ's own ministry as prophet, priest, and king is to be exercised by the threefold contemporary ministry of Word, sacrament, and pastoral charity.[39] There is also an explicit acknowledgment of the close relationship between the priest's own spiritual life and the ministry to his flock:

> Therefore, an intimate bond exists between the priest's spiritual life and the exercise of his ministry. . . . The ministry of the priest, precisely because of its participation in the saving ministry of Jesus Christ

> the head and shepherd, cannot fail to express and live out his pastoral charity which is both the source and spirit of his service and gift of self. (*PDV*, 24)

I cannot hear these words without thinking of Paul, in relation to his own communities. His love for them, his prayer for and with them, his promotion of community life, his parental care of them, and his collaboration were all part of his own spiritual life.

Finally, if Paul might be confused by some of our language about his ministry, now more than two thousand years removed from his day, I think he would nonetheless approve our attempt to read his letters with care and to find in them a source of exhortation and encouragement as priests. As we begin the second decade of the third Christian millennium, I think we have reason for hope. If we priests can begin to act more like Paul in our ministry, despite some embarrassing and monumental failures on our part, I think we can go a long way to help restore confidence in the priesthood that has been badly shaken by recent controversies.

Chapter Three

The Biblical and Patristic Roots of the Ministry of Leadership

That priests are leaders by virtue of their position should be self-evident.[1] The nature of this leadership rooted in its biblical and patristic foundations is less evident. The purpose of this chapter is to explore this topic. Although it is extremely broad, I believe we make inroads through five steps. First, we begin with a few observations on leadership in the church today. Second, we will summarize some aspects of leadership language in the Bible and the example set by Jesus and Paul. Third, we will examine eight essential characteristics of leadership distilled from a biblical perspective, concentrating mostly on the NT. Fourth, we will add a few choice insights from the patristic period. Finally, we will comment on the challenges of priestly ministry today in light of the biblical and patristic vision.

Leadership in the Church Today

Most priests are aware of the critical questions that are current in leadership circles, especially in the church. Compared to my days as a seminarian more than forty years ago, many priests are apprehensive about the prospect of becoming a pastor. Exercising leadership, especially in administration, has become such a headache that many priests prefer to "play second fiddle" rather than take center stage.

Yet paradoxically, seminaries are now faced with a new challenge. The priest shortage in North America and Europe has meant the need to place younger or more recently ordained priests in the position of pastor or administrator. Some seasoned priests earnestly desire to retire early, while others seek out the enviable position of "senior priest," by which they can exercise priestly ministry without the pressures of administrative decision-making. ("Let the young bucks deal with it!" some have opined.) So, bishops and vocation directors often urge seminaries to beef up instruction on practical leadership and administrative skills, something that generally occurred *after* ordination in bygone eras, if frequently only by osmosis rather than any formal training.

Two other factors are especially relevant to the topic. One is the persistence of divisions within the church and within many presbyterates and religious communities. The US bishops' document Basic Plan for the Ongoing Formation of Priests mentions these divisions several times and rightly calls for a return to the biblical ideal of unity in the church, especially seen in Paul's eloquent First Letter to the Corinthians.

The other factor is what some perceive as a failure of leadership in general in our day. Each field, be it politics, business, education, journalism, or religion, has seen its share of scandals on the part of those charged with leadership. Some voices ask, who can lead us today? Who really has the capability of addressing the complexity of our contemporary world? And more important, who has the integrity?[2]

If ever there was a time for good leadership, it is now. The Bible and the church fathers can offer some sage advice on this matter.

Leadership Language in the Bible and the Example of Jesus and Paul

One expert on leadership has written, "Leadership is one of the most observed and least understood phenomena on earth."[3] What is it really? The ability to lead others. The ability to inspire, to guide, to direct, to unify. It is in fact easier to observe than to define, perhaps because it is more a gift or a charism than a skill. Leaders are born, not made. And yet leadership is not only a natural gift but it can also be a formally designated role.

One of the most impressive images of leadership in the OT is the metaphor of the shepherd. It sprang naturally from the agricultural context of the time. A leadership title used primarily of kings, in the OT leadership is all about shepherding the people of God (2 Sam 5:2; Ezek 37:24).[4] The position entailed great responsibility and accountability. Ultimately, the OT describes the failure of Israel's leaders to put this image into practice honestly and effectively. (So, lack of good leadership is nothing new!) The prophets often excoriate the failure of Israel's leadership (e.g., Jer 23:1-2; Ezek 34:2-10). That is why in Ezekiel God himself finally promises, "I myself will be the shepherd of my sheep" (Ezek 34:15).

The starting point for any discussion of NT leadership is Jesus. The NT picks up on the OT vision of shepherding the flock. Jesus fulfills the role perfectly. He is the "good shepherd" who properly tends the flock (John 10:1-18). Indeed, he seeks out the lost sheep (Luke 15:4-6). When he reaches out in tenderness and mercy, it is because he perceives that the people are "like sheep without a shepherd" (Mark 6:34; Matt 9:36). They lack a compassionate leader. We could also recall here the image of the *Mandatum* celebrated every Holy Thursday. It commemorates one of Jesus' most memorable acts: washing the feet of his disciples (John 13:1-15)—the archetypal model (*hypodeigma*, John 13:15) of leadership that unexpectedly transforms a master into a servant. So, for Jesus, leadership is about shepherding, compassion, and service.[5]

Even in the most christologically exalted presentation of Jesus in the NT, that of the "High Priesthood" of Jesus Christ in the Letter to the Hebrews, the notion of service still shines forth. Although as High Priest Jesus is truly in an exalted position at God's right hand (Heb 1:3; 8:1), nonetheless his ministry is one of making atonement for his people. As High Priest he is chosen from among human beings (Heb 5:1), so that he can identify with our predicament, yet he "learned obedience from what he suffered" (Heb 5:8). Even as High Priest, Jesus serves those he loves and suffers for their sake.

We should also emphasize, however, that there is inherent authority and power in this NT portrait of Jesus. Authentic leadership is not only a charism. It carries with it inherent power and authority. In the gospels, Jesus strikingly affects people because he acts with power (*dynamis*) and teaches with authority (*exousia*), in contrast to the Jewish leaders (e.g., Mark 1:22; Matt 7:29). In fact, one could say the quality of Jesus' leadership exhibits power and authority beyond all expectation, which made it both effective and dangerous. It had a way of putting on notice those who pumped themselves up with inflated notions of power and authority, but it would also lead to his crucifixion. True leadership, then, can lead to rejection.

Most interesting in this NT presentation is the insistence that Jesus desired to share his leadership of God's people with his disciples (*mathētēs*, "learner"). He gathers disciples around him and organizes a new "family" (*ekklēsia*, "assembly") who relate to one another more as brother and sister than as master and slave, and he sends them out on mission (*apostolos*, "apostle").

Multiple passages show Jesus sharing his own power with his disciples (e.g., Luke 9:1; 10:19; Acts 1:8). He authorizes them to do the same things he does. This is remarkable, for it demonstrates that leadership can be passed on to others; it can be shared. Just as striking in the NT is the absence of standard secular leadership language and models from the Greco-Roman world as the norm for the Christian tradition. Yes, leaders are mentioned, both secular and religious, but they are not usually the ideal proposed to followers of Jesus.[6] Instead of the language of secular leadership, Jesus speaks in word and deed of surrender, discipleship, and servanthood. Just to quote one key text, remember what Jesus says in Matthew's gospel:

> You know that the rulers of the Gentiles lord it over them, and their great ones are tyrants over them. It will not be so among you; but whoever wishes to be great among you must be your servant, and whoever wishes to be first among you must be your slave; just as the Son of Man came not to be served but to serve, and to give his life a ransom for many. (20:25-28)[7]

These words find their truest meaning in the cross, which paradoxically becomes the model for Christian leadership.

If Jesus' position is countercultural in the context of his day, St. Paul's is also. Not only does Paul avoid the secular leadership language of his day but he too speaks of apostleship, service, and servanthood.[8] He constantly reminds his congregations that their call (they are the "elect," the "saints") is to model themselves after Jesus (Phil 2:5-11), whom he also imitates, especially as symbolized by the cross. He drew considerable attention to the sufferings that accompanied the leadership of his churches (e.g., 1 Cor 4:9-13; 2 Cor 11:21b-29), and he paradoxically spoke of power that comes from weakness (2 Cor 12:10). This is not the teaching of one who lords it over people but one who works hard in their midst and inspires by example. No wonder that the general word Paul uses to describe ministry in the church is *diakonia* ("service"). Like Jesus, Paul also shared ministry with others. We might consider him a precursor of collegiality. He regularly speaks of "coworkers" (*synergoi*) and uses other similar expressions (e.g., partner, fellow servant, fellow prisoner, fellow soldier). For Paul, leadership clearly included others, and he called on others to accept such positions for the good of the church.

Paul also acknowledges that a certain inherent authority goes with his leadership position. He emphasizes that his apostleship, given not by Jesus of Nazareth (whom Paul had never met in the flesh) but in a revelation of that same Jesus as the risen Lord, is as comparable in authority as that of the "pillars" of the church (Gal 2:9). The authority inherent in this position comes from the authentic exercise of a call initiated by God alone. It is not invested merely with earthly status, for this can never suffice when leading "the church of God" (1 Cor 1:2; 10:32).

In general, then, leadership in biblical terms is service-oriented, which in practice means acting more like a shepherd than a CEO. While it contains inherent aspects of power and authority, these are expected to be exercised in a "pastoral" manner that differs in kind, not just in degree, from secular forms of leadership.

Eight Essential Biblical Perspectives on the Ministry of Leadership

My summary of the biblical data is admittedly somewhat arbitrary and is not comprehensive. However, I believe at least eight essential characteristics emerge from a careful reading of the data. Each of them can be couched in the form of "both/and" propositions, which I also take to be a very "catholic" principle. The ministry of leadership according to a biblical perspective is

- both charismatic and structured,
- both a divine call and a human response,
- both christological (rooted in Jesus Christ) and pneumatological (guided by the Holy Spirit),
- both diverse and unified,
- both local and universal,
- both "lay" and "ordained,"
- both service-oriented (inwardly) and evangelically oriented (outwardly), and
- both cultic and ethical.

We will take each of these in turn.

First, leadership in the Bible exhibits both *charismatic* and *structured* elements. This is true for both the OT and the NT. Charismatically, in the OT one need only think of individuals like Moses, Deborah, David,

Solomon, Jeremiah, Isaiah, Esther, and many others to realize the power of personal charisma in propelling individuals into leadership positions. Generically, positions like judges, prophets, priests, kings, and sages were often occupied by individuals who can best be described as possessing innate gifts for the tasks they fulfilled. Of course, over time, even charismatically oriented roles such as the prophets acquired a structured form. The cult prophets, for instance, were organized in a manner that made it virtually a profession, and the role of sages in establishing schools for the education of boys is well attested. Even kingship, which lasted only a few hundred years in Israel, had both its charismatic and structured dimensions. The question of legitimate succession propelled the latter.

In the NT, leadership, not surprisingly, contains both elements as well.[9] Scholars often gravitate to the letters of Paul to illustrate the charismatic dimension of leadership. Paul's famous chapter on the gifts (*charismata*) of the Spirit is explicit (1 Cor 12:1-31). Using the image of the body (*sōma*), which held rich meaning in his culture, Paul eloquently explains how each part of the body brings its unique gift to the uniform, healthy functioning of the whole. He uses the image to speak of the many charisms in leadership in his churches: wisdom, prophecy, healing, mighty deeds, discernment of spirits, speaking in tongues, interpretation of the tongues, and so on. Some scholars assert that Paul's approach means that his churches were thus organized in a strictly egalitarian fashion, in which each gift was equally valued. But that may overstate the case.

In the very same chapter of First Corinthians, Paul uses the metaphor of "less honorable" or "less presentable" parts of the body (1 Cor 12:22-23), noting that they are necessary yet not as dignified as other parts of the body. The metaphor is applied to ministries; some are more significant than others. More important, when it comes to speaking of specific ministerial leadership roles, Paul acknowledges a certain hierarchical ordering:

> And God has appointed in the church first apostles, second prophets, third teachers; then deeds of power, then gifts of healing, forms of assistance, forms of leadership, various kinds of tongues. (1 Cor 12:28; cf. Eph 4:11-12)

I think the plain sense of this text admits to a reading of structured ministries precisely because of the context of First Corinthians. Paul was most concerned with divisions within the church at Corinth. Not only were there factions surrounding some of the well-known leaders within the community but some members were being carried away with these lesser "gifts" and downplaying the more important ones. It is not an accident that Paul lists apostleship first. For him, it was a preeminent call from the risen Lord and a badge of authority.[10]

Further evidence of structured leadership in the church occurs in later NT books, even in the Pauline corpus. The Pastoral Epistles, which portray Paul writing to his beloved coworkers Timothy and Titus, speak of bishop-presbyters and deacons and also mention the appointment of others to share in the community's leadership. These letters display the more organized aspect of ministry that eventually evolved into our tripartite structure of bishop, priest, and deacon in the sacrament of holy orders. But even here we should note that the undisputed Pauline letters speak of *episkopoi* and *diakonoi* in the church at Philippi (Phil 1:1), although the precise meaning of these terms—usually translated "ministers"—is uncertain.[11]

The NT, then, exhibits both charismatic and structured dimensions of ministry. While there was an increasing tendency to institutionalize leadership as time went on, and to delineate it more clearly, the charismatic dimension never disappeared entirely.[12] Indeed, both provide a kind of system of "checks and balances" essential to the exercise of good leadership.

Second, in the Bible leadership entails both a *divine call* and a *human response*. This statement is probably so obvious that we scarcely need to examine it. Yet there is an aspect worth emphasizing, rooted in the idea of a vocation. The biblical aspect of vocation is self-evident and is at the basis of our Christian faith. God actively called Abraham and promised that he would be "the father of many nations," but Paul rightly emphasizes that Abraham responded without hesitation to this divine call, and that is why he is upheld as a model of faith (Gen 15:5-6; Rom 4:9). Divine calls are also at the basis of other prominent OT figures, like Moses and the prophets (Samuel, Jeremiah, Isaiah, Ezekiel, etc.). Yet each call demanded a response. The human instrument is left free to reject the call, but when properly answered, the call is the basis for the ministry of leadership that follows.

In the NT, of course, this dynamic of call/response is prominent. Jesus called the Twelve (and, later, the seventy-two) and sent them out on mission (e.g., Mark 3:14-19; 6:7-13; Luke 10:1-12). The risen Lord Jesus called Paul to be a special apostle to the Gentiles, and he too, despite his prior history as a chief persecutor of the church, responded favorably and became its most devoted advocate. Although little is said explicitly about the specific roles of Christian prophets and sages in the early Christian community, the notion that their ministry was also rooted in a divine call is at home in this environment (e.g., 1 Cor 12:10, 28; Eph 4:11). In short, leadership was understood to emerge from acceptance of God's call to serve the community in distinct ways.

One caveat is crucial to this category. Just because one asserted a divine call did not necessarily assure acceptance of that assertion. Discernment of the authenticity of such calls is part of the testimony of both the OT and NT. Officials in the community must distinguish authentic calls from false ones. While determining authenticity is not always an easy affair, it is an aspect of vocation that cannot be ignored. The early church knew that "false apostles" and "false prophets" were a real possibility that had to be avoided (2 Cor 11:13); thus, the necessity of discerning authentic calls to leadership. (This practice continues today in "formation programs" for leaders in the church.)

Third, leadership in the NT is both *christological* (rooted in Jesus Christ) and *pneumatological* (guided by the Holy Spirit).[13] Jesus Christ is the source of all ministry and leadership in the church. He is the one and only great High Priest (Heb 4:14) who calls the church, the body of Christ, into existence and gives us our inherent identity as a priestly people. All "priestly" ministry is thus derivative of and participative in the eternal ministry of Jesus Christ.[14] But the Holy Spirit, too, is part of this process.

The Spirit enables us to become adopted children of God and to address God intimately as "*Abba*, Father" (Rom 8:14-17). The Holy Spirit is also the source of the many gifts that are for the good of the community and that help sustain the body of Christ (1 Cor 12:1-26). It is also the Spirit, in the Johannine image of the Paraclete, who enables Christian leaders to accomplish the great works begun by Jesus (John 14:12). The dignity of lay ecclesial ministry comes from baptism into Christ through water and the gift of the Holy Spirit in the first sacrament we ever receive. The dignity of ordained ecclesial ministry also comes from Christ, through the laying on of hands and reception of the Holy Spirit bestowed in the sacrament of holy orders. In other words, the christological and pneumatological foundations of leadership are intimately bound together and work toward the same end.

Fourth, leadership in the church is both *diverse* and *unified*. The mystery of the "one" and the "many" is most clearly expressed by Paul in First Corinthians, using the "body" imagery described above (first point). Here, however, the intention is different and is not exclusively related to that Pauline passage. The diversity of ministries in the church exists precisely because of the multiple needs that people have. Acts provides a prominent example in the establishment of the diaconate, because the Twelve could not meet the needs of all in the community (Acts 7:1-6). For Paul, each diverse gift (whether apostleship, prophecy, teaching, healing, or even administration, which [as an administrator myself!] I like to point out is low on the list [1 Cor 12:28]) brings something special that meets needs in the community. Yet every gift does not exist for its own end. It is an expression of what is ultimately needed for a unified body, the body of Christ.

The proper criterion for the use of these diverse gifts is whether it builds up or tears down the body. Additionally, we need to avoid ascribing to diverse gifts a value beyond their inherent dignity. As Paul says, the one value beyond all others is the quality of love (1 Cor 13:1-13). Unfortunately, in the history of the church, this point has been difficult to practice precisely because we often evaluate "different" ministries as either "better" or "worse" than others. After the Second Vatican Council, this struggle became evident in sometimes tense discussions of the respective value of ordained and lay ministries. This discussion is misguided if it pits one against the other, or if it leads to an exaltation of one over the other. Both are necessary in the church, and both are valid forms of leadership. Celebrating diversity while respecting the unity necessary to maintain the church's life remains as much a challenge today as in the early church.

Fifth, leadership is both *local* and *universal*. This is because the church exists on both levels. Some may have the tendency to emphasize one over the other, but both are essential. Originally, "church" (Greek, *ekklēsia*; Hebrew, *qahal*) meant an assembly, a group of individuals called together for a purpose. When Paul speaks of the "church" or "churches," he usually has in mind local communities of the faithful, the "saints," who gather regularly to celebrate their new life in Christ. Leadership was exercised in that context. Leaders emerged from within the community or were called out of the community for broader service. Many of Paul's coworkers ministered to their own native communities, but several of them accompanied Paul on his missionary journeys far and wide and came to serve him in a much larger capacity (like Timothy and Titus). For that matter, although one sees the conscious development of a sense of the "universal church" in later NT documents like Matthew (16:18; 18:17) or Ephesians (1:22-23; 5:23), Paul's important ecclesiological concept of "the body of Christ" hints at the universal level of this reality.

(Paul obviously never speaks of "bodies of Christ," even though he speaks of "churches.")

Keeping the balance between local and universal notions of church can be quite challenging on the parish level. Ministry takes place on the local level, for that is where people's needs are met. They know their pastor, their pastoral life director, their deacon, their religious education director, their hospital minister, and these are the people to whom they turn in need. Yet these very leaders are also the ones charged with communicating to their flock the larger perspective. We all belong to an entity much greater than ourselves, much more extensive than our parish. We are church, the body of Christ. This is also why our theology emphasizes the union of the priests and deacons with their bishop, and bishops with the college of bishops and the pope.

Sixth, leadership is both *"lay"* and *"ordained."* When applied to the biblical data, of course, such terminology is anachronistic. What is meant by them in a biblical sense is that there is the generic identity of discipleship that is bestowed on everyone in the community who answers the call of faith, and then there are the more specific roles of leadership within the community that have evolved into ordained positions (or other specific leadership roles). Jesus calls everyone to be a disciple. All Christians find their identity in this call. Moreover, Jesus Christ bestows on the entire community the identity of a priestly character: "you are a chosen race, a royal priesthood, a holy nation, God's own people, in order that you may proclaim the mighty acts of him who called you out of darkness into his marvelous light" (1 Pet 2:9; also 2:5). The very idea of "lay ministry" is rooted in this fundamental truth, affirmed eloquently by the US bishops in their statement Co-Workers in the Vineyard of the Lord.[15]

Yet we must also acknowledge that the NT envisions ministry as exercised by individuals chosen from among the general population and set apart for special office. The exercise of the gesture of the "laying on of hands" became associated with such offices and became a central feature of ordination ceremonies (Acts 6:6; 2 Tim 1:6; cf. 1 Tim 5:22). Ministry will always exhibit both dimensions.

Seventh, leadership is both *service-oriented* (*inwardly*) and *evangelically oriented* (*outwardly*). What this statement means is that leadership in ministry is simultaneously oriented toward building up the life of the community internally (1 Cor 14:12, 22) and taking the gospel message to the ends of the earth externally (Matt 28:16-20). Paul provides an excellent example of both orientations. On the one hand, when writing to the Corinthians, he is adamant that the many diverse gifts being exercised in the community are all for the purpose of promoting the life of the community. Nonetheless, Paul insisted, on the other hand, that his mission always carried him to farther fields. And he reminded his communities to be mindful of one another and to work toward fostering the faith as broadly as possible (e.g., 1 Thess 1:7). When he called them to imitate him as he imitated Christ (1 Cor 11:1), it was an exhortation to this dual orientation that exercised care for the community and the necessity of evangelizing others.

Eighth, leadership is both *cultic* and *ethical*. In one sense, this point flows directly from the previous one, but its focus is different. We cannot minimize the importance of the liturgical and sacramental life of the community. Those in holy orders, in particular, are identified as cultic individuals, charged with liturgical and sacramental duties specific to their call. (Priests are supposed to be "bridges" between the divine and human spheres.[16]) Again, if we use Paul's letters as an example, one sees a constant concern for the quality and frequency of prayer in the community (Rom 12:12; Phil 4:6), for the manner of respectfully celebrating the sacraments—especially the Eucharist (1 Cor 11:17-33)—and the need to uphold the gospel (Gal 1:6-9). In essence, the internal spiritual life of the community must be a priority for Christian leaders.

But ministry does not stop there. Equally important is emphasizing the ethical dimensions of Christian life. Day after day, ordinary people confront complex decisions that often have ethical dimensions. Leadership demands the ability to meet head-on such issues. When Paul answers the Corinthians' questions that have come to him by personal report from Chloe's people (herself a leader) and by letter, he does not shrink from addressing the many mundane and ethical issues that they bring, for example, eating idol food, scandal because of immorality or lawsuits in the community, marital difficulties, care for the poor, and so on. He also used the collection for the poor in Jerusalem as a means of reminding his congregations of their charitable duty toward others (1 Cor 16:1; 2 Cor 8:1-24). The Letter of James offers a similar perspective. The spiritual health of the community can be seen not only in its verbal expression of faith but also in its charitable deeds (Jas 2:14-26). Cult and ethics, word and deed, liturgy and life, prayer and justice—these go hand in hand in Christian life and ministry. Leaders should be attentive to both dimensions.

While these eight characteristics are not exhaustive, they are, I believe, foundational for the exercise of leadership in the church. Now that we have examined a biblical perspective, we turn to the contribution of the church fathers.

Patristic Insights

The patristic material is also extensive and disparate, so we must again restrict ourselves to certain key themes. I focus on three themes from the church fathers regarding ministry, accompanied by a few quotations:

- the continuation of the pastoral vision of the NT
- an increased emphasis on skills and training for leadership
- the realization of the challenges and difficulties of ministry

The church fathers naturally devoted an enormous amount of time to reading and commenting on the Sacred Scriptures. Many of their insights regarding ministry are found within homilies or commentaries on specific books of Scripture or particular biblical passages. It is not surprising, then, that the fathers exhibit a tendency to try to perpetuate the NT vision of ministry. For them, leadership in the church is still about service and shepherding the people of God. This is my first point. Theirs is truly a pastoral orientation. As time went on, the issue of preserving the unity of the community became prominent, especially as controversies erupted over doctrinal issues, something already evident to some degree in the NT (the Pastoral Epistles).

A quotation from St. Ignatius of Antioch can illustrate this pastoral perspective. When he wrote to Polycarp, bishop of Smyrna, he advised,

> I urge you, by the grace with which you are clothed, to press on in your race and to exhort all people, that they may be saved. Do justice to your office with constant care for both physical and spiritual concerns. Focus on unity, for there is nothing better. Bear with all people, even as the Lord bears with you; endure all in love, just as you now do. Devote yourself to unceasing prayers; ask for greater understanding than you have. Keep on the alert with an unresting spirit. Speak to the people individually, in accordance with God's example. Bear the diseases of all, as a perfect athlete. Where there is more work, there is much gain.[17]

Note the pastoral tone in this letter. Notice, too, the advice to attend to spiritual and physical needs, to promote unity, and to minister out of love. These continue the NT perspective.

Another aspect in the same vein is the recognition of the dual human and divine dimensions of leadership in the church. St. Augustine, who wrote considerably on the topic, emphasizes this in two passages, one of which reflected his trepidation at becoming a bishop.

> What I am for you terrifies me; what I am with you consoles me. For you I am a bishop; but with you I am a Christian. The former is a duty; the latter a grace. The former is a danger; the latter, salvation.[18]

And speaking of pastors, he wrote,

> For every man without exception is weak. And who is any man placed over you except someone just like yourself. Your pastor is in the flesh, he is mortal, he eats, sleeps and awakens; he was born and he is going to die. In himself he is, when you think of it, simply a man. But it is true that you make him something more by giving him honor; it is as if you were covering what is weak.[19]

In many ways, then, the fathers reiterated the biblical vision of leadership we outlined above. They were attentive to the "both/and" dimensions of ministry.

Second, as time went on, and especially as the church grew and became more influential and more complex, the ministry of leadership began to emphasize skills and training for leadership positions. Much of what the fathers write about Christian leaders focuses on bishops, priests, and deacons, for by that time the threefold office of holy orders was being more clearly delineated.[20] More than mere acceptance of a call to ministry was needed. Inherent abilities and skills were also requisites.

A quotation from St. Gregory the Great illustrates the point made by several fathers about the need for proper training in ministerial leadership:

> No one is so bold as to teach an art unless he has first mastered it by careful reflection. How rash, it is, then, for the unskilled to take up the pastoral office, when the government of souls is the art of all arts. Everyone knows that the wounds of the soul are more difficult to heal than the wounds of the body. Yet oftentimes those who know nothing at all about spiritual things set themselves up as physicians of souls, while those who are unacquainted with pharmacy would blush to be called doctors.[21]

But it was not only skills but also formal education that the fathers emphasized. In our own day, this has become (happily, in my judgment) a theme in ministry, under the rubric of ongoing formation, emphasized in both the US bishops' Basic Plan and *PDV*.[22] Church leaders need training in every era. St. John Chrysostom, for instance, calls attention to the importance of good education for priests:

> It is important that priests should be learned. If they are not, the church suffers greatly. This explains why, along with other qualities, such as zeal for well-doing, meekness, and a blameless life, the Apostle [St. Paul] mentions learning when he uses the word: Teacher. . . . I am not referring to the kind of learning which makes a man vain and boastful or which is clothed in artificial elegance. . . . I am speaking of the learning, which is fed on strength of mind, which is full of prudence and common sense. Such learning is not based on mere rhetoric and eloquence, but on ideas; its foundation is not in happy phrasing, but in truth.[23]

In addition to learning, of course, there were constant reminders of the necessity of holiness in the lives of the church's leaders. Calls for upright living, a regular and deep prayer life, chastity (even in times when celibacy was not the norm), humility, and ascetical practices, such as almsgiving and fasting, are frequently mentioned.

In short, the patristic period affirmed leaders but promoted expectation of proper training for the task, something that would resurface in later church history with formal programs of initial and ongoing formation, such as those designed by the United States Conference of Catholic Bishops (USCCB) and approved by the Holy See.

Third, the fathers emphasized the serious challenges and difficulties that accompany ministry. They understood that leadership was not easy; ministry entailed many challenges and difficulties. It is hard work. (Remember Paul speaks in Ephesians [4:12] of the "work of ministry"!)

St. John Chrysostom, who wrote a vast amount of literature on ministry, speaks of the hardships that accompany priestly ministry:

> When I speak of the hardships of the priest's life I am not referring to those who succeed by favoritism, who are seeking only an easy life and looking for a sinecure in the priesthood. I do not refer to them. I speak of those who keep careful watch over your souls, who are more interested in the welfare of their subordinates than in their own needs and comfort. . . . It is impossible to enumerate all the worries that are entailed in preaching and in the duty of teaching. . . . Hence the soul of the priest is like a ship tossed about by the waves; it is assailed from all sides, by enemies and friends, by relatives and strangers. . . . If he manifests emotions he is accused of tyranny; if he uses moderation, he is called a weakling. His life consists of reconciling the two extremes of leaving himself open to neither hatred nor contempt.[24]

No one said ministry was supposed to be easy. The fathers understood the demands of leadership.

In light of challenges in pastoral ministry, the fathers of the church are also particularly conscious that some pastors were not up to the task. Their language sometimes harks back to the OT prophetic lament at the lack of good leadership. That is why one encounters a frequent call for ministers with integrity. St. Jerome, who can be downright caustic in his remarks, comments, "The mere fact of being a dignitary in the church will not make you a Christian."[25] He also wrote to remind a man who had been chosen for the special ministry of priesthood about just how difficult the challenge he accepted would be:

> I hear that the choice of the whole city has fallen upon you. I hear that the bishop and the people are in perfect agreement. Do not forget, however, that *it is easier to become a priest than to deserve to become one.*[26]

I think it fair to say that Jerome's words have a certain timeless quality to them.

Integrity in ministry is also essential. One needs to put into action what is proclaimed by the office one has. The office does not make up for what is lacking in nature. And because of the de facto position of leaders, they must be held to a rigorous standard. As Jerome writes,

> The priest of Christ should be so blameless in his conduct that even the critics of religion will be unable to find fault with his life.[27]

The consistent testimony of both the Bible and the writings of the fathers is the terrible harm that can be done when leaders do not put into action what they preach and teach. In our day, that is why the sexual abuse scandal was so devastating. It tarnished the trust that should emanate between leaders and the ones they serve. St. Bernard of Clairvaux once said to the pope, "Either show yourself a shepherd to your people, or cease to claim the title."[28] And in words that almost sound modern, St. Gregory the Great notes,

> No one does more harm in the church than he who gives bad example and at the same time bears a name and exercises an Order which implies sanctity. No one will presume to correct such a person, and the evil effects of his bad example are made all the worse, when honor must be paid to a sinner because of this reverence which is owed to Holy Orders.[29]

This stance, of course, is reflected idealistically in our contemporary ceremony for the ordination of deacons. While handing them the book of the gospels, the bishop exhorts the candidates:

> Receive the Gospel of Christ,
> whose herald you have become.
> Believe what you read,
> teach what you believe,
> and practice what you teach.[30]

This remains an essential expectation for ministry in every era.

In summary, the patristic period upheld the biblical vision of pastoral leadership but also expanded its application, especially in terms of training and the exhortation to live up to the ideals of what is, at its heart, a very challenging life.

Conclusion

This broad yet somewhat selective overview begs the question, how does the biblical and patristic vision speak to the ministry of leadership in the church today?

If some are fearful of assuming leadership roles in the church today, this is understandable. Leadership is not easy, and there is a lot at stake. Leaders *should* feel some trepidation at what they assume. None of us is really worthy of the ministry to which we are called. Shouldering the cross is always difficult, yet God continues to call forth leaders, because in every age the Lord's people require shepherding. And God still works through us weak, vulnerable, human instruments. Someone once said, the question to ask of future priests should not be, are you tough enough to endure? The real question is, are you weak enough?

The ministry of leadership in the church is all about the cross. It is more about pastoral service than accruing honors and admiration. It is more about shepherding people than bossing them around. It is more about surrender, being taken to places where you would rather not go (like Peter, when he is told to feed the sheep [John 21:18]), than forging your own path. It is more about washing feet than being put on a pedestal.

Although I think it is a good exercise for all ministers to read secular literature on leadership, periodically returning to this biblical and patristic vision is useful and, in fact, vital. It helps root us in ministry. It helps keep the focus, like some internal compass, on service. As in the patristic era, we recognize in our day that skills and education are indispensable. But we also remember that at the very foundation of ministry is the divine call to serve, to love, to suffer, and to lead. It is the call to be a good shepherd.

Personally, as a Christian leader, I find the vision outlined here both an inspiration and an unsettling challenge. The church needs leaders who have integrity, have innate abilities to serve others, promote unity and not division, accept self-sacrifice as a way of life, are willing to be trained and to learn new skills, have the knowledge and ability to teach the truth of our faith, are full of compassion, and, above all, are humble about the role they fill. This is rather a grand vision. But most of us who have accepted it can testify that anyone willing to pick up this cross and follow in Jesus' footsteps will find that it is entirely worthwhile. If it is a cross to serve as a leader, it is also a special joy.

Conscious of my own limitations as a leader in addressing this topic, I conclude with some humble words of St. Gregory the Great with which he concluded a book on pastoral norms:

> And now, my good friend, spurred on by the need of self-reproach, in my efforts to point out for you what the pastor should be, I have painted for you a beautiful portrait, I who am only a mediocre artist. I have been directing others to the shore of perfection, while I myself was still tossed about on the waves of sin. But, I beg of you, amidst the wreckage of this life, keep me afloat with the plank of your prayers, in order that, though my own weight carries me down, the hand of your merits may hold me up.[31]

Chapter Four

Priesthood: The Contribution of Hebrews

The word that one most often encounters when reading about the Letter to the Hebrews is "mysterious."[1] It is an apt description for this neglected letter of the NT, which is at once both intriguing and difficult to understand. To read Hebrews is to enter into an astonishing world of divine beings and hyperbole. One gets the sense of standing on the threshold of the cosmos. The very first words of the letter set this cosmic tone: "In times past, God spoke in partial and various ways to our ancestors through the prophets; in these last days, he spoke to us through a son, whom he made heir of all things and through whom he created the universe" (Heb 1:1-2, NABRE).

Yet there can be no doubt that this letter, more than any other writing of the NT, has contributed to the Catholic Church's understanding of the priesthood. Its unique presentation of Jesus Christ as the great High Priest has inspired Christians through the ages to reflect upon what God has given the world in the gift of his own Son. In this chapter I propose to explore the fundamental contribution of Hebrews and how it might apply pastorally to the priesthood in the third Christian millennium.

This chapter comprises four parts: the context of Hebrews and why it matters; the principal message of the letter regarding Jesus Christ, the High Priest; the influence of Hebrews on the church's theology of the priesthood; and proposed reflections on the pastoral application of this letter today.

The Context of Hebrews and Why It Matters

If Hebrews has generally been a neglected book of the NT, recent publications in English have begun to remedy this situation. There are now several outstanding English commentaries and monographs on the letter that provide a rich collection of resources from which to seek guidance as one enters the world of Hebrews.[2] At the outset, I should clearly state some essential presuppositions concerning this letter, many of which are shared by a majority of contemporary scholars.

Although the date, authorship, provenance, and destination of Hebrews are contested, many believe it was written sometime between AD 60 and AD 100 by an educated, anonymous, Jewish Christian author, who is addressing a community in danger of experiencing the defection of some of its members from the faith (apostasy). Written in elegant Greek (the best in the NT), Hebrews has only the loose form of a letter and is best described in its own terms as a "message of encouragement" (13:22, NABRE; "word of exhortation," NRSV). Many scholars consider it a sermon or a homily.

Regardless of whether this is the most accurate description of its genre, it is evident that Hebrews exhibits considerable rhetorical refinements that are equally at home in skilled oratory or sermons.[3] It also provides an extraordinary example of the inventive interpretation and reapplication of the OT, typical of highly trained rabbinical practice. While the novel interpretations at times can mystify the modern mind, there can be no doubt of the respect of the author for the Word of God, which indeed is "living and active, sharper than any two-edged sword" and "able to judge the thoughts and intentions of the heart" (4:12). The argument of Hebrews is thoroughly rooted in the OT traditions of Israel, even if the author is sometimes unclear about the precise location of the source(s) he quotes or mentions.[4] He is thus conversant with the traditions of Israel but sees them in a new light, refracted as it were, through a trinitarian[5] and christological prism that brings out new shades of understanding previously hidden.

Yet this highly doctrinal orientation masks a more subtle insight. The author's highly developed theological stance is not done for its own sake. Throughout the letter there are indications that the real reason for this perspective is, in fact, exhortative. As Frank Matera has noted in his excellent *New Testament Theology*, as important as Hebrews' christological perspective is, it is "ultimately at the service of exhortation."[6] The author desires to exhort, to encourage, to strengthen, and to bolster a community being tested, most likely because of persecutions and the temptation to renege on the faith in the face of danger.

Thus in chapter 2 of the letter, when Christ's priestly identity is already stated, his suffering is acknowledged precisely because "he is able to help those who are being tested" (2:18). The letter reinforces this perspective at several points with such exhortations as "Let us hold fast to the confession of our hope without wavering" (10:23). Moreover, the final chapter is also exhortative and is oriented eschatologically toward our heavenly future: "For here we have no lasting city, but we are looking for the city that is to come" (13:14). In Hebrews, eschatology and exhortation merge to keep the focus on hopeful anticipation as we make our way toward perfection, a prominent theme in Hebrews, following Jesus the High Priest himself.[7] Hebrews can consequently be considered a document of hope, something that Pope Benedict calls attention to with great frequency in his encyclical *Spe Salvi* (In Hope We Are Saved, 2007).[8]

Although we cannot be more precise about the historical context of the first recipients of this message, we can accept that a proper understanding of Hebrews comes from this context of encouragement.[9] Its doctrinal stance is intended to support those in times of trial. As we shall see, this impacts on our own contemporary understanding of the priesthood as well.

The Principal Message: Jesus Christ, the High Priest

Scholars are generally agreed that the main contribution of this fascinating NT book is its unique and highly developed notion of Jesus Christ as the great High Priest (Greek, *archiereus*).[10] This theme, however, is rooted in a more overarching christological understanding. Hebrews begins with the announcement of Jesus as the Son of God, a high Christology that shows Jesus as higher than the angels, divine beings who surround God and act as his messengers.[11] Jesus is now the messenger "far superior to the angels" (1:4, NABRE). Although Hebrews implicitly acknowledges Jesus' divine sonship in terms of incarnation, it is the exaltation after the sacrifice of the cross that is most relevant. His sonship is intimately connected with his priesthood.[12] As a faithful Son whose identity comes from his Father, he is nonetheless made a priest, a man called, set apart, and imbued with holiness, to make intercession for humankind.[13] Jesus suffered death, Son though he was, and in doing so was made perfect through suffering (2:8b-10). He offered himself as the sacrificial victim. He tasted death for all (2:9b) and was one like us in everything but sin (4:15). His experience, then, was intimately close to our own, which enabled him to both understand us and assist us in our struggles. The letter explicitly states,

> Therefore he had to become like his brothers and sisters in every respect, so that he might be a merciful and faithful high priest in the service of God, to make a sacrifice of atonement for the sins of the people. Because he himself was tested by what he suffered, he is able to help those who are being tested. (2:17-18)

This is the first comprehensive statement about Jesus the High Priest in Hebrews, and it both concludes a section devoted to exhortation and the example of Jesus' self-abasement and subsequent exaltation, and begins setting forth an extensive exploration of this High Priest who is in every way superior to what had come before (Heb 3–10).

Jesus the High Priest

Since the design of the letter is quite complex and our scope and space are limited, I will summarize as succinctly as possible the high priestly theology of Hebrews.[14] Hebrews begins with the assertion that Jesus, as God's faithful and obedient Son, is superior to Moses, the faithful lawgiver and servant of God (3:1-6). When he describes Jesus' priesthood (4:14–5:10), it is in these terms.

- He exercises his ministry from heaven, where he has already passed to exaltation and sits at God's right hand (4:14; also 1:3, 13; 8:1; 10:12; 12:2).[15]
- He sympathizes with our weaknesses because he is exactly like us, having been taken from among human beings, but without sin (4:15; 5:1).
- He has not chosen his own identity but was called by God and sent on mission (5:4; 3:1).
- Just as the High Priest of old entered the holy of holies on the Day of Atonement and offered sacrifices for the sins of the people (9:7), so Jesus Christ has entered a heavenly sanctuary, having offered sacrifices for sin, offering himself as victim (5:1; 9:12, 14, 25; 10:10).
- He learned obedience through suffering (5:8).
- His sufferings made him "perfect" and the source of salvation, redemption, purification, forgiveness, sanctification, and perfection for all (5:9; 10:18, 22).

- As High Priest chosen and exalted by God his Father, he is our forerunner (Greek, *prodromos*, 6:20).
- His royal priesthood has made him mediator of a new and better covenant (7:22; 8:6, 13; 12:24).[16]
- In essence, Jesus' priesthood both fulfills and yet exceeds and abolishes the OT cult in favor of a new cult (7:18; 8:13-14; 9:14; 10:9).

This is an impressive and comprehensive view of Jesus' priesthood.

The Figure of Melchizedek

Melchizedek's role in this scenario is crucial. Jesus' royal priestly identity is not bound to Israel's historical priesthood, which was tied to the figure of Aaron and the tribe of Levi, which God set apart for priestly service. Unlike the Levitical priesthood, which was passed on through generations by family lines and tribal identity, Jesus' priestly identity is traced to the mysterious figure of Melchizedek by way of Psalm 110:4, which features prominently in the author's exposition: "You are a priest forever according to the order of Melchizedek" (Heb 5:6, 10; 6:20; 7:17, 21).[17]

Melchizedek is an obscure and mysterious figure about whom little is known (Gen 14:22). He is said to be "King of Salem" (likely, Jerusalem) and "priest of God Most High" (Heb 7:1) who blessed Abraham (Abram) and brought out bread and wine for him after Abraham defeated certain kings and rescued his nephew Lot (Gen 14:17-20). Abraham, in turn, rewarded Melchizedek with a tenth of his goods. Melchizedek's association with Abraham, the ancestor of Aaron and Levi, the source of Israel's inherited priesthood, gives him chronological and honorific precedence. As with so many characters in the Bible, Melchizedek suddenly appears onstage for his cameo performance and just as suddenly disappears offstage. The author of Hebrews, however, draws attention to this brief appearance and makes the most of it.

> His name, in the first place, means "king of righteousness"; next he is also king of Salem, that is, "king of peace." Without father, without mother, without genealogy, having neither beginning of days nor end of life, but resembling the Son of God, he remains a priest forever. (Heb 7:2-3)

Melchizedek is consequently the perfect foreshadowing of Jesus' unique identity. This elusive figure provides several essential elements to

Hebrews' Christology, in particular: divine rather than human origins; a royal and priestly identity not tied to human lineage yet fully human; and high priestly status that mediates cultically between God and humanity and provides blessing, hospitality (bread and wine), and peace (Hebrew, *shalom*). What is left unsaid but perhaps can be presupposed in the background is that the High Priest in Israel, by virtue of his breastplate containing the names of the twelve tribes, was representative of the whole people. Hebrews clearly envisions Jesus as possessing a universal role for his people as High Priest. His once-for-all sacrifice of his own body (7:27; 10:10) continues to intercede for his people from his heavenly throne (7:25).

In this theology of the High Priesthood of Jesus Christ, Hebrews holds together certain elements that should in normal parlance be seen in tension. Jesus is both priest and victim. He is both the one who offers the sacrifice and the sacrifice being offered. He is fully human in his identity, especially in his ability to identify with our human state, and yet he is exalted above even the angels and is enthroned forever in a heavenly sanctuary. His sacrifice was made once for all, yet his intercession on behalf of his own people never ceases. We have already received the salvation and redemption achieved by this sacrifice, yet there is more to come in the eschatological age. He is made perfect, yet perfection for his people remains a future goal and an undimmed hope. Jesus' high priestly ministry both fulfills and annuls the old cult. In these tensions perhaps we could say that Hebrews is eminently a "catholic" writing in its ability to embrace the "both/and" dimensions of life.[18] They are not contradictory, but they remain in tension.

It is also interesting to see what is left out of this scenario. Curiously, Hebrews never picks up on the image of bread and wine associated with Melchizedek. The eucharistic overtones of this imagery are unmistakable. Many scholars conclude that Hebrews does not mention the Eucharist at all, though some experts take the phrase "sacrifice of praise" (13:15) as an allusion to the sacrament.[19] Another notable lack is the use of shepherding imagery, which we have come to strongly associate with ordained ministry. Only near the end of the letter is Jesus called the "great shepherd of the sheep," in the only passage that also explicitly mentions the resurrection (13:20). But unlike in John's gospel, the image is not developed.

One also notes that two of the three traditional "powers" of the priesthood (Latin, *munera*)—teaching (*munus docendi*), divine worship (*munus liturgicum*), governing (*munus regendi*)—are not developed to any great degree.[20] The prominence of the high priesthood imagery overshadows the royal and teaching (prophetic) dimensions of the priesthood of Jesus Christ in favor of the cultic, sacrificial office. The seeds of these latter two offices of the priesthood are present, but they remain in the background.

Since an argument from silence is always tenuous, we should not draw too many conclusions from these anomalies, other than to say that they do not feature prominently in the Christology of Hebrews. The focus remains nonetheless on the High Priesthood of Jesus Christ, the exalted Lord, the Son of God.

This unique NT teaching is as broad as it is deep. While maintaining continuity with the OT traditions of the priesthood, Hebrews embarks on its own novel path to breathtaking christological innovation.

The Influence of Hebrews in the Church's Theology of Priesthood

One cannot exaggerate the influence of the Letter to the Hebrews on the Roman Catholic Church's theology of the priesthood. From its liturgical rites of ordination to its catechism and to official documents on the priesthood, the church has utilized the theology of Hebrews to great effect, explicitly and implicitly.[21] We should note, however, a striking truth. In the development of its theology of the priesthood, the church has gone where Hebrews itself never went. Nowhere in Hebrews (or in the NT, for that matter) is there an application of the High Priesthood of Jesus Christ to the ministerial priesthood! Indeed, when leaders in the community are mentioned in Hebrews, the terminology used is much vaguer. They are called leaders (Greek, *hēgoumenoi* [13:7, 17, 24]), and no description of their duties is given. They are not called priests, a term that in the NT is never applied to Christian leaders but only to OT figures, Jesus being the sole exception.[22] As Albert Vanhoye summarizes,

> By its imposing volume, the priestly christology of the Epistle to the Hebrews brings out very clearly the most important point of the Christian position in regard to the priesthood: there is only one priest in the full sense of the term and this priest is Christ. Christ alone has been able [to] fulfill effectively the essential function of the priesthood, which is to establish a mediation between God and [humankind]. He is the sole mediator. . . . A single new priest therefore succeeds to the multitude of Old Testament priests.[23]

This is the most profound teaching of Hebrews. Priests are by definition intermediaries between God and humanity, the spiritual and the secular. They are by nature called to a special holiness, set apart for service, which allows them to perform their cultic rites, their sacral duties, as intermediaries. They are supposed to be avenues to the divine. Whereas in the past there were priests (plural) to take on this role, now in Jesus Christ there is but one priest, the great High Priest who as God's Son fulfills this role perfectly. He established free access to God for all in a way only a faithful Son could do by self-sacrifice to his Father's will. Albert Vanhoye's words again hit the mark:

> Christ is not a member of a priestly family and on his cross he is far from fulfilling the requirements of ritual purity! If access to the sanctuary was formerly reserved to the high priest alone, now, on the contrary, all are invited to go forward with assurance by the way Christ opened up with his own blood (10:19-20).[24]

This special priesthood cannot be copied. It is permanent and it is uniquely tied to the person of Christ, the only NT priest.

Yet, for valid reasons and—from a faith perspective—under the guidance of the Holy Spirit in the ongoing development of theology, the church came to apply much of the terminology in Hebrews tied to Christ's identity as High Priest to the ministerial priesthood by way of a sacramental character that is bestowed upon priests with its origin in Christ himself. The priesthood today, or originally the "presbyterate" (from Greek *presbyteros*, "elder"), is a real participation in the one, unique priesthood of Jesus Christ.[25] We will now briefly examine some of the church's teaching in two of its most important documents on the priesthood, *Presbyterorum Ordinis* (1965) and *Pastores Dabo Vobis* (1992).[26]

Vatican II's Decree on Priestly Ministry and Life

The most obvious message of the application of Hebrews in *PO* is that the ministerial priesthood is modeled entirely after the priesthood of Jesus Christ. The document cites or quotes Hebrews explicitly some eleven times. Using the letter as its inspiration, what is striking is the direct and immediate application that is made to the ministerial priesthood. *PO* makes the following main points:

- Priests live on earth but mediate heavenly matters by offering gifts and sacrifices for sins; they are chosen from among human beings yet remain their brothers (*PO*, 3; Heb 5:1).

- Our priesthood is an imitation of Christ's (*PO*, 3; Heb 2:17; 4:15).
- Like Christ, priests should exercise hospitality, kindness, and sharing of possessions (*PO*, 8; Heb 13:1-2, 16).
- The priesthood is a universal service, valid for all peoples at all times (*PO*, 10; Heb 7:3).
- Christ's own holiness as the great High Priest makes up for the lack of holiness on the part of priests (*PO*, 12; Heb 7:26).
- Priests are called to enter God's sanctuary with sincere hearts, put the Word of God in practice, and share the wisdom of God (*PO*, 13; Heb 10:19, 22; 13:9-10).
- Priests should be men of faith, just as Abraham was a model of faith (*PO*, 22; Heb 11:8).

This use of Hebrews obviously does not provide a total theology of the priesthood, but we should note its fidelity to the spirit of Hebrews, especially in the balance between the humanity of the priests and their sacral duties. Jesus Christ is the model; he is the one who provides the sanctity we ourselves can never provide.

John Paul II's Apostolic Exhortation on Priestly Formation

PDV quotes or alludes to Hebrews more than a dozen times. Its pastoral orientation, however, comes across even more quickly than in *PO*. In the opening paragraphs *PDV* immediately connects the title in Hebrews of Christ, "the great shepherd of the sheep" (13:20), to God's promise recorded in Jeremiah to give shepherds for the flock (Jer 3:15; 23:4) and to the image of the "Good Shepherd" from John's gospel (John 10:11; cf. 21:15-19).[27] Like *PO*, this document also emphasizes the human dimension of the ministerial priesthood, and it does so utilizing two quotations from Hebrews (5:1; 4:15), stating explicitly at the beginning of chapter 1, "The Letter to the Hebrews clearly affirms the 'human character' of God's minister" (*PDV*, 5).

This is a significant indicator of the document's pastoral character, I believe, because *PDV* is, as I mentioned in chapter 1 above, the first official teaching of the church to emphasize human formation as one of the four main pillars of priestly formation and, in fact, as foundational to forming good priests.[28] There is no question that Jesus is the model, for the text of the apostolic exhortation says, "The priest, who is called to be a 'living image' of Jesus Christ, head and shepherd of the Church, should seek to reflect in himself, as far as possible, the human perfection which shines forth in the incarnate Son of God" (*PDV*, 43). This orientation in *PDV* is quite remarkable, not only for its emphasis on the human qualities needed for priestly ministry,[29] but also for its fidelity to Hebrews, which in fact blends well the human and divine aspects of the ministry of Jesus the High Priest.

In addition to this basic stance, *PDV* also applies Hebrews quite directly to the ministerial priesthood in three other important ways:

- Ministerial priests are configured to Christ, shepherd and head of the church, and participate in mediating the direct access to God Christ has achieved as High Priest; Christ fulfilled the OT roles of mediation previously performed by kings, priests, and prophets; ministerial priests now share this threefold ministry (*PDV*, 13; Heb 8–9; esp. 9:24-28).
- Priestly vocation is a mysterious call by God's grace; it must be answered with full freedom; Christ makes up for our weaknesses even as we are called to perfection (*PDV*, 20; Heb 7:26).
- Christ is the definitive Word of God; priests should be formed well to faithfully communicate the true wisdom of God (*PDV*, 53; Heb 1:1-4).

While these statements are consistent with the teaching of Vatican II, much of which is quoted or referenced in the apostolic exhortation, it is noteworthy that *PDV* develops much more thoroughly a theology of the priesthood that puts flesh on the bones of the council's teaching. It provides a far more extensive understanding. While it is replete with doctrinal insight, its pastoral sensitivity is equally apparent, a style that blends well with the character of Hebrews.[30]

Pastoral Applications

Having looked at Hebrews itself and the two principal church documents on the priesthood, we now turn to our own pressing pastoral question. What lessons can be learned from the Letter to the Hebrews that can be applied to Catholic priests today? I point to six principal teachings that I think are particularly pertinent to our contemporary situation.

The Unwavering Focus on Jesus Christ

First and foremost, the unmistakable focus on Jesus is preeminent in Hebrews. The call to perseverance in the faith is accompanied by the invitation to keep our eyes fixed on Jesus, "the pioneer and perfecter of our faith" (12:2). Nothing could be more important today in the life of priests. Not only is Jesus our model for the priesthood and its perfect embodiment, but in a contemporary yet traditional theology of the priest as "another Christ" (Latin, *alter Christus*), Hebrews is all the more important.

Priesthood is all about Christ. He is the only real priest. We priests act *in persona Christi Capitis* (in the person of Christ the head [of the church]) but really it is Christ who acts in us (Gal 2:20).[31] We are not literally but sacramentally other Christs. Thomas Aquinas said it best: "Christ is the source of all priesthood: the priest of the old law was a figure of Christ, and the priest of the new law acts in the person of Christ."[32] The expectation that priests should represent Christ concretely in people's lives is not merely pious theology. It is rightly intended to be a way of *being* and not merely a way of *doing*. We are given a share in the sacred power (*sacra potestas*) of Christ the High Priest.[33] It is ultimately a call to integrity and authenticity to the mysterious call of our priestly vocation, to be conformed perfectly to Christ who molds us, shapes us, and gives us our very being. But we must also remember, although it is not Hebrews that speaks to the issue, that our priesthood is not the only type given to the church. Vatican II strongly reminds us of the priesthood of the faithful, rooted in other NT documents, which also should profoundly shape our own living out of the ministerial priesthood we have received.[34]

Given the high Christology and theology of Hebrews, we priests especially could well reflect upon how we can better incarnate this modeling of Christ as we go about our ministries.

A Unique Priesthood, Source of a Vocation

A second application stems from the unique emphasis on the *kind* of priesthood Jesus had. Unlike the priests of the OT, it was not hereditary. It was not automatic because one was born to it. It was rooted in the mysterious call of his Father, in the mold of Melchizedek who had no lineage but was a chosen king and priest. Our theology of priesthood rightfully emphasizes the mystery of a vocation (*PDV*, 34, 36). It is a call, not self-chosen but a call to which we respond.[35] Interestingly, the only place Jesus is called an "apostle" is in Hebrews (3:1). He shares with us a divine call that he received from his Father and a divine mission that he accepted. Jesus was sent on mission from his Father. Priests, in turn, are called and sent by him on mission. Our identity and our ministry are bound up with the mystery of God at work through human resources, calling ministerial priests into being. This mystery of the vocation is not entirely in our control, but it gets tested and requires discipline, both of which Jesus experienced.

The Balance between Human and Divine

A third lesson concerns the balance between the human and divine, the sacred and profane, that one finds in Hebrews. On the one hand, as we have noted, it has one of the highest Christologies of the NT. In its understanding of Christ the High Priest, it exalts him in a way far above any human aspirations. On the other hand, the letter insists that even Christ was like us in all things but sin. Even this High Priest, unique Son of God that he is, is chosen from among men and can identify with our frailties, our sufferings, our limitations. Priests are at one and the same time called to a particular holiness (not higher!),[36] while acknowledging our human limitations. While we can never perfectly imitate Jesus as High Priest, we can try to better integrate the human and divine aspects of our ministry. Even while we proclaim the gospel message to others, we remain conscious that we ourselves are not the "masters" of the Word but its servants (*PDV*, 26). Even while we dispense the sacraments and mediate God's grace to others, we are mindful that we ourselves need to receive the same divine aid and be touched by the same healing power of God (ibid.). This dynamic tension between the human and divine in the ministerial priesthood is ever present.

Priests as Pastoral Theologians

Fourth, Hebrews can teach us about the wisdom of being "pastoral theologians," for that is what I think the author was, and that is what we are called to be. The subtle blending in Hebrews of profound doctrinal depth, and sublime theological understanding about Jesus Christ himself, served to inspire, encourage, strengthen, and challenge the people for whom the message was first written. It does the same for us. Hebrews reminds us of a truth about the priesthood emphasized in Vatican II and reinforced in *PDV*, namely, the intimate connection between our own priestly identity and spirituality and the people we serve. *PDV* calls it "an intimate bond that exists between the priest's spiritual life and the exercise of his ministry" (24; cf. *PO*, 12). As I read Hebrews, I believe one sees evidence of this bond. The deep and wise reflection on the ministry of Jesus the High Priest helped the author to reinterpret the OT traditions in a way that also nourished his threatened community. We should not be reticent to put our theological insights to work as we seek to become more effective pastoral theologians.

Eschatological Perspective

A fifth teaching in Hebrews stems from its eschatological orientation and the context of trial and tribulation that is an undercurrent in the letter. The theology of Hebrews, profound as it is, was not developed for its own sake by a systematic theologian. It was pronounced as a message of encouragement to a community under stress, fraught with the danger of apostasy in light of impending persecution or severe trials. It also strives to exhort the faithful to remain steady in their stance of faith as they journey toward perfection. The goal is the heavenly Jerusalem (12:22). As with all eschatologically oriented documents, Hebrews is intended to impart hope to its hearers/readers. The message is obviously phrased in various ways but always with a combination of challenge and encouragement:

- Just as Jesus was tested in suffering, so he can identify with us when we undergo the same (2:18).
- Because we have this secure High Priest who has already accomplished our salvation, "Let us hold fast to the confession of our hope without wavering, for he who has promised is faithful" (10:23).
- "Endure trials for the sake of discipline" (12:7).
- "So strengthen your drooping hands and your weak knees" (12:12, NABRE).

Given what the priesthood and the church have endured in recent years, we can properly see ourselves as a people in need of such advice, as we too journey toward perfection. As Pope Benedict XVI has reminded us in his encyclical *Spe Salvi*, hope and faith go together intimately and, along with the virtue of love, sustain the life of the church on our pilgrim journey.

Priest as "Victim"

Sixth and finally, just as Jesus was both priest and victim, priests today should reflect on the radical nature of our call to serve others. This message, of course, is rooted in Jesus of Nazareth's own teaching that he came to serve and not to be served (Matt 20:26-28; Mark 10:43-45). But for Hebrews, Jesus as victim is tied to his offering of his blood and his flesh, his sacrifice on the cross, and his subsequent vindication in the resurrection and exaltation at God's right hand.

We priests today, naturally, do not make the same sacrifice, even though we make it present through the power of the Holy Spirit in the celebration of the Eucharist daily.[37] But analogously, we are called to self-abnegation, surrender to the will of the Father, and to follow the call of discipleship even though it may lead to suffering. We need to become, metaphorically speaking, "victims" in the sense of surrender to the Father's will. I see two equally important sides to this expectation, outward and inward. Outwardly, a priest's participation in the suffering of Jesus the High Priest should help us identify and empathize with those who suffer, just as his experience enabled him to be one with humanity in our trials and tribulations. Inwardly, priests are called to enter into the passion of Christ the High Priest by our acceptance and endurance of the difficulties and the suffering that comes our way. Both means incarnate the practice of Christ the High Priest.

Sadly, the language of high priesthood (*alter Christus*, *sacra potestas*, etc.) and the exalted nature of priesthood sometimes lead to entitlement rather than selfless service. Some priests seemingly lack the capacity for true empathy with those who suffer. Others, when things are simply not going their way or they meet great challenges in pastoral ministry, give up, lose hope, or walk away. Even worse, perhaps, is falling into the trap of clericalism, which is a distortion of the true priesthood. Priests sometimes begin to see themselves as the privileged class, and there are always people willing to put us on a pedestal. This is a corruption of the call to priesthood in the mold of the High Priest, Jesus Christ. It is an inherent danger in a high theology of priesthood. But, in my judgment, Hebrews maintains the balance. Priesthood is about ministry, serving others in the person of Christ. It is simultaneously a humbling and an exhilarating experience.

Conclusion

This "fascinating and unsettling" book beckons us in the third Christian millennium to carefully examine where we have come from and where we need to go as church and as priests of God.[38] This NT letter, the only document from its unknown author and the only source of our theology of Christ the High Priest, does not give us every aspect of priesthood or ministry as our understanding has developed through the ages. There are other dimensions covered by different NT perspectives, such as the shepherding imagery from the Johannine literature, the threefold hierarchical ministries (bishop, priest, deacon) that evolved from the Pastoral Epistles, the spousal imagery that comes from the Pauline tradition, the practice of celibacy or the call to simplicity of life that come from the teaching and example of Jesus, more developed thought on Jesus as prophet and king, and so on.

Yet one can scarcely imagine understanding the priesthood without Hebrews. As Albert Vanhoye says, "The more we meditate on the Epistle to the Hebrews the more we are awestruck by the riches which it offers us."[39] It places our whole understanding on a firm foundation, the person of Jesus Christ himself. We should glory in this fact. And it is entirely appropriate that we reflect in awe, as we did during the Year for Priests, on the great gift that the priesthood is for the church and for the world.

While it is a time to support the priesthood and priests and to give thanks to God for priestly service, it is not a time to make of priests something we are not. If we are "other Christs," it is only as pale reflections of the real Priest. As members of the same pilgrim church, we journey with all the faithful, who share in the same priesthood of Jesus Christ, albeit in a different way,[40] toward that heavenly Jerusalem to which Jesus beckons us. This is, however, a time to renew ourselves in the one priesthood of Jesus Christ. Let us heed the words of Hebrews itself:

> Remember your leaders, those who spoke the word of God to you; consider the outcome of their way of life, and imitate their faith. Jesus Christ is the same yesterday and today and forever. (13:7-8)

Chapter Five

A Biblical Spirituality of Celibacy

Priestly celibacy remains one of the most debated and "hot-button" topics on the Roman Catholic priesthood.[1] In recent decades, it has been (wrongly, in my judgment) blamed for the sexual abuse crisis, and it has been regularly denigrated as unnatural and virtually inhuman, despite the fact that there is no scientific evidence connecting celibacy itself with sexual aberrations. Many people, and even a few bishops, have called for an open discussion about the practice of mandatory celibacy, something that the late Pope John Paul II and his successor, Pope Benedict XVI, have resisted firmly. This context must be acknowledged, but the purpose of this chapter is neither to defend nor attack the current practice of the Roman Catholic Church regarding celibacy. Rather, the purpose is to show that there is, in fact, a firm biblical justification for celibacy that can be informative and helpful, even in the context of the contemporary heated discussions of the topic. Although, from a biblical standpoint, celibacy is not inherently connected to priesthood, nonetheless celibate priests can live authentic and spiritually enriched lives by better understanding the distinct gift they have received in celibacy.

I propose to examine a biblical spirituality of celibacy in four stages. In the first stage I will provide some introductory comments and issue a few cautions to draw attention to the limits of this perspective. The second stage will evaluate the passages in the Bible that are typically referred to when discussing celibacy. This will include a negative assessment as well as a positive one, noting that some passages, in fact, do not pertain to celibacy. The third stage will outline what I consider to be basic elements of a biblical spirituality of celibacy. The fact that the Bible has very little to say about celibacy explicitly does not mean that there is no biblical basis for it. The final stage offers a brief conclusion oriented toward the future.

Introduction and Cautions

As indicated in the introduction to this book, we Sulpicians work in initial and ongoing formation of priests. Some years ago, while reviewing our own recruitment strategy, we sponsored a short anonymous survey of priests from around the country to help give us data on priests' concerns. The response was quite good. A topic that arose was certainly celibacy. One response, in particular, sticks in my mind. This priest said in so many words, "Celibacy is a joke. No one can live it. The only reason we have it is for purely economic reasons." The comment struck me as quite dismissive and shallow. While there are legitimate questions one can raise about *mandatory* celibacy, there are surely more profound reasons for it, even historically, than mere economics. Thus my search for some biblical foundations.

At the outset I went to various Bible dictionaries to seek out what they might have to say about celibacy. I began with one of the foremost Bible dictionaries of the twentieth century, the formidable multivolume *Anchor Bible Dictionary*. It is a standard in the field and very helpful. To my surprise, here was the complete entry under the topic of celibacy: "Celibacy. Votive abstention from marriage and sexual relations—unknown unless alluded to in Matt 19:12."[2] A remarkable entry! Even granting a traditional Protestant approach to the topic of celibacy, dating from the time of Martin Luther and the sixteenth-century Reformers, I think this perspective is too limited.

While this chapter will not offer a full exegesis of the two most prominent biblical passages that speak of celibacy, it will orient the question in a broader fashion to the true biblical foundations of celibacy, while avoiding the pitfall of proof texting. To that end I will not quote important official church documents on this topic or seek out references in the extensive theological Catholic tradition. Rather, the task is to seek the biblical spirituality of celibacy.

Five cautionary remarks are crucial at the outset.

First, a Catholic approach to Sacred Scripture is not entirely consonant with the approach of most of the Protestant tradition and, in particular, the fundamentalist approach to the Bible. Even if the Bible had not one word to say about celibacy, that does not mean that we would think it illegitimate for the church to institute it. As Vatican Council II asserts, Catholics acknowledge both Scripture and tradition as one continuous source of divine revelation. These are not merely two separate entities but interrelated realities in a complex relationship in which one interprets and influences the other. Not everything Catholics believe needs to be found literally in Scripture, although I admit we have done our own share of proof texting from the Bible throughout our history.[3]

Second, not every passage in the Bible is self-evident. Some passages are very obscure and difficult to interpret. They can confound even the experts. Thus we should not expect in every case a clear-cut interpretation about what any given passage might actually have meant or means for us.

Third, some clarification of vocabulary is helpful. People sometimes confuse chastity with other concepts. Celibacy is not chastity, is not virginity, and is not merely continence. I once read an article in a magazine in which an Eastern-rite priest argued strongly that all baptized Christians are called to celibacy. He made a fundamental error that many have made before; he confused celibacy and chastity. All are called to chastity, including married couples. But not all are called to celibacy. For our purposes, celibacy is the voluntary forgoing of a marital relationship and the genital expression of one's sexual identity for altruistic reasons.

Fourth, if by celibacy, we mean mandatory, obligatory celibacy tied to the Roman Catholic priesthood (in the tradition of the West, obviously, since Eastern-rite priests are permitted to marry and have children), then we must admit immediately that the Bible is indeed silent on the topic.[4] First of all, the only priesthood mentioned in the NT is that of Jesus, in the Letter to the Hebrews. There is certainly no mention of celibacy there, and it is not tied to priesthood. But I would suggest that celibacy, from a biblical perspective, is actually a broader concept than that identified with the church's current practice of a celibate priesthood. In fact, the church's practice has ancient roots and evolved historically for complex reasons unrelated to the biblical perspective, but that again is another topic that would lead us astray.[5]

Finally, as others have asserted before, even if the church decided to change the current practice of mandatory celibacy for diocesan priests, the practice would still remain an essential part of religious life. Celibacy is part of the warp and woof of religious life.[6] It is consonant with a communal perspective and an asceticism that belongs, by definition, to religious commitment, whether of religious sisters, brothers, or priests.

Biblical Passages to Consider

The biblical data are limited but can be divided into two parts. The first will briefly note three passages that are sometimes (wrongly) considered to have something to say about celibacy. Then we turn our attention to two passages that I believe do pertain to celibacy. In the interest of space, the passages will not be reproduced in their entirety; the key parts of the passages will be referenced. One should consult the Bible directly for full references.

Passages Not Pertaining to Celibacy

The first passage is 1 Timothy 4:1-3. First Timothy is likely a Deutero-Pauline letter written at a later time than Paul, perhaps by a disciple. The style of the letter is that of a senior apostle (Paul) writing to his younger colleague (Timothy) to give him advice about his ministry. The passage in question speaks of some problems in the community with false ascetical practices that Paul warns against. The most pertinent words for our purposes are these: "They forbid marriage and require abstinence from foods that God created to be received with thanksgiving by those who believe and know the truth. For everything created by God is good" (vv. 3-4).[7]

It is not clear who "they" are, but what is clear is that these opponents are teaching a false asceticism that is contrary to the gospel Paul preached. (Indeed, this was sometimes a problem in the undisputed letters of Paul also.[8]) Most important, these frauds are prohibiting marriage and the consumption of certain foods on the basis of some false assumptions about what is or is not permissible for those who follow the gospel. Whatever the forbidding of marriage is about, it is not celibacy. Rather, it more likely pertains to some extreme distaste for marriage on the grounds of sexual prudishness or perhaps pertaining to eschatological expectations. Whatever the actual circumstances, this passage does not address celibacy.

A second passage is Luke 20:34-36. The most pertinent words for our inquiry are as follows: "Jesus said to them, 'The children of this age marry and remarry; but those who are deemed worthy to attain to the coming age and to the resurrection of the dead neither marry nor are given in marriage'" (vv. 34-35). The context of the passage is important (vv. 27-40). Certain Sadducees, who denied the belief in the general resurrection of the dead accepted by the Pharisees, are trying to trap Jesus by asking a question about a woman who had married multiple times in this life. When she died and finally went to heaven, they ask Jesus, whose wife would she be?

In essence, Jesus sidesteps the question of marriage in favor of asserting that the life after resurrection does not mirror this earthly life at all. There is no institution of marriage in heaven. His commendation of those who do not marry is not about celibates in this life but about those who will attain the resurrected life in the kingdom to come. The issue, as the context indicates, is actually about the resurrection of the dead, not marriage or celibacy. Only by analogy could one say that this passage might suggest that celibacy is a foretaste of the eschaton, an understanding that does develop in later theology.

A third passage is Revelation 14:1-5. It concerns the 144,000 companions of "the Lamb" who are saved and found worthy of God's kingdom. The most pertinent words for us are, speaking of these saved ones, "These are they who were not defiled with women; they are virgins and these are the ones who follow the Lamb wherever he goes" (v. 4). Again, this is not about celibacy. As verse 5 clearly points out, the reason these limited number of chosen ones (not to be taken as a literal number but symbolic, relating to the traditional, historical tribes of Israel) are saved is not because of literal virginity but because "[o]n their lips no deceit has been found; they are unblemished." This is symbolic language for refraining from idolatry, the traditional sin that plagued Israel throughout its history. (Keep in mind the OT connection of idolatry with sexual promiscuity, e.g., Exod 32:1-6; Hos 4:13-14.) They are the "firstfruits of the human race" who are "ransomed" to be with God and the Lamb (i.e., the victorious Christ; v. 4). The passage, then, has nothing to do with celibacy but with remaining righteous and steadfast in the face of persecution. Those who do not succumb to idolatry will be rewarded with life in the kingdom of the victorious Lamb.

Now, if these three passages are not pertinent to celibacy, as such, there are two passages that are.

Passages Pertaining to Celibacy

The first passage is found in a gospel, the famous passage about eunuchs, Matthew 19:3-12. The passage is primarily about marriage and divorce, a hot topic in Jesus' day. Some Pharisees try to trap Jesus, perhaps by getting him to align himself with the liberal school of the day that permitted a man to divorce his wife for almost any reason, or the more conservative school that indicated there should be serious reasons for divorce. Judaism tended to frown upon multiple divorces but recognized instances in which marriages fell apart. Surprisingly, Jesus aligns himself to neither school. Instead he prohibits divorce of any kind. One of the more secure teachings of the so-called "historical Jesus" was that he prohibited divorce. That was extraordinary in his day. Matthew's community (or the evangelist himself) struggled with this, since the famous exception clause ("unless the marriage is unlawful," v. 9) is slipped into this passage. The exact meaning of the Greek word used (*porneia*) is disputed, but it could refer to infidelity or adultery or perhaps some form of sexual immorality. We cannot linger on this question or the complexities of this entire passage. Many books have been written about it, and this is not the place to rehearse them. Our goal is to examine the section on eunuchs rather than to discuss marriage and divorce.[9]

The most noticeable thing after Jesus speaks his mind is the reaction of the disciples. They declare incredulously, "If that is the case of a man with his wife, it is better not to marry" (v. 10). In other words, marriage sounds too complicated! We might as well stay single and save ourselves a lot of trouble. (After what I have seen of many marriages, I can sympathize with the perspective. For any celibate priest or brother who thinks marriage is the "silver bullet" or nirvana, he should take a good look at the struggles of married couples. For instance, they sometimes experience loneliness as deeply as anyone else.) To this objection (or is it abject resignation?), however, Jesus responds with the words most important for our context: "Not all can accept [this] word, but only those to whom it is granted. Some are eunuchs from birth; some were made so by others; some because they have become eunuchs for the sake of the kingdom. Whoever can accept this ought to accept it" (vv. 11-12, my translation).

A number of essential details about this passage confirm, in my judgment, that it does indeed concern celibacy:

> Notice that Jesus calls for a higher standard throughout the passage. Married couples are called to observe their marital obligations permanently. A small number of utterly dedicated "eunuchs" are called to forgo marriage and genital relationships for a higher purpose also, the kingdom.
>
> The image of the eunuch, unflattering though it may be, has two sides to it.[10] Clearly it implies that sexual urges have been checked. One "neuters" or "has neutered" naturally or forcibly one of the strongest urges of the human race, sex. This also ironically frees one for other things. The image

of the eunuch has a positive side to it. One thinks, for instance, of the high places some eunuchs held historically in the retinue of kings and emperors. They were often men of high rank and great influence. In some contexts they were charged with guarding a king's most sacred possessions, his harem. There is, then, a type of generativity that can be associated with the image.

Nowhere does the passage denigrate sexuality or marriage. In fact, Jesus goes out of his way to hark back to the ideals of Genesis 2, which shows God establishing marriage as a sacred institution (Matt 19:4-6). Jesus is not upholding celibacy (the eunuch image) as better than marriage.

Jesus says that being (becoming) a eunuch is not for everyone. It is quite restricted.

It involves free choice. One must accept this call.

It is also a gift ("to whom it is given"). For Matthew, the passive voice here evokes God as the source of the gift. God grants celibacy to some, and they are free to embrace it.

This free choice involves a higher purpose, "for the sake of the kingdom." In Matthew's judgment, all disciples are called to put the kingdom first, but a small number of disciples can choose celibacy as a means of expressing utter devotion to the kingdom.

In short, this passage contains several elements that provide a good spiritual foundation for celibacy properly understood in its context.

The second passage is 1 Corinthians 7. It is quite long, and we cannot be detained by an extensive look at it. We will concentrate on the essential verses that address our topic (vv. 6-9). It is interesting that, as in the case of the Matthean passage above, this one addresses celibacy in the context of marriage and divorce. The entire chapter speaks to sexual issues that the Corinthians have asked Paul to address. He does so both with an eye to what Jesus taught and to his own perspective that he freely shares.

After giving married Corinthians advice to give themselves to their spouses freely, and adding that it might be good for purposes of prayer to abstain from sexual relations once in awhile—and by mutual agreement—Paul goes on to add the lines that are most applicable to our discussion: "Indeed, I wish everyone to be as I am, but each has a particular gift from God, one of one kind and one of another. Now to the unmarried and to widows, I say: it is a good thing for them to remain as they are, as I do, but if they cannot exercise self-control they should marry, for it is better to marry than to be on fire" (vv. 7-9). Isn't Paul earthy? He recognizes the real potent force of sexual desire, but he also calls people to be prudent and to exercise self-control. Paul is ever the realist and advises those who cannot hold themselves in check sexually to embrace marriage.

Now several observations are pertinent with regard to celibacy:

> Note that Paul nowhere condemns sexual relations within marriage, nor does he exalt celibacy over and above marriage. They are separate ways, different, but both from God.
>
> A real question is what Paul means by "as I am." Is he single and never married? Is he a widower who now abstains from remarriage, as some scholars maintain? It was unusual in Judaism for men not to be married, but since Paul was fairly young at his conversion, perhaps he never married. Personally, I think the evidence favors that Paul was never married. There is no direct evidence in Scripture or elsewhere that he was married.[11]
>
> But why would he exhort people to imitate him in this choice of a non-married state if he recognizes that marriage is a legitimate gift of God? Paul's reasons are not because celibacy is better, a higher calling, or allows one freedom to do ministry. Rather, the context of 1 Corinthians 7 indicates that Paul's eschatological expectations about the coming of God's kingdom are powerfully present. He wants everyone to remain as they are because Jesus' return is around the corner, so to speak. He does not want them to change their lives because change can increase their anxiety. Thus Paul is not exhorting people to celibacy as such but to following one's individual gift (Greek, *charisma*), about which he will talk at length in later chapters (1 Cor 11–12). Consequently, we can say that for Paul celibacy, rare though it might have been in his day, is a valued gift from God given to some so that they can fully devote themselves to the proclamation of the gospel in the context of awaiting the arrival of God's kingdom.

To the above material, I want to point out something else that is often overlooked. Celibacy is not unique to Christianity. Judaism, in fact, exhibits some awareness of the practice of voluntarily refraining from marriage and sexual relations for other purposes. Jeremiah, the famous seventh-century-BC prophet, is the most prominent example. God instructs him that he is to remain unmarried precisely so that his life can be a witness to Judah about their infidelity (Jer 16:1-2). Through Jeremiah God will bring punishment and barrenness on this stubborn people. But paradoxically, Jeremiah's celibacy is also intended to call the people back to fidelity with God. His celibacy is intended to bear another kind of fruit.

Other examples of voluntary sexual abstinence include the ban on sex for warriors prior to entering battle (see 1 Sam 21:4-6); sexual abstinence in conjunction with divine revelation (Exod 19:15); and the taking of life-long Nazarite vows to avoid wine, leave one's hair uncut, and abstain from sex in order to be utterly dedicated to God (cf. Judg 13:5-7; 16:17; cf. Num 6:2). Some two centuries before Jesus, one group of Jews, the Essenes, went into the desert near the Dead Sea and invoked celibacy as a basic rule for their community. The Dead Sea Scrolls found at Qumran most likely bear witness to this phenomenon, by which adherents felt they could preserve authentic Judaism while awaiting the eschatological battle that would lead to God's ultimate victory over evil. In all these and other instances (e.g., certain pagan practices and Hellenistic philosophies in NT times) celibacy is seen as voluntary and an ascetical practice that could have other benefits. Celibacy was usually viewed as a temporary practice rather than permanent.

Now that we have examined the biblical background, we turn to some observations about a spirituality of celibacy.

Basic Elements for a Biblical Spirituality of Celibacy

This essay is meant to be suggestive rather than comprehensive. Nonetheless I think five areas are crucial to developing a spirituality of celibacy. First, however, I recall four "learnings" from the biblical data, limited as they are.

(1) It is important to note that Jesus, the one to whom we trace our beginnings as Christians, was himself celibate. There is no scriptural evidence that he was ever married. To the contrary, his life seems to have been devoted entirely to God. Absolute fealty to God is uppermost, and abandoning all human endeavors to be utterly devoted to his heavenly Father is quintessential. Furthermore, his foremost apostle Paul (who never met Jesus in the flesh but only as the risen Lord) remained celibate. Celibacy has some strong biblical warrants in Jesus and Paul. One can hardly overlook the fact that these two monumental figures loom large at the very beginning of Christianity.

(2) While the Bible does not explicitly connect celibacy with priesthood, the biblical perspective shows that celibacy is perfectly consonant with it. Indeed, the Bible shows that celibacy is well suited to certain individuals, at certain times and in certain circumstances, precisely because it aids in the specific mission to which God calls them. The Roman Catholic priesthood, as it has evolved over time, is one of those special realities.

For religious priests, in particular, celibacy is part and parcel of what it means to tie oneself freely to a community to give witness to a prophetic ministry of utter devotion to God.

(3) The biblical data suggest that celibacy is countercultural and highly restricted. It is not and has never been intended for everyone. It is a unique gift from God that requires free acceptance of it. If it goes against the grain of a given culture (ours is clearly no exception), that is part of its heritage. Celibacy calls one to look elsewhere for a deeper purpose and goal in life. Celibacy calls one to look beyond. Importantly, celibacy also offers no guarantees. It creates the possibility of closeness with God, of single-minded devotion to God's kingdom, of becoming truly an *alter Christus* in a special way, but it does not guarantee it.[12] In fact, our contemporary situation shows how far removed from the ideal those who embrace celibacy can actually be. Furthermore, if celibates are expected to help lead others to see this deeper reality of God's reign, then they must experience it for themselves, and this is part of the real challenge of this way of life.

(4) Finally, I would note that celibacy is not a gift that can function alone. It must be hinged to some other values that, in fact, are tied explicitly to religious life in the evangelical counsels. I mean values such as prayer, developing a closeness to God and to Christ, obedience to transcendent values and to higher authorities, and simplicity of life (poverty). Celibacy cannot be sustained on its own. Like any good garden, it needs to be watered and fertilized to produce.

What, then, can constitute the biblical underpinnings of celibacy in our day? I point to five aspects of the biblical perspective where we ought to look: theological, christological, pneumatological, eschatological, and ecclesial. The first three are consciously grouped successively because they constitute a trinitarian approach that should be foundational in Christian life, especially the religious life and the priesthood. The Trinity is the primary model of relationship. The threefold Godhead is the quintessential "family," the essence of self-donation in love and friendship to which all are called but which should especially be a hallmark of celibate life.

(1) The theological foundation of celibacy is to be located in utter devotion to God and God's kingdom or rule. Celibates must make God the absolute in their lives.

(2) The christological foundation of celibacy is rooted in the person of Jesus Christ himself. Not only is he the prime model of celibacy by the witness of his life, public ministry, and death but he is also the one whom

celibates strive to incarnate. Becoming an *alter Christus*, another Christ, is at the very heart of celibate life. In word and deed, we are called to imitation of Christ, perfectly and without reservation. This implies befriending Christ, becoming intimate with him in prayer, the sacraments, and the Word of God. Indeed, so transforming should this christological power be that we should be able to cry out with Paul, "I have been crucified with Christ; yet I live, no longer I, but Christ lives in me; insofar as I now live in the flesh, I live by faith in the Son of God who has loved me and given himself up for me" (Gal 2:19-20).

(3) The pneumatological foundation is rooted in the Holy Spirit. According to Paul, celibacy is a gift of the Holy Spirit. The Holy Spirit is the enabler, the font of our ability to live the celibate life. Celibacy means becoming "supple in the Spirit," able to bend and adapt and be transformed by the breath of God.[13] Celibacy cannot be lived alone apart from the Spirit.

(4) The eschatological foundation brings us back to a prophetic dimension of celibacy that is also consonant with religious life. Celibacy is primarily intended to be a symbol. It is liminal and it calls us to live "on the edge." It is profoundly countercultural and viewed by many as out of step, when in reality, it is intended to call us to a more transcendent awareness that there is much more to life than we experience here and now. Prophets embrace a countercultural attitude that is intended to spark in people the hint that God is about more than success, power, money, prestige, and the like, measured in this world's terms. Celibacy can only thrive if it is viewed with an eye to the future, the ultimate future of God's eschatological victory over evil, sin, and death.

(5) Finally, there is an ecclesial dimension to celibacy that is also rooted in Scripture. Celibacy is an institution of the church. From one angle it is appropriate to say that celibates do, in practice, become spouses of the church. The Scriptures note that marriage is an analogy for the love between Christ and the church (Eph 5), and the church has now adopted this in relation to the celibate priesthood.[14] This became particularly prominent in the work of Pope John Paul II.[15] Nonetheless, I must point out that nowhere is it developed in Scripture, especially in relation to the priesthood. It is intended rather as an analogy, a symbol. As such, it has utility but also limitations. As with so many analogies, if one carries it to extremes or interprets it too literally, it can dissolve before our very eyes. More important is to be reminded that celibates relate to the church, the people of God, in terms of service. There is a freeing aspect to single-minded devotion to ministry. Celibates choose to make living for others

and serving them the priority in their lives. In this fashion, they are "married" to the church, the people of God. This is a practical result of a more theological commitment. But we should never allow this to mean that celibacy is a superior way of life. It is not, and the Bible nowhere assesses it thus. It is, rather, a unique calling for those who can accept it.

Conclusion

So where does this information lead? This chapter does not address the Western church's insistence that its priests be celibates. That is a separate question. Rather, I have tried to show that there is, in fact, a biblical foundation to celibacy, freely chosen as a gift from God given to a select few who accept this mysterious invitation from God to follow an unusual path to serve the kingdom of God. Just as the lifestyle of John the Baptist (another celibate in the New Testament) and Jesus himself was an exception to the norm of their day, so will celibacy always be an exception in any era. Yet there is an ongoing validity to the celibate life. It is a witness to an alternative that places the kingdom of God above all other values. It is surely not an easy gift to accept. Even less is it an easy life to live. Yet people—women and men—have been doing it for centuries, whether in religious communities or as an individual commitment. Given the proper spiritual foundations, celibacy becomes a potent sign in the world that God can enter the human arena in most remarkable ways. God can also use certain human instruments who freely accept the invitation to live exclusively for the kingdom for creative ministry. Priests participate in this unique ministry and are sustained in it precisely by our close relationship with Christ, the High Priest.

Chapter Six

"Eunuchs for the Sake of the Kingdom": What Kind of Image?

Perhaps one of the most jarring images from the gospels is Jesus' apparent reference to celibacy through the notion of "eunuchs who have made themselves eunuchs for the sake of the kingdom of heaven" (Matt 19:12). In all my years of priesthood I have never once heard a priest or bishop announce to a congregation that he is a eunuch, for obvious reasons. Eunuchs are castrated men. In most people's eyes they are pitiable. They are not really men at all; they are incomplete, impotent, effeminate, and ultimately outcasts. So why would Jesus have used this image at all? Or did he? And what does the notion of eunuch have to do with celibacy? Is it an image that can say anything about the priesthood today, centuries removed from its historical context?

This chapter seeks to explore the notion from a biblical perspective but with a view to its possible pastoral relevance to the complex question of celibacy in the Roman Catholic priesthood. We proceed in three stages. The first briefly examines the biblical passage itself from the perspective of modern biblical scholarship. The second surveys the image of eunuch in the ancient world to glean some aspects that may provide some explanation of why Jesus would have used the image. The final part proposes reasons why this metaphorical image may still have value for priests today but not because of an inherent connection to priesthood.

Biblical Background to Matthew 19:12

The passage must first be placed in its context in Matthew's gospel. The text on eunuchs occurs in the context of Jesus' teaching on marriage and divorce (Matt 19:3-9), which is given in response to a question from some Pharisees on whether divorce is permissible. In rather stark terms, Jesus forcefully responds that monogamous marriage is inviolable and that divorce (with one exception, "unfaithfulness" or "an unlawful marriage" [Greek, *porneia*]) is not permissible.[1] This answer causes his disciples to respond despondently. The full text of the subsequent exchange provides our context:

> His disciples said to him, "If such is the case of a man with his wife, it is better not to marry." But he said to them, "Not everyone can accept this teaching, but only those to whom it is given. For there are eunuchs who have been so from birth, and there are eunuchs who have been made eunuchs by others, and there are eunuchs who have made themselves eunuchs for the sake of the kingdom of heaven. Let anyone accept this who can." (Matt 19:10-12)

Without desiring to repeat in detail what numerous scientific studies of this passage have concluded, I can summarize what scholars generally say about it.[2]

First, to the question of the authenticity of the saying as coming from Jesus' own lips, as it were (*ipsissima verba*), most scholars conclude affirmatively. For example, John Meier, whose magisterial study of the historical Jesus is incredibly thorough, concludes that it is a genuine saying of Jesus.[3] Moreover, he situates the image of the eunuch with Jesus' own self-identification as a celibate. Although Meier says we cannot know for certain why Jesus himself chose not to get married but to remain celibate, he calls Jesus' celibacy "a parable in action."[4] It was intended to symbolize something deeper, something associated with the kingdom of heaven.[5]

A second task is to understand the passage itself in its Matthean context. Because of its intimate connection with the preceding teaching of Jesus on marriage and divorce, some scholars have denied that the passage is, in fact, about celibacy. They propose that the passage prohibits remarriage after divorce rather than celibacy. While it is clear that the topics are intertwined in this teaching of Jesus, there are good reasons to reject this position. The image of the eunuch can hardly serve appropriately as a model for staying single after divorce, since eunuchs, by definition, cannot properly consummate a marriage or procreate.[6] Furthermore, choosing to become a eunuch (the third of Jesus' three options) does not describe a divorced person, as such. The freely chosen state of becoming a eunuch is different from anything else in the passage, and its tie to the kingdom of heaven places it in a distinct category apart from Jesus' teaching on marriage and divorce.

But what does the passage mean? Jesus mentions three types of eunuchs:

- born eunuchs (through some happenstance of nature)
- eunuchs forcefully castrated (whether by accident or intention)
- eunuchs who choose to be so "for the sake of the kingdom of heaven"

The first two categories were well known in rabbinic circles (with slightly different terminology). This dual definition became the standard description within Judaism of the phenomenon of eunuchs. The third category, however, is novel. It is as if Jesus rejects the disciples' reaction to the hard saying prohibiting divorce and remarriage by thinking that it would be so much simpler to stay single! Not so, Jesus says. His demanding perspective on marriage and divorce carries over to an equally or even more demanding perspective on what it means to purposefully stay single, to embrace a life of celibacy. To be celibate by choice is not an easy way out: "Let anyone accept this who can" (Matt 19:12).[7]

A comment must be made on the phrase translated here as "for the sake of the kingdom of heaven." A crucial question in interpretation is the Greek preposition *dia* (which with the accusative case usually means "on account of" or "because of" or "for the sake of").[8] It is causal. The reason for embracing the unusual condition of being a eunuch, then, lies outside the individual. It is a free choice yet one imposed by the intense desire to focus only on the kingdom of heaven. Note, however, that the choice is not *in order to enter* the kingdom but *because* of it. Celibacy is not a requirement of the kingdom, but the kingdom is the reason some choose freely to become "eunuchs."

It should also be noted that almost no scholars think that Jesus intended the image to be literal. Despite some rare exceptions in the history of Christianity (e.g., Origen of Alexandria in the third century AD), Jesus did not mean that some must castrate themselves *literally* to accept this teaching. Rather, it is a metaphor, and a strong one at that. Before turning to this dimension, we will find it instructive to summarize some further background to eunuchs in the Bible and antiquity.

Eunuchs in the Bible and Antiquity

The OT is fairly uniform in its teaching about eunuchs.[9] Eunuchs were generally despised and seen as unfit to properly belong to the people of Israel. The book of Deuteronomy is quite explicit: "No one whose testicles are crushed or whose penis is cut off shall be admitted to the assembly of the Lord" (Deut 23:1). The reasons for this position are not difficult to grasp. To be a eunuch was to make it impossible to procreate and thus fulfill God's commandment to be fruitful and multiply (Gen 1:28). Moreover, Judaism had a high respect for the unblemished human body (as well as those of animals).[10] Only the unblemished were cultically or ritually pure and thus worthy of sacrifice. By definition, eunuchs were terribly blemished and consequently not worthy of the cultic purity of God's people (e.g., Lev 22:18-25). Eunuchs were also included among those prohibited from being members of the priesthood because of their physical deformity (Lev 21:17-21).

Yet this viewpoint does not tell the whole story. Later writings of the OT show a more nuanced position. Trito-Isaiah, for instance, includes eunuchs in a vision of universality when all will be gathered together under God's lordship:

> Do not let the foreigner joined to the LORD say,
> "The LORD will surely separate me from his people";
> and do not let the eunuch say,
> "I am just a dry tree."
> For thus says the LORD:
> To the eunuchs who keep my sabbaths,
> who choose the things that please me
> and hold fast my covenant,
> I will give, in my house and within my walls,
> a monument and a name better than sons and daughters;
> I will give them an everlasting name
> that shall not be cut off. (Isa 56:3-5)

Even more remarkable is a saying from the wisdom literature:

> Blessed also is the eunuch
> whose hands have done no lawless deed,
> and who has not devised wicked things against the Lord;
> for special favor will be shown him for his faithfulness,
> and a place of great delight in the temple of the Lord. (Wis 3:14)

Exactly what explains this more positive assessment in these postexilic texts is unknown. Perhaps the piety of these eunuchs overshadows their physical defects. Or perhaps, after the experience of the exile, where doubtless some male captives were castrated in order to serve as slaves, the Israelites realized that people were more than their physical makeup.[11]

In any case, the example of the Ethiopian eunuch in Acts (8:26-38) shows that by NT times, being a eunuch did not prohibit one from participating in the kingdom of God or in the new faith. Yet what does any of this have to do with the priesthood?

Some recent biblical studies have pointed to a fruitful direction.

Roles of Eunuchs

Most scholars agree that ancient Egypt, Greece, and Rome did not have the practice of eunuchs except by way of Oriental influence. In the ancient Near East, while it is true that eunuchs were generally looked down upon as inferior and damaged human beings, over time they nonetheless assumed important roles, especially within royal courts.

The Hebrew word for eunuch (*saris*) is often used for royal or court officials, a type of military officer, or a palace attendant. To translate this word, the Septuagint uses the Greek word *eunouchos*, which literally means "keeper of the bed."[12] While it is true that the OT in general looks down upon eunuchs, nevertheless their presence cannot be denied. One recent study of the Hebrew Bible has yielded some interesting observations, which I summarize with several points.[13]

First, the image of the eunuch is surprisingly uniform in the ancient world. Studies of various ancient cultures have shown that the roles eunuchs played, especially in life within the royal household, were quite stable. The primary reason that eunuchs were valued was for their faithfulness and loyalty. It is also true, of course, that some eunuchs were ambitious, devious, and even treacherous, but as a group they were seen as special servants of royalty who could by and large be trusted to be loyal.

Second, across ancient cultures eunuchs were viewed as "liminal" characters.[14] Their unique physical status made them perfect "go-betweens" for men and women. In fact, it may not be an exaggeration to claim that their liminality, their almost marginal identity as not-quite-men but also not women, was their primary source of power. Their unique status gave them a certain respect as "boundary crossers," people who could operate in different environments without posing a threat.

In the book of Esther, for example, they are described as "watchers of the threshold" and in some cases they apparently became instrumental in the transition from one monarchy to another.[15]

Finally, their ability to serve their royal benefactors in trusted positions made them often useful for sensitive diplomatic or political missions. They could function as trusted messengers who could be counted on to negotiate delicate matters without compromising their loyalties.

In sum, while eunuchs often provoked a certain revulsion or even derision among people, they nonetheless rose to function in prominent positions in royal courts and became known as trusted and loyal servants whose services were greatly valued.

This brief synopsis of the value of eunuchs from a historical perspective leads us to the next step, the connection with the priesthood.

Eunuchs and Priesthood

The most obvious point to begin with is that there is no obvious connection between eunuchs and the priesthood whatsoever! In fact, as noted above, the OT excluded eunuchs from the priesthood altogether, since they were, by definition, physically damaged and thus not cultically pure.[16] While it is true that some pagan religions apparently allowed eunuchs in their priesthood, the reasons for this are not clear, and their functionality is hazy, unless it was perhaps for reasons of asceticism.

More important, Jesus' eunuch saying in Matthew is addressed to *all disciples*, whether male or female. Celibacy is an extreme ascetical practice that is not intrinsically related to priesthood. It is only by later church tradition that the Roman Catholic Church has tied celibacy to the priesthood.

One aspect of the theology of a celibate priesthood that has developed in recent years in a distinctive direction, especially during the papacy of John Paul II, is the notion of priests functioning as "spouses" for the church rather than accepting literal spouses.[17] This has become a prominent metaphor today, but one should note that it is not inherently contained in Jesus' call to become eunuchs because of the kingdom of heaven.

So how is it possible that Jesus can speak of "eunuchs because of the kingdom" and that the church connects this image explicitly with a celibate priesthood? I believe the answer to this question lies in five separate realities.

First, based on the fact that most scholars accept Jesus' "eunuch" saying in Matthew's gospel as an authentic *logion*, a likely reason for Jesus having invoked it is precisely because it is so jarring, so radical, so unexpected. The image is a subtle acknowledgment that he was viewed as a marginal person.[18] His own status as a single Jewish male already marked him as outside the norm. Celibacy, though not unknown in Judaism (e.g., the prophet Jeremiah), was highly unusual.[19] Jesus' marital status marked him as, at least, eccentric. It fit with other caricatures of Jesus among his contemporaries that made him look irresponsible and unattractive. He was accused also of being a "drunkard or a glutton" (e.g., Matt 11:19; Luke 7:34), especially in comparison to his ascetical relative, John the Baptist. Moreover, the choice of his friends and acquaintances (tax collectors and prostitutes!) made him even more susceptible to ridicule (e.g., Matt 9:11; 11:19; Luke 5:30; 7:34; 15:1). In short, identifying himself as a voluntary eunuch further delineated his liminality and thus confirmed his unique identity as the "Son of Man" whose mission did not fall within normal religious expectations. His special status as eunuch (= celibate) thus became an essential part of his identity. It also makes the witness value of this position all the more significant. Liminal figures are obviously marginal. In the context of societies organized around power, marginal figures stand out. Yet they can sometimes function well as prophetic voices in a spiritual wilderness (allusions to John the Baptist intentional).

For the church, it became standard to apply this same status to priests. Priests are by nature liminal figures. We are outside the "norm" of society. We are also boundary-crossers, in the sense that we should be able to identify with both women and men in the existential challenges they face in their daily lives.[20] Just as in Jesus' day choosing celibacy was considered by far the exception, and a strange one at that, so in today's highly sexually charged Western society celibacy is seen as, at least, exceptional and perhaps abnormal. But we must be careful in these distinctions. Celibacy can be seen as "nonnatural" (in the sense that it is not the norm), but it should not be seen as "unnatural" (i.e., against nature).[21] Yet the choice does indeed often lead to ridicule or mockery, something that Jesus obviously experienced himself.

A second and related aspect of this image is its ascetical value. Becoming like a eunuch in the voluntary abstinence from genital expression is a kind of "poverty" or "fasting" that indicates a freely chosen ascetical lifestyle. Indeed, some scholars have used such expressions to describe the deeper meaning of celibacy.[22] As an ascetical practice, it has become part and parcel of consecrated life, where it is enshrined as one of the three vows (chastity, poverty, obedience).[23] Indeed, such asceticism fits well with Jesus' own chosen lifestyle and his teaching to put the kingdom of God above all else (Matt 6:33).

Third, the eunuch image—historically speaking, as noted above—also has an inherent connection with trusted, faithful, loyal servants. Eunuchs had the reputation of being faithful servants to their royal masters. The fact that some of them were devious and conniving did not overshadow the overall impression of their fidelity and loyalty.[24] This special status obviously fits well with the expectations of the church's priests. We are called to be good and faithful servants. We are also called to serve the Lord unswervingly, focused only on accomplishing the Lord's will by faithful service to his people.

Fourth, for Jesus as well as for priests today, celibacy—becoming eunuchs for the kingdom of God—is a voluntary choice, not something into which we can be coerced.[25] This is an essential aspect of being eunuchs that is different from the historical reality of eunuchs, who were either born that way or were forcefully castrated for other reasons. This free choice brings with it certain expectations. It does not mean giving up one's entire sexual existence or being asexual. Eunuchs also had their sexual feelings and desires. But sometimes giving into these tendencies could lead them into court intrigue in ways detrimental to their livelihood.

Voluntary eunuchs, however, freely abandon this aspect of their humanity in service to another cause to which they are wholeheartedly devoted. Keeping one's intense sexual desires, attractions, and impulses in check is not easy. It requires great discipline. It does not mean that temptation will never come our way. But acting on them to gratify one's sexual needs genitally is not an option for the voluntary eunuch. Yet another aspect of this issue is the question of how we live out our "generativity" as celibates. To become an authentic self-fulfilled human being does not require literal sexual fulfillment. For that matter, becoming a "parent" does not necessarily mean literally fathering or giving birth to children. Many adoptive parents, some of whom are perhaps incapable of conceiving or giving birth, are exemplary parents, entirely devoted to their "children" and thus well fulfilled in terms of generative urges. For the eunuch, too, generativity must come through other means. For those devoted exclusively to the Lord's service through the celibate priesthood, this means sexual abstinence and single-minded devotion to God.

It might be noted that there is no evidence that eunuchs by their very nature led unhappy, misdirected, or totally unfulfilled lives because of their physical (or in the case of voluntary eunuchs, purposeful) liability. On the contrary, many literal eunuchs led successful and productive lives, often being rewarded significantly for their loyal service to their royal masters. Likewise, despite some popular misconceptions, male celibates today are no less successful or happy than many married men.[26] A negative judgment to the contrary is often based wrongly on the assumed priority of sexual desire over and above any other human inclination. When celibates first accept the gift God gives them, they may not have all of the aspects of this life together at once. Celibacy also requires growth. It must be struggled with, prayed over, and endured. But if it truly is an authentic gift from God, then one's identity ultimately becomes secure in this lifestyle.

Fifth and finally, the church's contemporary teaching on the connection between celibacy and priesthood utilizes this biblical perspective but develops it with deeper theological reflection. Although it is beyond the scope of this chapter to expound the full teaching on celibacy, one can note that *PDV* (29) highlights the free nature of this call to celibacy and emphasizes that it is also a gift from God, a charism that comes to a chosen few. This is quite consistent with Jesus' outlook. The apostolic exhortation goes on to point out the "nuptial meaning" of this celibacy, which points to its generative purpose in a different direction than is normally the case in human existence:

> "This perfect continence for love of the kingdom of heaven has always been held in high esteem by the Church as a sign and stimulus of love, and as a singular source of spiritual fertility in the world." In virginity and celibacy, chastity retains its original meaning, that is, of human sexuality lived as a genuine sign of and precious service to the love of communion and gift of self to others. This meaning is fully found in virginity which makes evident, even in the renunciation of marriage, the "nuptial meaning" of the body through a communion and a personal gift to Jesus Christ and his Church which prefigures and anticipates the perfect and final communion and self-giving of the world to come: "In virginity or celibacy, the human being is awaiting, also in a bodily way, the eschatological marriage of Christ with the Church, giving himself or herself completely to the Church in the hope that Christ may give himself to the Church in the full truth of eternal life." (*PDV*, 29, citing *Lumen Gentium*, 42, and *Familiaris Consortio*, 16, respectively)

While this passage does not summarize all that can be said about celibacy today, it does reinforce much of what has been said above. Celibacy can be and is a valuable gift, given only to some, for a higher service. One cannot overlook the fact, also, that celibacy does have a practical side effect in terms of availability for others. While this is not a primary motivation for requiring celibacy of priests, it in fact serves the ministry well.

Conclusion

So how should we deal with the image of the eunuch today? It is not a comfortable image. It will never be an attractive one either. It clearly serves as a metaphor for certain ascetics, among whom are priests, with a strong biblical foundation in the teaching of Jesus. Yet I think it highly unlikely that priests are suddenly going to embrace this image and announce it from the mountaintops. It is still viewed, and always will be, as too crude, embarrassing, or bizarre to make it an image to be evoked regularly or in a highly visible fashion. But my main goal has been to try to help celibate priests make some sense out of our celibacy as a reality that comes to us from the teaching of Jesus.

I believe Jesus' saying about eunuchs for the kingdom still has value for us today, even if we will never trumpet the notion of the eunuch too loudly. More important is the witness of our lives as happy, fulfilled, faithful, and effective celibates. Insofar as the church applies the image to the priesthood, the metaphor calls attention to the unique status of priests as ascetical and liminal figures who can serve others because of the kingdom of God and not because of any desire for personal gain. By using such an extreme example for a radical and prophetic call to the values of the kingdom of God for those relatively few who can truly accept it, celibacy is an unparalleled gift to the church. In the image of the eunuch we are reminded of the highly exceptional nature of the priesthood. It, too, is not the norm. Priests are exceptional figures called to embrace an ascetical lifestyle that calls them to focus intensely and with single-minded devotion on the values that derive from God's perspective, and not the world's (cf. Mark 8:33; Matt 16:23).

One scholar succinctly summarizes the value of celibacy rooted in Jesus' own teaching and vision of the kingdom of God:

> Thus, Christians may be celibate, not because they are deprived, deformed, or in some way "strange," it is because they are so taken up by the overwhelming presence of God's Lordship that they are existentially incapable of married life. This does not make their life any

> easier, but like Jesus, they are "eunuchs because of the kingdom of heaven," and they ultimately point to that value beyond all values, God's Lordship in the lives of all men and women—married and celibate.[27]

While this may not make us feel any more inclined to loudly proclaim ourselves eunuchs, it does, I hope, reinforce the ongoing value of celibacy for the life of the church. Even if the Roman Catholic Church were to change its practice of mandatory celibacy, that in no way would diminish Jesus' view that there will always be some few liminal characters who will receive the gift of voluntary celibacy for the service of the kingdom of God.

Chapter Seven

The Priest as Poet: Reimagining the Priesthood

Reimagining is not exactly an elegant word. Yet it has become frequently used in recent decades. In religious circles it is a word that means a new and creative way of looking at the present in order to shape the future. Hence one can speak of reimagining church or reimagining parish. The challenge of the future requires the creative use of imagination to raise our sights and focus our vision in order to address the present problems of church and society.

Given the shortage of priests and the challenges faced by priests in the twenty-first century, reimagining the priesthood may be a useful tool to rekindle the spark of ministry that has sometimes been overshadowed by the dark revelations of recent years. This chapter focuses on one possibility for reimagining the priesthood—priest as poet.

An Image Rediscovered

One day some forty years ago, when I was a seminarian, a professor assigned the class to read some rather difficult material from the writings of Karl Rahner. Rahner, one of the greatest Catholic theologians of the twentieth century, was (and is) notorious for being difficult to understand—the bane of a seminarian's existence. I was quite effectively avoiding the inevitable task of doing my assignment by perusing the rest of the book of Rahner's essays, when I ran across a title that caught my eye, "Priest and Poet."[1] I was amazed to find such a fascinating topic in the midst of the otherwise dry theological topics of the book. An explanatory note indicated that Rahner had written this essay as a foreword to a fellow Jesuit's book of poems on the priesthood. As I read the essay, while it still proved to be a challenge to comprehend, I found an oasis in my desert! It gave me a memorable image that has abided over the years and that I have developed to use on priest retreats—"priest *as* poet." Time and again I have returned to this image and found it refreshing. What I have to say is geared specifically to priests, but much of it could apply to anyone engaged in the ministry of the Word, especially bishops or deacons.

Why the Poet?

What makes "poet" an apt image of the minister? In what ways does it connect with the current theology of priesthood? What can it offer the future of ministry in general and the priesthood in particular? These are some questions that give direction and focus to the reflections in this chapter.

The primary definition for a poet in the dictionary is one who writes poems. But the secondary definition is more telling for our purposes: "one who is esp. gifted in the perception and expression of beautiful or lyrical."[2] A poet is primarily one who deals with *words*. This focus on the word is the foundational insight of the notion of priest as poet. This broader description of the poet is the crucial starting point for reflection. Indeed, Rahner begins his essay with the observation, "To the poet is entrusted the word." He notes here the NT's emphasis on the ministry of the Word (Acts 6:4). This sense of the poet, not as writer of poems but as one who effectively uses the power of language to express reality, puts us in the heart of the ministry of the Word.

When the council fathers of Vatican II wanted to describe the ministry of priests in chapter 2 of their Decree on the Ministry and Life of Priests, they first enunciated the concept of "Priests as Ministers of God's Word" (*PO*, 4). The initial statement of this chapter says, "The People of God is formed into one in the first place by the Word of the living God, which is quite rightly sought from the mouth of priests." Priests are intimately bound to the Word of God and are to be effective expositors of it by their preaching. As the document says further,

> the priest's preaching, often very difficult in present-day conditions, if it is to become more effective in moving the minds of his hearers,

> must expound the Word of God not merely in a general and abstract way but by an application of the eternal truth of the Gospel to the concrete circumstances of life. (4)

Pastores Dabo Vobis, Pope John Paul II's exhortation from the 1990 synod on priestly formation, more recently has bolstered this image.

> The priest is first of all a minister of the word of God. He is consecrated and sent forth to proclaim the good news of the kingdom to all. . . . For this reason, the priest himself ought first of all to develop a great personal familiarity with the word of God. Knowledge of its linguistic or exegetical aspects, though certainly necessary, is not enough. He needs to approach the word with a docile and prayerful heart so that it may deeply penetrate his thoughts and feelings and bring about a new outlook in him—"the mind of Christ" (1 Cor. 2:16). (26)

Ultimately the Word of God changes one's vision and gives direction to one's life. Consequently, studying, praying with, and meditating upon God's Word is a task inherent to the priesthood and to the duty of all ministers of the Word.

Qualities of the Poet

For the image of the poet to be useful for priesthood, we should be able to describe some of the qualities of poets that would be appropriate to the priesthood. Of course, poetry is a gift. Poets are born, not made. Yet poets possess qualities and exercise skills that are able to be acquired or at least imitated by others. I propose five such skills that are central to the task of the poet.

(1) The primary skill that poets develop is the keen power of *observation*. Poets hone their vision so that they are able to see more deeply than most people into everyday occurrences. As Samuel Johnson, the eighteenth-century author and lexicographer, once said, "To a poet nothing can be useless."[3] When poets see a sunset or the late afternoon play of light on a forest, they see more than scientific phenomena. Their observations penetrate to a deeper level where they see hidden connections and insights. Poets often struggle for this vision, but they achieve it by means of concentration and diligence. Flannery O'Connor, the American Catholic writer of fiction, described it thus:

> The poet is traditionally a blind man, but the Christian poet, and storyteller as well, is like the blind man whom Christ touched, who looked then and saw men as if they were trees, but walking. This is the beginning of vision, and it is an invitation to deeper and stranger visions.[4]

Poets, then, are people who *see* more than meets the eye and are able to express what they see to others. John Ruskin, the great art critic and philosopher, pointed out the power of this kind of sight:

> The greatest thing a human soul ever does in this world is to *see* something, and tell what it saw in a plain way. Hundreds of people can talk for one who can think, but thousands can think for one who can see. To see clearly is poetry, prophecy, and religion,—all in one.[5]

(2) Poets are profoundly in touch with the *essential experiences of human existence*, such as life, death, sex, love, violence, war, hatred, God, and mystery. Poets have the ability to plumb the depths of the mundane and to see humanity in all its minute details. This is particularly true of the sadder dimensions of human experience. Historically, poets have often been people who have led rather tragic lives, for instance, Edna St. Vincent Millay, Anne Sexton, Edgar Allan Poe, and Maya Angelou. Perhaps their personal experience of human emotion gives them a sixth sense to dig deep into the wells of human souls. Although one need not see this experience of harsh realities as a prerequisite for a good poet, surely suffering, the darker side of life, has a way of molding an individual's abilities to perceive profound human experiences and to speak of them in depth. At the very least, poets have an empathetic ability to enter into others' suffering without being overwhelmed by it.

(3) Poets understand the *power of words*. They paint pictures with words that allow people to see something as they have never seen it before. Words are not merely descriptive but help to create the reality they describe. Poetic vision sets ideals before people so that they can reach for the intangible. Little wonder that poets are often present at the start of a new presidency (e.g., Robert Frost, Maya Angelou). Joseph Conrad, another famous writer, described this aspect well:

> My task which I am trying to achieve is, by the power of the written word, to make you hear, to make you feel—it is, before all, to make you *see*. That—and no more, and it is everything.[6]

Another more recent writer wrote, when reviewing a book of poems by the great contemporary poet Mary Oliver, a description of the vocation of a poet with these words: "to urge the reader to bear witness to the world with unreserved fervor and thus to live more abundantly."[7] Poets help people live life to the fullest extent, something harmonious to Jesus' own ministry as described in the Gospel of John: "I came so that they might have life and have it more abundantly" (John 10:10b, NABRE).

(4) Poets emphasize *comparisons, contrasts, and parallels* in such a way that the familiar is understood in a different fashion. They have the ability to note similarities or incongruities in life so that analogies, similes, or metaphors may make life more understandable.

(5) Finally, poets are *mediators*. They stand between the rest of humanity and the mystery of life. They straddle the line between mystery and the mundane. They become true bridges that allow people to cross the boundaries from one reality to another. Poets provide new avenues for the divine to touch the human sphere through the power of words and for people to reach out to God through the same medium. This is an aspect of the church's expectation of priests as expressed in *PDV*:

> In order that his ministry may be humanly as credible and acceptable as possible, it is important that the priest should mold his human personality in such a way that it becomes a bridge and not an obstacle for others in their meeting with Jesus Christ the redeemer of humanity. (43)

Before seeing how these qualities apply further to the priesthood, a comment on how the Bible itself, as God's Word, embodies some of these qualities will be instructive.

Poetry and the Bible

Even a cursory glance at the Bible shows that there are large sections of poetry in it. Whole books, such as Psalms and Proverbs, consist of blocks of poetry, some of which is hymnic and was originally accompanied by musical instruments. Much of the wisdom literature is poetry, along with many of the prophetic books, such as Jeremiah and Isaiah. The NT also contains poetry, although on a much smaller scale than the OT. One can find poetic sections of the NT in the parables of Jesus (Mark 4:1-41 and Matt 13:1-53), in the Sermon on the Mount (Matt 5–7), or in the letters of Paul (e.g., Phil 2:6-11; Col 1:15-20).

How and why does poetry find its way into the Bible? There are doubtless complex reasons. For one thing, poetry helps people enter into sublime mystery. It opens doors and invites people to enter the realm where

God can be met on a different level. Since the Bible consciously wrestles with the mystery of God, it is no surprise to find poetry in it.

Another important idea is that poetry fosters memorization. Much of the Bible originated in oral tradition. Rhyme, rhythm, and repetition characteristic of poetry helped to preserve important traditions for future generations. Furthermore, poetry expresses basic truths in concise and formulaic fashion. This is especially true of the wisdom literature. The poetic form of the proverb allowed succinct observations about life to be encapsulated in an easily digestible format. Thus, the wisdom literature recorded the observations of the wise in their culture to instruct young people in the ways of God and the ways of the world.

Two brief illustrations are instructive. Proverbs 10:12 poetically and succinctly states a basic truth so profound that it is used by several other NT books: "Hatred stirs up strife / but love covers all offenses" (cf. 1 Cor 13:7; Jas 5:20).

Another passage from Proverbs compares by means of a poetic wisdom formula several common realities as expressive of mysterious aspects of the world:

> Three things are too wonderful for me;
> four I do not understand:
> the way of an eagle in the sky,
> the way of a snake on a rock,
> the way of a ship on the high seas,
> and the way of a man with a girl. (30:18-19)

Both examples provide memorable and pithy comment on deeper aspects of human existence. The poetry in the Bible is thus a means of appropriating the deeper truths of life and passing them on.

Poetry and the Priesthood

There are two ways that poetry particularly relates to the life of a priest as a minister of the Word. The first concerns prayer, the second preaching.

Poetry and Prayer

"The world is charged with the grandeur of God," wrote the Jesuit poet Gerard Manley Hopkins.[8] At the heart of any understanding of the relationship between poetry and ministry is the acceptance of poetry as a conduit of prayer. Prayer is the lifeblood of the priesthood. In the humdrum of everyday life it is prayer that keeps the priest's life in focus. Because God's grandeur fills the world, prayer finds a profound expression in the beauty of the word experienced in everyday life. Prayer and poetry go together because they are twin gateways into the mystery of God. To insist that priests and other ministers of the Word become poets, or at least engender a poetic vision of life as they go about their daily tasks, is to call them to deeper prayer. And prayer finds its expression profoundly in poetry. So essential is poetry to a prayerful vision of life that Karl Rahner comments, "In its inmost essence, the poetic is a prerequisite for Christianity."[9]

The basic Christian insight is indeed that "the Word became flesh and dwelt among us" (John 1:14). The poetry so evident in the prologue of John's gospel (1:1-18) enters into life in the mystery of the incarnation. Jesus Christ is God's poem given to the world. The poet innately grasps this essential truth: "the incomprehensible itself, as grace and mercy, has entered the human word."[10] And the proper response to this mystery is prayer in that sacred presence.

This same aspect is affirmed in *PDV* with regard to the role of priests in helping people explore the mysteries of human existence. The exhortation says,

> It is necessary that, following the example of Jesus who "knew what was in humanity" (Jn. 2:25; cf. 8:3-11), the priest should be able to know the depths of the human heart, to perceive difficulties and problems, to make meeting and dialogue easy, to create trust and cooperation, to express serene and objective judgments.
>
> Future priests should therefore cultivate a series of human qualities, not only out of proper and due growth and realization of self, but also with a view to the ministry. (43)

Poetry and prayer thus become avenues that help human beings arrive at a deeper awareness of their existence as creatures of God the Creator.

The Liturgy of the Hours

The Liturgy of the Hours is one aspect of prayer that sometimes gets neglected in the life of some priests, but this is unfortunate. True enough, pastoral duties, especially in a time of priest shortage, can be so predominant that priests become too tired and preoccupied to give much time to the Liturgy of the Hours, despite the ordination promise to do so.

Or the recitation of the psalms can become so routine that their inherent poetic beauty is lost on the one praying them. The Liturgy of the Hours celebrates the poetry of the Bible in an unparalleled fashion, especially in its use of psalms and canticles.[11] The book of Psalms is one place in the Bible that, in the form of poetry and song, humans speak their words to God rather than the other way around! The psalms are testimony to the breadth of human emotion in crying out to God in prayer. The psalms evidence effective prayer, whether one is happy or sad, alone or with others, fearful or courageous, sorrowing or rejoicing. The psalms are both individual and communal prayers, laments and songs of praise, hymns of thanksgiving and prayers of petition. St. Athanasius (d. 373) described the psalms beautifully in a well-known letter:

> Among all the books [of the Bible], the Psalter has certainly a very special grace, a choiceness of quality well worthy to be pondered; for, besides the characteristics which it shares with others, it has this peculiar marvel of its own, that within it are represented and portrayed in all their great variety the movements of the human soul. . . . For I think that in the words of this book all human life is covered, with all its states and thoughts, and that nothing further can be found in the human person. (11)[12]

The psalms, then, represent centuries of poetic reflection on the multiple situations of human existence and the recognition of God's relationship to people in the diverse contexts of their lives. In the psalms women and men who have reflected long and hard on the circumstances of their lives cry out to God in precise ways that correspond to their feelings. In times of oppression, they cried out in supplication for God's redemption. In times of sorrow they cried out in lament. In times of joy they cried out in praise and thanksgiving.

Viewing the psalms from their poetic foundation can help priests rediscover an aspect of the Liturgy of the Hours that has at least been undervalued in recent times—its poetic power. As Athanasius would phrase it, the psalms must "become like a mirror to the person singing them, so that he might perceive himself and the emotions of his soul" (ibid., 12). There can be, however, a stumbling block to appreciating the psalms to the fullest extent. The current translation of the psalms in the Liturgy of the Hours has serious limitations. Indeed, the translation of the psalms for the revised lectionary was such a controversial issue that it held up the recent revision of the OT of the New American Bible. Controversial or not, for private use, there are some fresh and crisp translations of the psalms that have become available that may rekindle the power of the Psalter in one's general prayer life.[13] If they help promote one's thirst for praying the psalms more from the heart, they are certainly worth considering.

Poetry and Preaching

The second area flows from the life of prayer. The prayerful priest is the one who can speak from the heart and thereby touch others' hearts. Preaching is where all of the aspects of priest as minister of the Word come together. Preaching is the very heart and soul of priestly ministry. It is also where a reimagining of priest as poet is most necessary.

One has heard rather consistently in recent decades of complaints about the quality of Catholic preaching. In my seminary days, Andrew Greeley, the priest sociologist, was one who had sounded the clarion call for better preaching on the basis of his sociological analyses. Moreover, it is clear that many members of newer, evangelical communities are disaffected Catholics, who state that among the reasons for leaving the Catholic Church was the lackluster preaching and the lack of any clear explanation of the Bible from the pulpit. Although polls have shown some growth in the appreciation of Catholic preaching from the pulpit, there is still considerable evidence of dissatisfaction. Experts have called for improvement in the quality of preaching among priests (and deacons). Many have called for more effective training in seminaries, which have responded by trying to beef up courses in homiletics and promoting better contact between homiletic and Scripture classes. Some find homilies too boring and unrelated to daily life. Others find little spiritual insight or enrichment. Still others complain about the content of homilies, finding too much pop psychology or moralizing or expounding of the preacher's most recent pet peeve, and too little clear and concise elucidation of the Scriptures as the Word of God. No one can deny, however, that in comparison to other means of modern communication preaching presents priests with a real challenge.

The fact is that many fine improvements have been made in seminary formation programs in the area of homiletics and also in Scripture study. But has it been enough?

Preaching is an enormously challenging task for priests. Not everyone is a gifted preacher. There will inevitably be differences in quality among preachers. Nonetheless, as long as preaching is considered a primary aspect of ordained ministry, there must be ways of shaping how it is accomplished. Reimagining the priest as poet may help.

Poets have some of those qualities most applicable to good preaching. Poets know the power of the word, are experts at observation, penetrate the analogies and incongruities of life, and inspire others to a deeper vision. They are deeply in touch with human life, with all its joys and sorrows. Poets effectively use human imagination in their art, yet they also communicate a transcendent reality beyond human appearances. Ultimately, poets—like good ministers—are effective mediators between the human and the divine.

One scholar, Walter Brueggemann, has summarized this challenge well:

> The event of preaching is an event in transformed imagination. Poets, in the moment of preaching, are permitted to perceive and voice the world differently, to dare a new phrase, a new picture, a fresh juxtaposition of matters long known. Poets are authorized to invite a new conversation, with new voices sounded, new hearings possible. The new conversation may end in freedom to trust and courage to relinquish. The new conversation, on which our very lives depend, requires a poet and not a moralist.[14]

Archbishop George Niederauer of San Francisco, who is trained in English literature, once gave a presentation to seminary formation personnel in which he quoted a poetic passage that summarized well this position:

> As evangelists we priests are mediators of meaning to a culture submerged in chaos and confusion. We speak of mystery and meaning to a people whose allegiance is to comfort and consumption. When we dare to name injustice and sin, we see with the poet's eye the drama of grace unfolding all about us. As bearers of the Word we have the transforming task of naming grace. To those who are disgraced, we name grace. To those diseased, we speak the name of the one who heals. To those without hope, we name the One who is light to all who are in darkness. If there is any authenticity to our preaching, we, like Bernanos' country priest, have slowly come to see that all is grace.[15]

The Directory on the Ministry and Life of Priests (DMLP)[16] emphasizes the delicate balance necessary for good priestly preaching. On the one hand, the priest is charged with transmitting the faith. Good preaching will have solid content, reflecting careful attention to the Scriptures themselves and to doctrinal truths essential to the life of the church. In this regard the document says,

> Preaching, therefore, cannot be reduced to the presentation of one's own thought, to the manifestation of personal experience, to simple explanations of a psychological, sociological or humanitarian nature; nor can it excessively concentrate on rhetoric, so often found in mass-communication. (45)

On the other hand, the document continues,

> In order to be effective and credible, the priest, within the perspective of the faith and his ministry, and with a constructively critical outlook, must be familiar with the ideology, language, cultural intricacies and the typologies diffused in the mass media and which, to a large part, conditions the attitudes of society. (46)

The American bishops themselves addressed this issue earlier in their excellent document Fulfilled in Your Hearing, a publication that still retains its usefulness despite the intervening years since its original publication.[17] They emphasize the role that the study of humanities plays in shaping the abilities of priests to preach:

> The great artistic and literary achievements of a culture are surely a privileged means of access to the heart and mind of a people. Regular and sustained contact with the world's greatest literature or with its painting, sculpture, and musical achievements can rightfully be regarded by preachers not simply as leisure time activity but as part of their ongoing professional development. The same can be said of attention to modern entertainment media—television, film, radio—or to theater.[18]

In effect they encourage priests to become poets in their own right. Preaching is an art, but artists must consistently improve their skills in order to become more effective. Flannery O'Connor once more offers a view of this process when she observes,

> When people have told me that because I am a Catholic, I cannot be an artist, I have had to reply, ruefully, that because I am a Catholic, I cannot afford to be less than an artist.[19]

What she says about Catholics in general applies to all ministers of the Word and even more directly to priests. We can be no less than artists. Poets are artists of the written word. They paint pictures with words that allow others to see that which otherwise would remain invisible, intangible, and difficult to grasp.

Preaching the Lectionary

An aspect of preaching that should not be forgotten is the role of the lectionary. The layout of the lectionary virtually demands a poetic vision in preachers. Finding legitimate connections between the readings as they are designed in the lectionary requires a sensitivity to imagery and themes, comparisons and contrasts. Effective preaching from the lectionary also demands that the priest take the time needed for prayerful reflection on the readings of the day. One must sit at length, carefully reading and observing the movements in the text, in order to perceive how the Word of God speaks today. This action, a form of *lectio divina*, should really be a part of the priest's daily spiritual life. The Eucharist provides the setting wherein the priest himself is nourished by the very sacrament he celebrates for his people, as Vatican II describes it:

> Those actions by which Christians draw nourishment through the Word of God from the double table of holy Scripture and the Eucharist hold a preeminent place above all spiritual aids. Everybody knows how important their continuous use is for the personal sanctification of priests. (*PO*, 18)

Regular and careful reflection on the lectionary readings can consequently sharpen one's poetic skills of observation.[20] It should also be noted that the Synod on the Word of God (2008) devoted a considerable amount of energy on the question of *lectio divina*, which is a favorite topic of Pope Benedict XVI. This topic was an aspect of the pope's post-synodal apostolic exhortation *Verbum Domini*, which appeared in late 2010.[21] Among the many interesting teachings in this lengthy document are the call for more *lectio divina* (86–87), meditation on the Scriptures, and the expressed desire for the design of a "Directory on Homiletics" as an aid to preachers (60). The exhortation also emphasizes throughout that the Scriptures are God's Word in human words, implicitly acknowledging the need to understand the value of the human communication to which the Bible bears witness and yet which also brings to us God's own message. If we preachers can answer the call to improve our preaching, we will go a long way to fostering the vision of appreciating God's Word proclaimed by this latest church teaching.

Conclusion

This chapter has explored only two areas where a rediscovery of the poetic might enliven priestly ministry. Prayer and preaching are obviously critical aspects of contemporary priestly ministry. A poetic vision alone is not going to rejuvenate priesthood or ministry in general. Obviously, a complex set of skills is needed for effective ministry. Yet, reimagining ministry and priesthood in the image of the poet may well breathe some new life into a tired body. To become a poet in the sense described here is not easy. Poetic vision, to some degree, is a gift and not merely a skill. It is not simply a matter of picking up a book of poems to read, although reading poetry is essential to developing one's poetic sensibilities. The task, rather, requires quiet time for reflection and reading, for meditation and prayer, for poetic rumination on the ebb and flow of life. Some good skills for keen observation and prayerful meditation can be learned. Most of all it requires allowing the Word of God to gestate deeply within our beings so that the poet within us can be born again.

Chapter Eight

The Priest as Sage: Retrieving a Neglected Model

The fiftieth anniversaries of the opening and closing of the Second Vatican Council (1962–65) are close at hand. As has occurred in the wake of other ecumenical councils in the church's history, it fostered considerable changes and discussion. Indeed much discussion continues to take place today about the nature and identity of ministry in the Roman Catholic Church. In particular, some literature after the council complained that the priesthood was being watered down by the proliferation of other "ministries." On the other hand, Vatican II fostered the growth of other ministries that have greatly enriched the church. As we move further away from the council and further into the third Christian millennium, one can rightly ask, What shape will priestly ministry take as the church moves forward?

There is, of course, no crystal ball that can give us the answer. Yet, Vatican II itself lends some direction. Tucked away in a small section of *Gaudium et Spes*, the Pastoral Constitution on the Church in the Modern World, is a quotation that is often overlooked. In the context of a statement praising human reason and the need to search for truth, the Constitution provides a vision of the need for wisdom to confront the world's problems:

> The intellectual nature of the human person reaches its final perfection, and needs to do so, through the wisdom which gently draws the human mind to seek and love what is true and good, and which leads

> it through visible realities to those which are invisible. The present age more than ever requires such wisdom to humanise its new discoveries. The future of the world is at risk if wiser people are not forthcoming. (15)[1]

What is said here of human beings in general applies even more specifically to those engaged in professional ministry, whether ordained or not. The rest of this chapter reexamines a neglected model of ministry, namely, the sage, which embodies the need for wisdom expressed in Vatican II.

Models of Ministry

Modern theology has shown the usefulness of "models." For example, theologians have proposed various models of the church, of ministry, and even of Jesus, which help to interpret aspects of these realities. The late Cardinal Avery Dulles (1918–2008), one of the finest American Catholic theologians of the twentieth century, contributed greatly to this conversation. His book *Models of the Church*, which I appreciated as a young seminarian, started the trend in looking for various heuristic "models" that could help explain some of the complexity of theological concepts today.[2]

There are also models of ministry. The traditional models that the church has used and especially applied to ordained ministries are the three biblical models of priest, prophet, and king. Each of these biblical figures represents an essential aspect of the ministerial priesthood as it finds its fullest expression in Jesus Christ, the High Priest. The model of priest focuses on cultic and ritual aspects of ministry. The model of prophet emphasizes both the ministry of Word, being the mouthpiece of God, and the ministry of social justice, calling people back to the ethics of covenantal life. Finally, the model of king stresses both the shepherding function and authority.

In his exhortation published after the 1990 synod of bishops on the formation of priests, *Pastores Dabo Vobis*, Pope John Paul II reinforced these three traditional models under the categories of prophet, priest, and shepherd. It is interesting to note, however, as I mentioned in chapter 1 above, that this document is not organized according to the three traditional categories of priest, prophet, and king, in the fashion of *Presbyterorum Ordinis*, for example, where the order is teacher, priest, and king (*PO*, 1, 4–6).[3] These notions are present throughout *PDV* but they are distributed in a novel way. Doing so allows for new emphases to come to the fore.

In particular, the pope explains the three traditional categories according to the three major areas of responsibility of the ministerial priesthood: word, sacraments, and pastoral charity. This changes the emphases significantly, but always within the framework of the threefold priestly character of the ministry of Jesus Christ.

With this background in mind, I propose that another biblical model exists that is consistently neglected and that I believe has contemporary significance for the way we view ministry, and closely matches the vision of *Gaudium et Spes* quoted above.

The Wisdom Tradition

Catholicism, more than Protestant traditions, makes use of the wisdom tradition of the Bible.[4] Books, such as the Wisdom of Solomon and the Wisdom of Ben Sirach, that are not found in the Protestant canon of Scripture are frequently used in the Catholic lectionary. A primary reason seems to be the practical orientation of these wisdom traditions. The wisdom literature of the Bible often addresses such basic human questions as the nature of the family; roles of parents and children; the problem of old age; the mystery of human love and sexuality; and common virtues like humility, obedience, honesty, truthfulness, loyalty, and kindness. These principles apply to virtually any human society, but they are also, in the Judeo-Christian tradition, characteristic of people of faith.

Another aspect of the wisdom tradition is the nature of the wisdom figures in Israel's history who were the caretakers of these ancient traditions.[5] Sages formed "schools" that preserved accumulated wisdom and taught it to children. While the wisdom schools seem to have been primarily a male institution, interestingly the wisdom tradition itself idealizes wisdom in the figure of a woman, "the wisdom woman" (Prov 1:20-33; Sir 24:1-31). This female figure is a personification of an aspect of God that is said to have been with God from the beginning and to have participated in the creation of the universe (Prov 8:22-31). She beckons to the hearer to come and acquire her knowledge so that life can be lived properly in accordance with God's will. The attraction of this image can be seen in two excerpts from the Bible. At the beginning of the book of Proverbs, we read,

> Wisdom cries out in the street;
> in the squares she raises her voice.
> At the busiest corner she cries out;
> at the entrance of the city gates she speaks:

"How long, O simple ones, will you love being simple?
How long will scoffers delight in their scoffing
and fools hate knowledge?
Give heed to my reproof;
I will pour out my thoughts to you;
I will make my words known to you." (1:20-23)

This is clearly a call to heed wisdom, but her origins in the God of all creation are seen even more clearly in an excerpt from Sirach:

Wisdom praises herself,
and tells of her glory in the midst of her people.
In the assembly of the Most High she opens her mouth,
and in the presence of his hosts she tells of her glory:
"I came forth from the mouth of the Most High,
and covered the earth like a mist.
I dwelt in the highest heavens,
and my throne was in a pillar of cloud.
Alone I compassed the vault of heaven
and traversed the depths of the abyss.
Over waves of the sea, over all the earth,
and over every people and nation I have held sway. . . .
Before the ages, in the beginning, he created me,
and for all the ages I shall not cease to be.
In the holy tent I ministered before him,
and so I was established in Zion." (24:1-6, 9-10)

This is a sweeping vision of the wisdom woman who preexisted with God, comes from God, participates in God's act of creation, and ultimately finds a home in Israel (Zion) in order to instruct God's chosen people properly in the ways of wisdom. Paradoxically, this feminine *ideal* of wisdom seldom appears in the biblical tradition in the *tangible* image of specific women.[6] Although women are also said to be vehicles for wisdom (Prov 1:8; 31:1, 26), they are overshadowed by the image of men, probably owing to the dominance of a patriarchal society. Despite this limitation of the biblical foundations of the wisdom tradition, the ideal of wisdom is assuredly a universal call shared by women and men alike (Prov 1:7; cf. Deut 31:12; Neh 8:2-3).

Some forty years ago Walter Brueggemann, a creative Protestant biblical scholar who continues to publish creative studies in biblical theology, proposed that wisdom literature provided an alternative style of ministry.[7] In contrast to the traditional models of priest, prophet, and king, he suggested that a wisdom model would focus on other aspects of ministry more suited to a pluralistic society. Brueggemann offered a tentative analysis of this model, but his suggestions tantalize further reflection when applied to the Roman Catholic priesthood today. I suggest this is a model worth retrieving from the dustbins of biblical history.

Aspects of a Wisdom Model

Despite the risk of being overly simplistic, it is possible to outline some basic aspects of the figure of the sage in the Bible. The wisdom figures were especially keen observers of human life.[8] One cannot read the accumulated sayings of the book of Proverbs, Ben Sirach, the book of Wisdom, or Qoheleth (the pessimist of the group) without recognizing their deep insight into human nature with both its strengths and its foibles. Moreover, this perspective on humanity shows up in an incarnational view of creation. Creation itself is the locus for God's revelation.

People sometimes wrongly view this basic orientation of wisdom literature as secular or antireligious. The biblical wisdom tradition rarely mentions such basic religious concepts as redemption, salvation history, or revelation. But it would be false to assume that these are totally absent from the wisdom tradition. They are a subdued or subtle assumption rather than an expressed belief. They are operative in the background of the wisdom traditions. Indeed, wisdom itself is not the mere accumulation of human wisdom over time but is a gift of God (Prov 2:6; cf. 3:5). "The fear of the Lord is the beginning of wisdom" (Prov 9:10; Ps 111:10; cf. Prov 1:7; Job 28:28). This continuous refrain in the wisdom literature is an acknowledgment that wisdom comes from God and not merely from human insight.[9] The true sage is one who "fears" the Lord, that is, humbly stands in respectful awe of the Creator who is the source of all life, all knowledge, and all wisdom. If the sages seldom overtly mention basic religious concepts that are so central to the law and the prophets, it is more because of a presumed background rather than oversight.

The Model of Priest as Sage

Applying the basic model of the sage to the contemporary setting is not a question of an absolute one-to-one correspondence. But within a general framework the wisdom literature provides an orientation toward ministry that I believe fits the context well today. I will begin by describing basic elements of this model and conclude with observations on how this model is inherently present in the vision of ministry, especially the priesthood, offered in *PDV*.

(1) Sages in Israel were generally the elders in the community. The Bible makes a connection between wisdom and age. However, they did not perceive this connection naively. While youths often were too hasty and impatient to achieve true wisdom, simply living a long life did not guarantee wisdom. Wisdom was primarily a gift from God, acquired in old age and refined in lengthy and careful reflection. But it could also be taught to young people, and for this reason they established schools in which the elders could pass on wisdom from one generation to another.

(2) The sage is especially a professional observer of human life. To discern where God is most visibly present and active in people's lives requires careful attention to detail and to judgment. People often call upon their priests precisely to help them discern what God is saying to them in their lives. The process of keen observation and discernment in human life is characteristic of the professional ministry. Pope John Paul II directly applied this to priesthood in an address to priests:

> We need heralds of the Gospel who are *experts in humanity* who have shared to the full the joys and sorrows of our day, but who at the same time are contemplatives in love with God. [10]

(3) The sage is a consultant rather than a guru. In Israel, sages did not provide all the answers to life's questions. Although they wrestled with very serious life questions, such as innocent suffering (Job) and futility in life (Qoheleth), they did not give answers. Instead, they reflect at length on the problem and draw people back to the mystery of human life. Sages did not flee to traditional religious language to provide easy answers to complex questions. A temptation today is for people to expect that their priests and professional ministers provide easy answers when what is really needed is more prayerful reflection and discernment on the complexities of contemporary life.

(4) Wisdom figures preserved the religious traditions of Israel more in the background than in the foreground. They were not antireligious or antispiritual. Instead, they recognized that overtly religious language could sometimes deceive and give one false security. Ultimate faith in God did not mean abandoning the powers of human reason. One might say from a modern perspective that the sages resisted attempts to be fundamentalist in their outlook.

(5) The sages were extremely pragmatic and pastoral. Their concerns were those that affected daily life and responded to people's genuine pastoral needs. They invited dialogue within the context of a complex, pluralistic society. Much of the later wisdom literature of the Bible (e.g., Wisdom and Sirach) reflects both a dialogue with and an adaptation of secular Hellenistic culture. They helped to give people proper tools to cope with contemporary society.

The Sage Model and the Vision of Priesthood Today

While this model applies appropriately to all forms of professional ministry, I believe a particular application can be made to the priesthood today. Pope John Paul II's pastoral exhortation *Pastores Dabo Vobis* grew out of the 1990 synod on the formation of priests. While it does not address every aspect of priesthood, I believe it provides an interesting and challenging view of the priesthood that can orient us to the future. Although it is probably unintentional, *PDV* inherently contains many elements of the wisdom model described above. I will point to five of its significant features.

One feature that *PDV* mentions explicitly is the context of contemporary priestly ministry—*pluralism* (51). Pluralism is reflected in both society and the church. In the midst of such pluralism priests as well as other ministers need to have abilities to reflect on the complexities of modern life with some sophistication and to dialogue convincingly with a wide variety of people. The sages of ancient Israel were experts in such a context. Much OT wisdom originated in the influence of other cultures but was adapted for use within the religion of Israel. Wise adaptation demands careful discernment so as not to dilute the truth one seeks to protect.

A second feature is the foundational type of priestly formation called for by *PDV*—*human formation* (43), which was treated more formally in chapter 1 above. Significantly this is the first category treated under the "areas of priestly formation." Without appropriate human formation, the priest becomes more of a stumbling block for people rather than a "bridge . . . for others in their meeting with Jesus Christ the Redeemer of humanity" (*PDV*, 43). The call for basic human formation in the priesthood is an incarnational principle at home in the wisdom tradition. God chooses to be revealed within the context of human experience. Basic insight into human nature becomes also an avenue for exploring God in relation to the world. The sages of Israel were indeed "experts in humanity" who knew "the depths of the human heart" and attempted to accurately describe the experience of being human.

The catalogue of human qualities and virtues that *PDV* lists for priests, accompanied by an "intense spiritual life," sounds idealistic but expresses many of the common qualities and virtues exalted by the wisdom tradition. In a leadership role *PDV* calls the priest to embody

> faithfulness, integrity, consistency, wisdom, a welcoming spirit, friendliness, goodness of heart, decisive firmness in essentials, freedom from overly subjective viewpoints, personal disinterestedness, patience, an enthusiasm for daily tasks, confidence in the value of the hidden workings of grace as manifested in the simple and the poor (cf. Ti. 1:7-8). (26)

The third feature is the emphasis on *intellectual formation* of priests (51). *PDV* is quite insistent on this point. The complexities of modern life, especially in the area of moral theology, demand not less but more intellectually sophisticated priests. Again, biblical wisdom figures offer a model. The incessant questioning and the ceaseless search for ways to understand life's deep mysteries inspired the sages of Israel to an endless quest for truth. Sometimes it led to discouragement as in the case of Qoheleth, but more often it exhilarated them to seek further. Intellectual curiosity is not a panacea; it does not guarantee answers. But such an approach recognizes the limits of human reason while always moving it beyond the status quo.

The fourth feature is the related attitude toward *ongoing formation* (*PDV*, 70–81). Despite a sometimes lackadaisical attitude among some priests toward ongoing education, *PDV* notes how necessary this aspect of formation is for priests today. *PDV* gives enormous attention in its final chapter to the need for priests to submit to ongoing formation. *PDV* points out that "[p]ermanent or ongoing formation, precisely because it is 'permanent,' should always be a part of the priest's life. In every phase and condition of his life, at every level of responsibility he has in the Church, he is undergoing formation" (76). This is beyond mere educational efforts. Rather, *PDV* envisions formation in its broadest sense, the holistic formation of the entire person. Priests need continual renewal in order to avoid either burnout or irrelevance. This too is an attitude of the wisdom schools. The sages viewed persistent striving after wisdom as a lifelong task. One can never cease being a learner.

The final feature is the Holy Father's call in *PDV* for priests to truly become *presbyters*, "elders" in the "noblest and richest sense of the word"

(26). As the wisdom figures of old were respected for age and experience and accepted the task to train others as their successors, so do priests today need to become elders in their pastoral communities and for one another. *PDV* explicitly encourages older priests to take on the task of shepherding younger priests. The wisdom schools functioned in just such a fashion, assuring that the collective wisdom of the group would be learned and passed on to future generations. The modern term perhaps is "mentoring," but the goal is the same. This is not a simplistic desire to have older priests share from their experience. As one elderly Sulpician seminary professor put it, "Sometimes experience is nothing but old ignorance." The intent is rather to have priests who have deeply reflected on the experience of priesthood assist more recently ordained priests with their own adjustment to it.

A Neglected Model

Models are useful insofar as they can be applied to concrete situations. Every model has its strengths and its limitations. My contention is not that the wisdom model of ministry should supplant the more common and traditional models of priest, prophet, and king (shepherd), whether for priests or other ministers. Nor does it cover all aspects of ministry, ordained and nonordained. Instead I suggest that this neglected biblical model can be useful in our own day for reflection upon the lived experience of ministry. Priests will still need to be cultic, sacramental leaders who call people to justice and who also exercise an authoritative leadership in the community. Other ministers, too, will need to maintain their various roles in service to the poor, counseling, visitation, teaching, etc.

But all ministers of today and of the future will also need to develop the attitudes, the skills, and the knowledge that enlivened the sages of old. Far from becoming a guru, the wise minister will more humbly exercise ministry as an "elder," whose leadership does not come from an imposed *external* authority but from a recognized *internal* authority. With the features described above, the exercise of ministry in the wisdom model can effectively be an exercise in humble service to the community.

Some might see in this model a danger of reinforcing an unhealthy form of individualism in the priesthood or in other ministries. The temptation for a "lone ranger" kind of ministry is certainly real. Yet, the wisdom figures of Israel were not prima donnas who exercised their talents alone. They belonged to schools of wisdom in which their individual reflections could be tested and weighed against the wider biblical tradition and the experience of the community.

The wisdom model of ministry is inherently humble (Sir 3:18). Even within the biblical perspective, the wisdom figures did not obtain the flashy, center stage kind of publicity that was more common to the priestly, prophetic, or royal figures. Their claim for divine authority was never so bold. Their authority came from their personal achievements as much as from their office, although they consistently taught that wisdom was ultimately a gift from God. They were the sacred realists and faithful skeptics of their day. They reflect an inductive tradition rather than a deductive one. Perhaps that is why it is so appropriate that, with regard to the priesthood, *PDV* itself does not explicitly call for a wisdom model for priests but more subtly reflects it in the content of its teaching.

In light of the contemporary search for models of ministry, the "priest as sage" alone will not resolve all our ministerial questions and challenges. Nor will it renew the priesthood singlehandedly or solve the complex issues that currently confront professional ministers. It can, however, provide a functional model for exercising a ministry that, in the vision of Vatican II, calls people to greater wisdom as we advance further into the third Christian millennium and the challenges that have yet to be revealed.

Chapter Nine

The Priest as Teacher: Reassessing a Familiar Role

It is likely that few priests reflect in depth on the teaching role of priestly ministry, unless they are specifically engaged in higher education.[1] Yet the ministry of teaching (the *munus docendi*) is one of the three essential characteristics of priesthood (the other two being the ministries of sanctifying [*munus sanctificandi*] and governing [*munus regendi*]) in accordance with the priesthood of Jesus Christ, exercised as priest, prophet, and king.[2] By ordination, priests share in this threefold ministry as cooperators with their bishop in fulfilling Jesus' priestly ministry today. Some forty years ago, when I was a seminarian, my attraction to the special ministry of formation done by the Sulpicians centered on a strong desire to teach the Word of God. I really wanted to teach professionally. As sometimes happens in the real world, my priestly desires took a detour. Out of the last thirty-five years of ordained ministry, I have had exactly three years of full-time teaching without administrative duties, and two of those were before I joined the Sulpicians, a community of diocesan priests specifically dedicated to teaching and forming priests. Never make your personal plans too firmly; the Holy Spirit (and one's superiors!) often has other ideas.

I hasten to add that I am not complaining. Priesthood is a call to service. I have always tried to respond to the desires of superiors with regard to my specific duties as a priest. Yet my interest in the teaching ministry of priests is more than academic. My personal desire to be an effective teacher as a priest has directed my own ministry in multiple ways, and I will try to bring these to bear on my analysis.

This chapter comprises five categories. The first addresses the biblical foundations of the teaching ministry. The second offers some observations about the role of the *munus docendi* in the context of the other two *munera*. The third comments on *Pastores Dabo Vobis*, John Paul II's post-synodal exhortation on priestly formation, and its particular contribution to the topic. The fourth will briefly review the nature of the teaching office. Finally, I offer a creative attempt to coordinate the *munus docendi* with the four pillars of priestly formation as they might look in terms of implications for both initial and ongoing priestly formation.

Biblical Foundations of the Teaching Office

One might easily think of beginning our biblical discussion with the teaching office of Jesus. It is, after all, foundational to the church's theology of the priesthood. Jesus Christ is the source of all priestly ministry. But to do so, actually, would miss an important prior step. Jesus himself entered the scene of human history in another context, one in which the Hebrew Bible (OT) featured prominently. So we begin there in searching for appropriate biblical foundations of the teaching office of priestly ministry.

Old Testament Background

Hebrew has two main verbs for teaching (*limmēd* and *hôrāh*), each with a slight nuance.[3] The first word indicates a kind of formal instruction whereby an individual drills certain knowledge into the minds of hearers. The second word is a more formal expression for priestly instruction (whence the word Torah, "instruction," which we normally understand as the law [of God]). The actual methods and content of teaching in the OT are not described in any detail, although the wisdom literature mentions settings for boys or young men that might resemble a school. My interest in the OT background, however, is not primarily for this purpose. Rather, when one looks at how teaching is described in the OT, three things stand out.

First, God is the one who provides the words. One thinks, for example, of some of the great proclaimers in the OT, like Moses (Exod 4:10-15), Isaiah (Isa 6:6-9), Jeremiah (Jer 1:7-9), or Ezekiel (Ezek 3:1-4). Indeed, in the OT only God is the true teacher. God provides both the content of the instruction (usually statutes, commandments, and ordinances or prophetic messages) and the means (usually placing the right words in the mouth of the one who teaches them). To illustrate, let's recall the protest of Moses in Exodus:

> But Moses said to the Lord, "O my Lord, I have never been eloquent, neither in the past nor even now that you have spoken to your servant; but I am slow of speech and slow of tongue." Then the Lord said to him, "Who gives speech to mortals? . . . Is it not I, the Lord? Now go, and I will be with your mouth and teach you what you are to speak." But he said, "O my Lord, please send someone else." Then the anger of the Lord was kindled against Moses and he said, "What of your brother Aaron, the Levite? I know that he can speak fluently; even now he is coming out to meet you, and when he sees you his heart will be glad. You shall speak to him and put the words in his mouth; and I will be with your mouth and with his mouth, and will teach you what you shall do." (4:10-15)

Second, since God is the true teacher, everyone else is a learner. Even the "teachers" must be instructed before they teach. As the psalmist regularly cries out, "Make known your ways to me, O Lord; teach me your paths" (Ps 25:4, my translation; cf. Ps 25:12; 32:8; 86:11). And as Job responds to his friends who try to justify his predicament, "Will any teach God knowledge, seeing that he judges those that are on high?" (Job 21:22).

Third, according to John L. McKenzie, the role of the teacher in the OT is, in both secular and religious senses, primarily as a "revealer," one who unveils God's will. This type of teaching, then, is not merely intellectual; it is moral and religious in nature; it is a teaching for life.[4]

This OT background on teaching is useful for one important reason. If we too facilely jump to the conclusion, which comes from our theology of the priesthood, that the priest is a teacher by being configured to Christ as a teacher, we forget a prior biblical foundation that served even the formation of the NT. In my reading of this OT perspective, the important point is that teaching is, or should be, a humble activity. God provides the content and method, something that might be easy to forget if we are impressed by the fact that we priests are ordained to teach authoritatively in the name of Jesus Christ. In some modern societies where teachers are held in great respect (e.g., in Asia), there can be a tendency to think of the position in exalted terms. The biblical foundations of any teaching ministry, however, bring us back down to earth. Priests as teachers must remain humble servants of the Word.

New Testament Background

Three important aspects immediately come to mind with regard to the NT background. First, Jesus is *the* Teacher in the NT. He is most frequently addressed as "Teacher" (Greek, *didaskalos*, or Hebrew, *rabbi*), a title of respect and honor, although, from the perspective of all four evangelists, not adequate as a christological title. Moreover, the NT most frequently includes "teaching" as a description of the ministry of Jesus. Matthew, for instance, portrays Jesus as teaching long, formal discourses with varied content. In summary passages Matthew also describes Jesus' ministry as "teaching, preaching, and healing."[5] Concomitantly, the disciples are primarily learners (the root meaning of the Greek term *mathētēs*, "disciple"). Even when they are commissioned for ministry, the disciples must receive their authority and message from Jesus himself.

Second, the NT makes a distinction between teaching (Greek, *didache*, *didaskein*) and preaching (Greek, *kerygma*, *keryxein*), although both are closely related activities. The synoptic gospels portray Jesus as preaching the kingdom of God, and this is also the object of the preaching of John the Baptist and the disciples of Jesus (cf. Matt 3:2; 4:17; 10:7). But the kingdom is also part of the content of the teaching of Jesus, such as in the parables (Matt 13:1-52), so preaching and teaching cannot always be separated neatly. Later NT documents (especially the Pastoral Epistles) emphasize that the content of teaching should be authoritative and guarded carefully. There is clearly a developing concern over authentic teaching ("sound doctrine"; 1 Tim 1:10; Titus 1:9; 2:1) and not letting it be corrupted by outside or devious influences.

Finally, one NT author seemingly relativizes the ministry of teaching, at least a bit. Paul, writing to the Corinthians, a community beset with divisions and factions, says,

> Now you [plural] are the body of Christ and individually members of it. And God has appointed in the church first apostles, second prophets, third teachers; then deeds of power, then gifts of healing, assistance, administration, various kinds of tongues. (1 Cor 12:27-28; my translation)

Despite attempts on the part of some scholars to view the Pauline churches as totally egalitarian communities, I think the plain sense of this passage is to recognize that Paul believed in a certain hierarchy of ministries in which apostles and prophets outranked teachers.[6] But note two things: (1) Paul himself fulfilled all these roles! And (2) they are not mutually exclusive positions. Apostles were sent to evangelize, and prophets spoke God's Word. Each of these is intimately bound to the generic ministry of teaching. All are aspects of the ministry of the Word.

Summary

This is not merely a pedantic exercise. Rather, it is foundational to an understanding of the priestly ministry of teaching. From a biblical perspective, several important points stand out. Teaching is an activity of God. Even the teaching of Jesus is a communication of his Father's message and in conformity to his Father's will. Furthermore, God chooses human vehicles to undertake the task of teaching, whether they be prophets or apostles or disciples, and whether they proclaim, preach, evangelize, or teach formally. In short, those called to the task of teaching participate in a divine mission as sacred handlers of the Word. They are mouthpieces for God.

"Teaching" in the Context of the Threefold *Munera*

When one thinks of the threefold offices of priestly ministry, what springs to mind? Doubtless we immediately recite the teaching that, by virtue of ordination, the priest is configured to Christ—priest, prophet, and king—and thereby shares in his ministry authentically and authoritatively. This is the order of the words in common parlance, at least as I often hear them. But word order and vocabulary can be a bit fluid, and with telling consequences. Let's take a closer look.

To begin, we go to *Presbyterorum Ordinis,* Vatican II's decree on the priesthood. In chapter 2 on "the ministry of priests" the threefold functions of the priesthood are treated in this order and wording:

> Priests as Ministers of God's Word (4)
>
> Priests as Ministers of the Sacraments and the Eucharist (5)
>
> Priests as Rulers of God's People (6)

In other words, the order treated by the Decree on the Ministry and Life of Priests is essentially prophet, priest, and king, or functionally, teaching, sanctifying, and governing.[7] This may at first seem trivial, but both vocabulary and word order can convey important nuances. For example, the title of the decree itself places the "ministry" of priests before their "life," meaning, I believe, all aspects of priestly life but especially the spiritual dimensions.[8] This is not accidental. A priest's personal holiness, as absolutely essential as it is for priestly ministry, is not the *goal* of our vocational call. Priesthood is about service, and ministry is intended to take priority over personal concerns. This point was reinforced in the title of a later document, the Directory on the Ministry and Life of Priests, issued by the Congregation for the Clergy in 1994.[9] I also believe it is why Vatican II emphasized the intimate connection of a priest's spiritual life and his ministry as a priest (*PDV*, 24 and 26).[10]

What would it mean if we took seriously this word order? Emphasis would rightly be placed on the role of prophet, thus giving precedence to the ministry of the Word and priority to the function of teaching. This is, in fact, what I think our theology does. Here is what *PO* says in describing this first task of priests:

> The People of God is formed into one in the first place by the Word of the living God, which is quite rightly sought from the mouth of priests [cf. Mal 2:7; 1 Tim 4:11-13; 1 Tim 1:9]. For since nobody can be saved who has not first believed [cf. Mark 16:16], *it is the first task of priests as co-workers of the bishops to preach the Gospel of God to all [people].* In this way they carry out the Lord's command "Go into all the world and preach the Gospel to every creature" (Mk. 16:15) and thus set up and increase the People of God. (4, emphasis mine)

The Latin text of the emphasized words reads, "primum habent officium evangelium Dei omnibus evangelizandi." It is the first duty of the priest to evangelize, that is, to teach and preach. The text also contains an explicit acknowledgment that the Word of God brings the people of God into being (remember God's Word at creation recorded in Genesis). Thus priests, as coworkers of the bishops, must first and foremost proclaim the Word, the gospel of God, to the people, and we must do so having first absorbed it ourselves.

Further confirmation of this precedence can be found in the ordination rite itself. The suggested homily of the bishop during a priestly formation mentions the ministry of Christ several times in reference to the ministry of bishops and priests, and each time the rite refers to Christ as "Teacher, Priest, and Shepherd."[11] When it proceeds to describe these ministerial duties, it preserves the same order of treatment, speaking of the "sacred duty of teaching in the name of Christ the Teacher."

The reason I emphasize this point is simple. For hundreds of years priests defined themselves primarily in terms of sacramental ministry. This identity, deeply rooted in Christ's ministry itself and obviously one of the three *munera*, became a focal point especially in the wake of the Protestant Reformation. Vatican II awakened in the church a dormant emphasis on the Word of God that reshaped, albeit in continuity with the church's ancient tradition, many aspects of our faith, including priestly ministry.[12] Vatican II allowed us to rediscover that priests are ministers of Word *and* sacrament. Now, in the second decade of a new century and the third Christian millennium, nearly fifty years removed from the ecumenical council, we are inheritors of this rediscovered perspective. Making a priority of the prophetic ministry of teaching and preaching is one of the ways we fulfill the vision fostered by Vatican II.

The Perspective of *Pastores Dabo Vobis*

Let's add another layer of understanding about the teaching office, this time with an eye on *PDV*, which has been a principal resource for this book. This document, as we have noted before, is assuredly the most important ecclesial teaching on the priesthood since the Second Vatican Council. Its influence has been wide-ranging. Most recently, it guided the outline and content of the USCCB's latest edition of the Program of Priestly Formation that governs priestly formation in the United States.[13]

When *PDV* finally addresses the threefold priestly ministry (26), it uses the following vocabulary and word order: "the ministry of word, sacrament and pastoral charity." Note the wording. In place of the expected vocabulary of prophet, priest, and king, we find word, sacrament, and pastoral charity. In my estimation, this subtle shift orients one's understanding of the threefold ministry in a new way. Word and sacrament clearly allude to Vatican II's primary description of the ministry of priests, but pastoral charity more clearly emphasizes the shepherding role over the ruling (or kingly) role. *PDV* describes the ministry of Word in this fashion:

> The priest is first of all a minister of the word of God. He is consecrated and sent forth to proclaim the good news of the kingdom to all, calling every person to the obedience of faith and leading believers to an ever increasing knowledge of and communion in the mystery of God, as revealed and communicated to us in Christ. For this reason, the priest himself ought first of all to develop a great personal familiarity with the word of God. Knowledge of its linguistic or exegetical aspects,

> though certainly necessary, is not enough. He needs to approach the word with a docile and prayerful heart so that it may deeply penetrate his thoughts and feelings and bring about a new outlook in him "the mind of Christ" (1 Cor. 2:16)—such that his words and his choices and attitudes may become ever more a reflection, a proclamation and a witness to the Gospel. (26)

These are heady words. But note that the priority of the Word is acknowledged in the first line. *PDV* goes on to emphasize how the priest must humbly exercise this ministry:

> He is not the master of the word, but its servant. He is not the sole possessor of the word; in its regard he is in debt to the People of God. Precisely because he can and does evangelize, the priest—like every other member of the Church—ought to grow in awareness that he himself is continually in need of being evangelized. He proclaims the word in his capacity as "minister," as a sharer in the prophetic authority of Christ and the Church. (26)

In a sense, *PDV* places this first priestly *munus* in its proper context. We are not masters of the Word of God but servants. In order to teach, to preach, to evangelize, to catechize, we ourselves must have absorbed its message. Just as important is *PDV*'s warning that priests exercise their ministry of teaching in the context of the church's magisterial role as teacher par excellence. The Word we proclaim is not our own. *PDV* says it this way:

> As a result, in order that he himself may possess and give to the faithful the guarantee that he is transmitting the Gospel in its fullness, the priest is called to develop a special sensitivity, love and docility to the living tradition of the Church and to her magisterium. These are not foreign to the word, but serve its proper interpretation and preserve its authentic meaning. (26)

Summary

There is a certain fluidity of vocabulary in the official documents concerning the teaching office of the priesthood, yet the primary focus is clear. The teaching office, described variously as preaching, teaching, evangelizing, catechizing, or being heralds, makes God's Word a priority in the priesthood. Priests are first and foremost ministers of the Word, prophets called to proclaim a divine message.[14]

A Brief Description of the Teaching Office

With this biblical background in mind, and before proceeding to the more creative task of coordinating the *munus docendi* with the pillars of priestly formation, I wish to succinctly summarize by means of twelve statements the main characteristics of the teaching office of the priesthood, using the biblical data and official church documents:

- The teaching office is a direct sharing of the ministry of Christ, the Prophet and Teacher, and is tied to the nature of the church itself (see 1983 Code of Canon Law (*CIC*), Book III, "The Teaching Office of the Church").[15]

- In the fulfillment of their vocation, priests are "cooperators" with the bishops, who are the first "teachers" in the diocese (*CIC*, 757; *PO*, 2 and 4; *PDV*, 23; DMLP, 47; *CCC*, 1562, 1595).[16]

- Priests are not masters of the Word but its servants (*PDV*, 26).

- The office of teaching is exercised not simply by words but by word and deed; the priest's ministry and life itself should teach by example (*PO*, 4).[17]

- The first task of the teaching office is to preach the gospel; thus there is the primacy of the ministry of the Word (*CIC*, 761; *PDV*, 26; Program of Priestly Formation, 23, 26).

- The office includes preaching, teaching, catechizing, and evangelizing (*PO*, 4).

- There is an intimate bond between the priest's personal spiritual life and the exercise of the ministry of teaching (*PDV*, 24, 26; The Priest and the Third Christian Millennium [PTCM], II.1).

- There is also a close bond between the Word and the sacraments; thus the ministry of priests is properly described as one of Word and sacrament (*PO*, 4).

- The homily is the most important of several forms of preaching because of its close tie to liturgy (*CIC*, 767; Basic Plan, p. 17).

- The content of the priest's teaching is not his own message; rather it is first and foremost the Word of God (the gospel of the kingdom of God) and the magisterial teaching of the church (DMLP, 45); thus priests teach in "*nomine Christi et nomine Ecclesiae*"[18]; thus a priest should exhibit loyalty and docility to the magisterium (*PO*, 4; *PDV*, 26).

- Priests should also have a missionary attitude, a willingness to spread the gospel far and wide (*PO*, 4; *PDV*, 32).

- Methodologically, the teaching office should be adapted to the hearers and the times in which one teaches (*CIC*, 769); all means possible should be used to communicate the Word (*CIC*, 761); priests should not teach abstractly but concretely (*PO*, 4); any form of fundamentalism or distortion of the message is to be avoided (PTCM, II.2).

While more could be said about the teaching office, these twelve statements derived from biblical data and the church's official teaching capture the essence of the priest's duties as prophet and herald.

Relating the Four Pillars with the Teaching Office

How can this teaching office intersect practically with the four pillars of priestly formation—human, spiritual, intellectual, and pastoral? While there is some inevitable overlapping of categories, I think certain distinctions will stand up under scrutiny; so I offer the following descriptions.

Human Formation

One of the more remarkable aspects of *PDV* is its emphasis on human formation as foundational to priestly formation. Priests must be "bridges" rather than barriers, and their humanity must be well formed. With regard to the teaching office, I suggest at least three qualities that must be nourished.

The first is the development of basic communication skills. Teaching, preaching, and evangelizing require ability to handle words. The ministry of the Word requires a knowledge of how good human communication works and the exercise of these basic skills. Public speaking ability should be assessed, and basics like learning good diction and enunciation, acquiring rhetorical skills and an understanding of rhetoric, and the handling of microphones should be examined. Also, the quality of our language should be examined. Are we using proper expressions to communicate this divine message? Are we avoiding ecclesiastical jargon? In the context of our multicultural world, of course, this area can quickly become problematic. At what point is someone's foreign accent a mere inconvenience that requires some getting used to, or a real hindrance to the communication of God's Word? It is also worth noting here the advice given by the Congregation for the Clergy on this topic: "Elegant accurate language, comprehensible to contemporary men and women of all social backgrounds, is always useful for preaching. Banal commonplace language should be eschewed" (PTCM, 20).

The second area is harder to assess. A priest must speak from the heart. He must enunciate an authentic word, one that emanates from the depths of his being. Basically, this value is important at the very beginning of a priestly vocation. Is what you see really what you get? Is the man authentic? Does he have integrity? Does he actually believe what he preaches, teaches, proclaims? In this regard, we should keep in mind the exhortation of the ordination ritual itself: "see that you believe what you read, that you teach what you believe, and that you practice what you teach."[19] Moreover, the task of teaching in word and deed means incarnating the message we speak in our lives.

The last area under this heading is a simple one. Being a good teacher requires true humility. This can have several meanings. On one level, it means that a person has the good sense to know what he does not know. Everyone's knowledge is limited. Can we acknowledge that? Or must we always be right and always have the last word? On another level, humility requires preaching and teaching authoritatively but not with arrogance. The priest who has to assert that people should believe what he says just because he's a priest and has the authority to teach does a grave injustice to the role. Yet another aspect is having an attitude of constant learning. This is a major emphasis in both *PDV* and the Basic Plan. Lifelong learning makes for the most effective teacher. It is essentially an exercise in humility.

Spiritual Formation

At least four qualities come to mind with regard to spiritual formation for the teaching office. The first is obviously the presence of a devotion to and love of the Word of God. This is emphasized in all the church's teachings regarding the role of the priest as minister of the Word, most recently in Pope Benedict XVI's post-synodal apostolic exhortation *Verbum Domini* (121). We must love the Word in order to serve it. Do we love Christ, the Incarnate Word? Does the Bible influence our daily life in any real way? Are we familiar with the Bible as a personal part of our life of prayer, in addition to the Liturgy of the Hours, which is sometimes prayed rather perfunctorily? Liturgically, are we both attentive to the best methods for the proclamation of the Word and open to its multiple meanings?

A related but also distinct aspect of love for the Word of God is the practice of *lectio divina*. As the Synod on the Word of 2008 and Pope

Benedict XVI's subsequent apostolic exhortation emphasized, this practice is very important for priests. Fortunately, this has become a more popular part of spiritual interests today, and not just among seminarians and priests but among laity as well. There are many different types of *lectio* available and spiritual traditions that foster them. Seminarians and priests should develop some good habit of *lectio* for their own lives, and seminary programs should foster familiarity with such methods and opportunities for practicing these skills. Nothing can develop greater sensitivity to hearing and absorbing the Word of God than prayerful meditation upon it.

It may seem self-evident, but as Andrew Greeley has been reminding us for ages, there is still a problem among Catholic priests regarding how to preach the Word of God effectively. One area of serious attention in any formation setting, then, should be the lectionary. How familiar are we with it? Do seminarians learn how to preach *biblically* from the lectionary context?[20] Do we use the lectionary as part of our own prayer on a daily basis? This practice, of course, can be related to *lectio divina*, but it could also be developed separately. In terms of ongoing formation, one area that seems to attract some attention for priests is attending workshops geared to highlighting the lectionary year, whether the specific gospel year or the liturgical season. Effective preaching and teaching God's Word would clearly be more effective if we pay attention to this context.

Finally, since the teaching office is directly linked to the role of Christ the prophet, some attention should be given to assessing our prophetic convictions as priests. Do we understand the biblical role of prophets properly? Are we comfortable with the church's own prophetic voice, especially in areas like teachings on social justice? Is there some level of comfort for the need to proclaim not just a message of love and acceptance but also a message of challenge and exhortation in contexts that demand it? The role of a prophet is not an easy one. It should never be assumed lightly. Nor should it become the sole focus of one's proclamation, although it has its place in the office of teaching.

Intellectual Formation

Three elements come to mind in this arena. The first element is most obvious. Exercising the teaching office requires not just basic intelligence but a real knowledge of the church's tradition and magisterial teaching. Seminary curricula, of course, address this area in a formal way. In the Program of Priestly Formation course requirements are set forth for all levels of priestly formation. Moreover, familiarity with the documents of Vatican II, the *Catechism*, and so on should be demonstrated prior to ordination. It should go without saying that a priest should be able to communicate these basic truths in a fashion that is both comprehensible to the faithful (on their level) yet faithful to the tradition. In my experience, I fear that this is an area that still needs improvement. At times, especially with more recent converts to the Catholic faith, what those in formation consider Catholic teaching is not necessarily so, and seminary faculties must sometimes foster some "unlearning" in order to promote a more nuanced learning.

A second area should be a well-developed sense of historical perspective. A priest lacking in historical consciousness, whether regarding the Bible or the church's own teachings, can do tremendous harm in his attempts to teach the faith. Knowing how truths developed over time and how the formulation of ancient truths has changed to accommodate changing contexts is crucial to teaching the authentic faith. Thus, a truly Catholic approach is nonfundamentalist.[21] In our day, this is another area where some concerns remain, for fundamentalism has gained as a cultural perspective, and there is a tendency for some to dismiss historical consciousness as a way to dilute the truth. In fact, it does the opposite; it confirms the truth by placing church teachings in their proper context.

The third area concerns the role of the priest as teacher and preacher by extension of the ministry of the bishop. Priestly ministry is not solitary even when it is exercised all alone in a distant parish. As all the documents pertaining to priestly identity and formation maintain, we are coworkers with the bishops in their ministry. When we teach, preach, evangelize, and catechize, we should ask ourselves if we are communicating the mind of Christ in line with the mind of the bishop. Of course, one could ask if the bishop himself is fostering the kind of unity among the presbyterate as he should, but our focus here is on our own priestly ministry. Are we in tune with the bishop's message? Do we see ourselves as exercising our teaching ministry as an arm of the bishop who is the chief teacher of the diocese? Are we truly coworkers with our bishop?

Pastoral Formation

As *PDV* indicates, pastoral formation is the arena in which all the elements should come together in a unified whole (57). In fact, integration of the four pillars and all aspects of priestly formation is the ideal. Pastoral application is where we find out if our ministry is effective or not. This is where our personal, spiritual, and intellectual formation should bear fruit. Again, I point to three areas of interest relating to the teaching office.

The first area is hermeneutics. Do we as priests know how to apply the texts of our faith (Bible and magisterial teaching) in a way that makes sense to people and addresses their real lives? This requires not only a knowledge of Scripture and tradition, as essential as these are, but also a deep familiarity with the local culture and congregations we serve. In the search for application, it is not sufficient to rely on cutesy stories or canned illustrations. Ideally, our application of the faith should come from keen observation of daily life, from observing the media, from reading novels and going to movies, from listening to music and noting societal trends, and most important from interacting with our people on a regular basis.[22] I am not sure how well this aspect of our ministry can be learned. It may be that some priests are simply better at blending these things together. Not everyone is a keen observer of human life. Not everyone has the ability to use metaphor and simile in a way that jars the imagination and enlivens the sensitivity to God's message today. But it is a skill worth promoting.

The second area concerns sensitivity to and familiarity with multicultural realities today. Increasingly, we live in a highly mobile and multicultural world. We cannot ignore this reality. In our American context, in particular, we priests have a duty to bring attention to the challenges posed to and by the new immigrants. Teaching today requires helping people gain a more universal vision, the kind of vision that Jesus Christ himself fostered in his day, and that becomes so apparent in the letters of Paul. Ideally, this perspective also means some personal acquaintance with what it is like to be a "foreigner" or a sojourner in a strange land. For some, this means study of a foreign language; for others perhaps short trips abroad. Most seminaries offer direct ministry to the poor and some have now taken to fostering special trips to underdeveloped countries, in addition to promoting the study of Spanish, in order to help seminarians gain a real sense of the universal church and a concrete experience of poverty. But opportunities also abound in this country. Some dioceses have relations with parishes in dioceses abroad, especially in Latin and South America, and sometimes US priests participate in ministry abroad for a time. These experiences enrich the pastoral situation of both participating dioceses.

Third, to teach like both a "shepherd" and a "prophet" is a real challenge. Pastorally, we should examine the ability of seminarians and priests to be adaptable in many different pastoral situations. The shepherd cares for and tends the flock. The prophet sometimes has to exhort, to cajole, and to be a thorn in the side. These are not always compatible skills, yet diverse pastoral situations require such responses. I think pastoral training programs, in both initial and ongoing contexts, should take both elements into account.

Conclusion

To draw this chapter to a close, I return to our *vocation* as priests. Our theology, exalted as it is, proclaims the priest as being configured to Christ, the head and shepherd of the church, and having the authority to act *in persona Christi capitis* (*PDV*, 18; DMLP, 7). The foremost ministry that derives from this calling is teaching—proclaiming God's Word in deed and in words. But I think it might be helpful if priests remembered a couple of biblical admonitions directly pertaining to the ministry of teaching. Paul cried out, "Woe to me if I do not proclaim the gospel!" (1 Cor 9:16b). And the Letter of James, in its inimitable fashion, gives a warning that I think should give anyone pause about assuming the teaching office too facilely. James forthrightly states, "Not many of you should become teachers, my brothers, for you know that we who teach will be judged more strictly" (3:1; my translation).

In my estimation, this is as it should be. As Jesus warns in Luke's gospel, "From everyone to whom much has been given, much will be required; and from the one to whom much has been entrusted, even more will be demanded" (12:48b). If that does not make us priests a little nervous, it should. We who answer Christ's call to follow him in this special vocation of the priesthood should do so humbly. For if we fulfill our task properly, it will be primarily because Christ himself—prophet, priest, and shepherd—is at work in us priests.

Chapter Ten

The Role of Scripture Studies in Priestly Ministry

This scene has probably been repeated in subtle ways at various times in seminary history. The seminarian, a fourth-year deacon preparing to return to his diocese for ordination, was tossing books from his shelves into a large wastebasket. When queried by a classmate as to his intentions, while a one-volume Scripture commentary was subjected to a similar fate, the quick response was, "Thank God, I'll never have to read another book again in my life!"

Though this case is admittedly an extreme example of anti-intellectual bias that periodically appears in the priesthood, it exemplifies an attitude that makes the topic of this chapter so difficult to address. The undercurrent of anti-intellectualism that flows through American Catholic thought has often received the attention of scholars, such as John Tracy Ellis or Andrew Greeley.[1] But there is very little historical or sociological evidence to address the topic at hand. Consequently, the direction this chapter will take will be based primarily upon my own experience of teaching scriptural studies in Roman Catholic seminaries. It will focus on the *ideal* role these studies can have on the intellectual formation of future priests.

The chapter consists of four parts. The first section will explore the role of Scripture studies in seminary formation in the recent past. The second section will set forth two influences on the current situation in biblical studies, the vision of Vatican II and the efficacy of seminary Scripture courses. The third section will enumerate ways in which scriptural studies in seminaries today and in the future can *ideally* have a major impact on future priests. The final section will draw on the Bible's own testimony.

Scripture Studies in the Recent Past

The critical study of the Bible is a relatively recent development, when compared to other technical fields. Although its roots are in the Enlightenment, it was only in the early nineteenth century that biblical studies began to make tremendous advancements that forever reshaped the way the Bible would henceforth be studied.[2] The application of modern critical scientific method to the study of the ancient Scriptures opened dozens of new pathways to their understanding. Linguistic advances, archaeological discoveries, and scientific method itself led to a microscopic examination of the biblical texts, especially in the intense search for the historical foundations of Christianity. Unfortunately, little of this scientific progress made its way into the common formation of Roman Catholic priests until the mid-twentieth century.

Several factors shaped this situation. First, the major figures behind the development of modern biblical study were Protestant. Although some Catholic scholars were also involved in the early formulation of critical theories about the Scriptures, the majority were Protestants. Indeed, since the time of the Reformation, the Bible had come to be seen as a means of self-definition between Roman Catholics and Protestants. Protestants emphasized the Bible while Catholics emphasized the sacraments and the teaching traditions of the church. This overly simplified and exaggerated means of self-definition endured until Vatican II, and its effect was to impede Catholic awareness of professional biblical study. A second factor was that much of the scholarship itself remained only on the level of scholarly dialogue between professionals. It took decades for research to sift down to the general public. Many Catholics remained blithely unaware of the professional study of the Scriptures, despite the official sanction given to Catholic scholars by Pius XII's encyclical *Divino Afflante Spiritu* (1943) to utilize the historical-critical method. A third factor was that seminaries themselves did not have a developed system of promoting Scripture study. Most Roman Catholic seminary training prior to Vatican II incorporated the study of the Bible only from the perspective of "proof texting," finding Scripture passages that justified traditional church doctrines or practice. Courses in dogmatic and moral theology took precedence over those in Scripture, and the Bible was seen only as an auxiliary resource to support these primary areas of study.

The situation was exacerbated by a critical lack of textbooks in the biblical field, and an exaggerated fear of so-called modernist trends in seminaries.[3]

Despite the seemingly bleak picture of the role of Scripture studies in Roman Catholic seminaries prior to Vatican II, there were pockets of hope that presaged a different approach altogether. To illustrate this assertion, I will focus on two figures from the past whose writings give a glimpse of a view of Sacred Scripture that can nearly claim to be contemporary.

The first figure is an Irish-born, French-trained, American Sulpician, John Baptist Hogan. More than 120 years ago, in 1891, Hogan began to publish a series of articles that led to a book titled *Clerical Studies*, which appeared in 1898.[4] Hogan, who was superior at St. John's Seminary in Brighton, Massachusetts (1884–89), was not formally trained in the area of biblical studies, having taught dogmatic and moral theology. However, he became a supporter of the new approach to biblical studies that was slowly making its appearance in American Catholic circles. He published his essays in book form because of their popularity and their application to the ongoing formation of priests in active ministry. Although many of the essays are bound by culture and time, reflecting a preference for advice on matters of dogmatic or moral theology, several sections are devoted to the study of the Bible. In fact, it was Hogan who established a series of biblical courses at St. John's Seminary before it became *de rigueur*.

Several observations about Hogan's *Clerical Studies* are noteworthy. The first is that he took a strong stand on the need for intellectual study in the life of a priest. In the face of protestations that sound all too familiar, he could assert, "In reality there is room, even in the busy existence of a priest, for much more serious study than is commonly thought" (v). He not only valued the importance of intellectual pursuits in the life of priests but also believed they were part of a priest's solemn duty.

Perhaps even more astonishing is the way in which Hogan viewed Scripture as central to priestly formation. For him studying the Bible was more than simply looking for proof texts. The Bible was *central* to the study of all theology, for he wrote,

> Theology in every shape—dogmatic, moral, ascetic, mystical—proceeds directly from the Inspired Word, and borrows from it at every step its substance and its form. It is from the Bible that sacred oratory derives its deepest thoughts and most striking utterances. (420)

This centrality of the Bible was coupled with his insistence that one must go beyond the mere literal translation of texts. He thus recognized a multiplicity of approaches to biblical texts that he felt were useful to priests. In some ways he may have been reverting to a medieval view of Scripture that evoked more profound spiritual meanings in biblical texts. Yet, his intention was oriented practically for priests in ministry. He wanted seminarians and priests to use the Bible with ease and to recognize the multifaceted dimension of the text. He drew attention especially to the literary forms found in the Bible. In this way Hogan exhibited a remarkably nonmechanistic view of the concept of inspiration, for he believed inspiration did not override the importance of literary style in understanding the meaning of the sacred text (471–74).

Granted that Hogan, like others of his era, was bound by many constraints, his commitment to the historical-critical approach to the Bible and his insistence regarding the centrality of the Bible in the life of the priest, mark him as a precursor of a post–Vatican II approach to biblical studies.

Nearly fifty years later, in 1939, an Anglican theologian by the name of Hubert S. Box edited a book of essays by various Anglican scholars on the topic of "the priest as student."[5] Despite its Anglican orientation, the book bears a remarkable resemblance to the earlier work of Hogan. Its applicability to the Catholic priesthood is, to my mind, quite apparent, as the following brief analysis will show.

Box devotes separate chapters to the need for priests to continue studies in such areas as Old and New Testaments; patristics; canon law; liturgy; and dogmatic, moral, and spiritual theology. The first chapter is devoted to the importance in a priest's life of study in general. While it presents the idealistic picture of a priest who devotes an essential part of his day to intellectual pursuits, it nonetheless sounds the realistic lament that "the most charitable judgment is constrained to say that practice does not quite march with theory" (3). The chapter is also filled with sage advice about how this study should be done. It strongly urges the need to read critically (29), and it specifically warns against the danger of reading *about* the Bible rather than reading the biblical text itself (27).[6] With the occasional exception of quaint British expressions, one can hear virtually the same advice today from any teacher of biblical studies!

Box's book contains further specific advice on biblical studies. The chapter on the NT warns against taking refuge in biblical fundamentalism on the grounds that it does not take the Bible seriously as a product of inspiration, "for it makes the writers of the books of the Bible to be little more than mechanical agents of God" (73). Furthermore, the book ties the importance of critical biblical study to the main task of a priest, that is, preaching the gospel. While recognizing the impossibility of preaching the Good News of Jesus Christ apart from a careful study of the Scriptures, the book also acknowledges the difficulty of the hermeneutical task, how to relate the Bible to the contemporary Christian's life (83). Even though it was written in a less hectic age, Box's book is not naive about the taxing demands of parochial ministry and the lack of time for reading that priests incessantly lament. Instead, the book gives the practical recommendation of carefully choosing the most important literary or theological works to read (367–68), and it appends a brief bibliography of important works to the end of each chapter.

These examples in the works of John Hogan and Hubert Box, from two recent periods of history, are sufficient to illustrate that, with regard to the role of studying Scripture in priestly ministry and formation, the more things change, the more they remain the same! Even prior to the major explosion of historical-critical study of the Bible, which occurred in seminary formation in the last half of the twentieth century, the significance of the formal study of Scripture for the life of a priest was indispensable. Before elucidating more clearly the gains of such study, we will take a brief look at three factors that have shaped the current situation.

Three Factors Influencing Current Scripture Study

Without doubt the most important factor that has shaped the current understanding of the Bible's role in the formation of priests is Vatican II itself. Even fifty years after the council, the church continues to explore ways of implementing the vision imparted by the council documents.

The Decree on Priestly Training explicitly calls for the centrality of Scripture studies in any formation program precisely because of the Bible's fundamental role in the history of the church. Alluding directly to Leo XIII's influential encyclical *Providentissimus Deus* (1893), the decree states,

> The students are to be instructed most diligently in the study of scripture which ought to be the soul (*anima*) of all theology. After a suitable introduction, let them be carefully initiated into the method of exegesis. Let them see the main themes of divine revelation and receive inspiration and nourishment from a daily reading and meditation of the sacred books. (*Optatam Totius*, 16)[7]

The council's urging of the central role of Scripture as the "soul" of theology is not simply to foster formal study of the Bible for its own sake. Rather, the Scriptures are central to the life of the priest because of their intimate connection with the task of preaching. One of the great outcomes of Vatican II with respect to a theology of priesthood is to reawaken in priests their central duty to preach the Word of God. The Decree on the Ministry and Life of Priests explicates this challenge as an extension of the first duty of a bishop:

> [I]t is the first task of priests as co-workers of the bishops to preach the Gospel of God to all . . . in every case their role is to teach not their own wisdom but the Word of God and to issue a pressing invitation to all [people] to conversion and to holiness. (*PO*, 4)

Vatican II also avoids the trap of a naive stance vis-à-vis hermeneutics, for it explicitly warns of the difficulty of preaching the ancient word in modern circumstances, and also acknowledges that the gifts (or lack thereof) of the preacher are an essential component of the preaching task (*PO*, 4).

It is important to note that Vatican II does not merely connect the centrality of Scripture (and consequently the need for proper training in this area) with the *task* of ministry. The vision extends to incorporating the Scriptures into the mainstream of a priest's total life. Speaking of seminarians, the Decree on Priestly Training declares,

> So let them be prepared for the ministry of the word, in such a way that they may acquire an even better understanding of the revealed word of God, take it to heart by meditating on it and express it in speech and conduct. (*Optatam Totius*, 4; cf. *PO*, 4)[8]

This recognition serves as a reminder that the efficacy of priestly ministry is bound to the ability of the priest himself to hear and be nourished by the Word of God. This is why it remains as true as ever to insist that there is no better means of proper Scripture study than reading the sacred text itself.

The vision proffered to seminarians and priests by Vatican II has had a major impact on the role the Bible plays in their lives.[9] A recent sociological study of priests ordained five to nine years supports this observation.[10] The results of this study point to the second factor influencing the current scene, that is, the efficacy of contemporary Scripture classes.

From the viewpoint of Scripture professors, this study contains some proverbial good news and bad news. The good news is that Scripture courses were rated among the two most helpful courses that recently ordained priests took during their years of seminary formation (13–14). The survey suggests that these courses in Scripture were quite effective in preparing them for priestly ministry and that they would have liked more courses in Bible. There was a curious downside to this interesting observation. Though reading the Bible ranked very high among priestly activities in the group surveyed, no biblical scholar was listed in the top three authors who most influence priests today, nor was any biblical magazine or commentary series rated extremely high in the list of most influential readings (v). Data of this nature are difficult to interpret, but there is sufficient evidence to indicate that awareness of the Bible's importance for contemporary priestly ministry has grown enormously since Vatican II. One finds evidence of this growth in programs or institutes for the ongoing education of priests. Workshops on Scripture or biblical themes remain popular with priests because they fill a need that is both ministerial and personal.

A third factor to remember is the Synod on the Word of God in 2008 and the subsequent apostolic exhortation of Pope Benedict XVI, *Verbum Domini* (2010).[11] Part of the context for this synod was the ongoing discussion about the value of scientific, or historical-critical, study of Scripture in comparison to older, precritical approaches, such as that practiced by the fathers of the church. Yet both the preparatory documents and the final papal exhortation affirm the ongoing value of scientific approaches to Scripture. At the same time, both sets of documents make it clear that there is an equally important value to precritical exegesis of Scripture, and especially to the ancient practice of prayerful meditation on the Scriptures, *lectio divina*. The historical-critical data are an important first step in Scripture study, but for them to bear fruit in the context of faith, they need to be followed up with more spiritually oriented approaches. Essentially, this position of "both/and" rather than "either/or" affirms the direction in priestly formation in Scripture that has been practiced in many priestly formation programs. I believe this balanced approach also provides impetus for encouraging priests to continue their scriptural studies and meditation throughout their entire ministry. The payoff is both personal and pastoral. Such combined study/prayer will help in personal spiritual growth, but it will also impact their preaching and their interaction with people on a pastoral level.

Pope Benedict succinctly summarized the value of this integrated approach with these words, addressed to seminarians but equally applicable to priests:

> Such attention to the prayerful reading of Scripture must not in any way lead to a dichotomy with regard to the exegetical studies which are a part of formation. The Synod recommended that seminarians be concretely helped to see *the relationship between biblical studies and scriptural prayer*. The study of Scripture ought to lead to an increased awareness of the mystery of divine revelation and foster an attitude of prayerful response to the Lord who speaks. Conversely, an authentic life of prayer cannot fail to nurture in the candidate's heart a desire for greater knowledge of the God who has revealed himself in his word as infinite love. Hence, great care should be taken to ensure that seminarians always cultivate this *reciprocity between study and prayer* in their lives. This end will be served if candidates are introduced to the study of Scripture through methods which favor this integral approach. (*Verbum Domini*, 82; emphases in original)

These three factors, then, Vatican II, the success of Scripture courses in seminary formation, and a reemphasis of prayerful reflection on Scripture, have influenced the contemporary situation. However, none of these factors provides an understanding of the specific skills that Scripture study can impart to priests for their active ministry and how it contributes to their intellectual formation. For this information, we will have to enter the world of the ideal.

Skills Imparted by Scripture Study

The following observations are based upon my own teaching experience and upon conversations I have had over the years with other Scripture instructors. I obviously make no pretense that these observations become incarnate realities in priests or seminarians. However, I believe that proper study of the Bible can greatly contribute to the intellectual and spiritual formation of priests, initial and ongoing, in at least seven ways.

(1) Perhaps the most fundamental skill that the formal study of the Bible can give to students is the ability to read critically. Any teacher of the Bible knows that the biggest challenge is getting students to read the biblical text itself and not simply to read *about* it. Exegesis demands first and foremost that one read the text very carefully, observing structure,

noting development of argumentation, and learning to ask the right questions of the text. Many seminary teachers today have observed that their students seem less academically prepared than in the past, especially in the area of literary skill. Lack of proper reading and writing ability seems more widespread than in the past, and there is some sociological data to confirm this general observation.[12] If biblical studies can contribute to improved performance in this area, the result would be significant for all fields of theological study. In an age where so much learning is accomplished by visual imagery (e.g., TV, video, movies, etc.), the ability to read critically is a lost skill that must be rediscovered. Modern biblical studies can foster the acquisition of this literary skill.

(2) A corollary to the above is the ability to increase one's power of observation and to develop more attention to detail in the reading process. Much of biblical exegesis involves the use of logic and fine attention to details in a text. These skills were at one time more developed with the formidable background of philosophical studies that preceded theology. Seminarians today have increasingly less background in philosophical thought, especially classical and scholastic philosophy. Biblical studies can at least help in making up for this lack. Many commentaries exhibit these skills and, if they are supplemented by appropriate classroom instruction in exegetical method, students can learn to pay more attention to detail both by example (good commentaries) and by practice (application of good exegetical method to biblical texts). Such skill is also essential in the realm of moral theology where so many contemporary moral issues are complex and intertwined with conflicting values.

(3) Biblical studies can also greatly contribute to the field of homiletics by promoting good biblical preaching. Vatican II mandates that the priest's first duty is to preach the gospel of Jesus Christ. We also saw above that, among priests recently ordained five to nine years, biblical courses were among the most satisfactory in seminary formation programs. The importance of good biblical preaching can hardly be overestimated. Donald Senior, a biblical scholar and president of the Catholic Theological Union in Chicago, some years ago addressed this issue of the relationship between biblical studies and preaching.[13] Not only did he call for more biblical courses in seminary formation but he also noted that students should be taught to read more literature in general. Biblical studies can enable seminarians to understand the power and function of rhetoric, and thus it can have a direct impact on the quality of preaching. As Senior points out, biblical preaching is more expansive, evocative, and visionary rather than didactic, moralistic, and trivial.[14] In this regard,

I think more should be done in seminaries to promote courses in preaching that are team-taught by biblical exegetes and homiletics instructors.

(4) A further intellectual benefit of biblical studies is to promote more cooperation between other areas of theological study and the biblical field. Father Hogan reminded seminarians and priests more than a century ago that biblical studies provided the foundation of virtually all areas of theology. Vatican II confirmed that vision and drove it to the very heart of the priesthood. Many books, especially in systematic and moral theology, begin with observations on the biblical material that relate to a specific theological topic. However, the task of taking the Bible seriously for its direction, rather than simply acknowledging its contribution cursorily, is challenging and not always apparent in theological works. Ideally, biblical studies should promote more dialogue between diverse areas of theology because of the Bible's foundational character.

(5) Biblical studies can also contribute intellectually by fostering a desire for ongoing education among seminarians and priests. Vatican II particularly noted the need for priests "continually to renew and foster this life and activity" (*Optatam Totius*, 22), and no field symbolizes this more than biblical studies. Every year the media publish stories about new archaeological finds in the Middle East or about new opinions about the gospels or the historical Jesus. The sheer number of significant discoveries in linguistics and archaeology in this century is indicative of the need for ongoing education in Scripture. The need for new Bible translations, commentaries, and resources should model for students the need for continual education and formation. Perhaps the popularity of biblical studies in the Hemrick-Hoge study is an indicator of the relevance that this field still holds for priests. If this attitude of ongoing formation can be transferred to other fields as well, biblical studies would make another significant contribution to the priesthood.

(6) Another area in which biblical studies can serve as a model of intellectual integrity is in ecumenism. Since Vatican II, perhaps no other theological field has contributed so greatly to ecumenical progress as biblical studies. If for centuries there was a large gap between Protestant and Catholic biblical scholarship, that gap was quickly closed in the period immediately following the close of the council. Scripture scholars have been involved in significant ecumenical dialogue, which has produced a body of literature that begins to address the scandal of Christian divisions.[15] Participation by Protestants in the Catholic Biblical Association and by Catholics in the Society of Biblical Literature is taken for granted; it symbolizes the progress that has been made in ecumenism

in the last forty-five years. Besides being of service to the churches on complex questions of history, biblical exegesis, and church practice, this model ecumenism shows that Christians have less to fear from one another than to be gained by cooperation.

(7) A final contribution of biblical studies goes beyond merely an intellectual dimension to a faith dimension. Biblical studies in the seminary represent an area where the intellectual and the spiritual can truly be wedded in a blissful union. As the teaching from the Synod on the Word of God emphasized, the ancient tradition of *lectio divina* holds a great promise to promote this unity. We should also remember that for the fathers of the church, there was an extremely close connection between the study of the Sacred Scriptures and prayer.[16] Biblical studies provide an arena where the blend between the intellectual and the spiritual can be most fruitful. Seminarians, if properly taught good exegetical method, can also learn that the study of Scripture can be intimately tied to the experience of praying the Scriptures. This is not to say that study and prayer are exactly the same phenomenon. Rather, the study of Sacred Scripture should be a related exercise, one that both prepares for prayer and leads to greater insight into the text for its spiritual message. Father Hogan had also admonished his readers to be aware of the different approaches they could take to Scripture, for he wrote, "for a priest engaged in ministry, the study of the Bible may be literary, or devotional, or doctrinal, or apologetic."[17] Yet he also believed that the newer methods of exegesis were not *de*structive of the faith perspective on the Bible but *in*structive. An advantage to this viewpoint is also to save the Bible from becoming the object of scientific scrutiny only from the perspective of the "university." Teaching biblical studies in seminaries, and maintaining the quality of biblical scholarship among seminary professors, helps prevent biblical study from being merely an academic exercise. Exegesis from the perspective of faith, and within the purview of the church, makes an important statement to the world. These sacred writings are canonical and inspired words that continue to shape the life of the church. Of course, this is an area where seminary instruction all too often fails. As Katarina Schuth, a noted expert on priestly formation programs, remarks, "in practice, theologate personnel have not determined clearly how to help students apply their academic knowledge to pastoral situations or to their interior life."[18] Yet, this could almost be a refrain about biblical study in any era of church history. The hermeneutical task is always the most difficult one to fulfill, but it is an area where intellectual and spiritual interests can fruitfully merge.

These seven skills are not meant to be comprehensive (despite the use of the perfect biblical number!). They are merely suggestive of the contribution that I believe biblical study has made, or ideally can make, to the formation of future priests. However, before concluding, it will be instructive to look briefly at what the Bible itself might say to this endeavor, lest we fall into the trap of only reading *about* it.

The Testimony of the Bible

If one was limited only to the book of Ecclesiastes, one might find a sympathetic voice to the seminarian's sentiment expressed at the beginning of this chapter: "much study is a weariness of the flesh" (12:12). Although the Bible has little to say about its own use, a few indications are given from which we can take our own cues. The wisdom tradition especially communicates the importance of pouring over the sacred writings, particularly emphasizing the Torah. The psalmist who expresses that "fear of the LORD is the beginning of wisdom" (Ps 111:10) also commends those who do not forget the Word of God (Ps 119:15-16) because "their delight is in the law of the LORD, and on his law they meditate day and night" (Ps 1:2). An even more potent image is found in the prophet Ezekiel (Ezek 2:9–3:3). God instructs the prophet to eat the scroll on which powerful words of woe and lamentation are written, but Ezekiel surprisingly finds that "in my mouth it was as sweet as honey." Interestingly, an essay in Hubert Box's book also makes reference to this passage and comments, correctly I think, on the meaning of eating the scroll: "It was only when Ezekiel had eaten the scroll—that is to say, when he had read, marked, learned, and inwardly digested God's word—that he was ready to teach."[19] The study of Scripture is truly a task of digesting the Word of God. When the author of Second Timothy writes that "all scripture is inspired by God and is useful for teaching, for refutation, for correction, and for training in righteousness" (3:16), it is not from a simplistic or fundamentalistic perspective. Rather, the purpose of such study of God's Word is to make the minister "competent, equipped for every good work" (2 Tim 3:17). Forming priests who are competent in every respect, in spiritual, intellectual, moral, dogmatic, and pastoral matters, is the task of every seminary faculty. The testimony of the Bible, then, is primarily to issue a challenge to seminarians and priests. Take up the Word! Eat it; digest it; incorporate it in your life; meditate on it day and night. Then you will become the competent minister of the Word you are called to be.

As this chapter has sought to demonstrate, the formal study of the Bible can greatly contribute to the intellectual and spiritual formation of priests in an ongoing fashion. We who seek to digest God's sacred Word in mind and heart and soul can inspire others to do the same and, in turn, give nourishment to all God's people. This is surely a task worthy of the future as much as it has been a testimony of the past. In joining "so great a cloud of witnesses" (Heb 12:1), we Sulpicians who specialize in the field of biblical studies also help to fulfill the vision of our founder, Jean-Jacques Olier, evoked at the beginning of this book, who first saw the need for professional training of future priests and responded to it with vision.

Chapter Eleven

Ongoing Priestly Formation: Option or Necessity?

One of the more vexing problems currently encountered in the priesthood is the lack of time. Priests are very busy today. Many wear multiple "hats" in their dioceses. Many others are pastors of multiple parishes, sometimes spread out geographically. With regard to ongoing priestly formation, which is my main "frontline" ministry when not engaged in administration, I encounter regularly the following two obstacles: time and resources.

In Europe and North America, where the priest shortage is most evident, the complaint is the lack of time and replacements. Priests who desire a minisabbatical of one to three months (let alone six months or a year!) often cannot get the release from their bishop to do so. Even finding a day here or there for personal renewal can be a challenge.

In the southern hemisphere, especially in Africa and South America, the priest shortage is also critical, but there is the added problem of fewer resources, financial or otherwise, to promote ongoing formation of clergy. So what is to be done?

During the Year for Priests (June 2009–June 2010), I participated in many convocations, colloquia, and study days for priests in which I found a great enthusiasm and thirst for further enrichment. In general, I could sense that the priests were interested in anything that could reinvigorate their ministry or give them even a little insight that they had not thought of before. It reinforced my own convictions about ongoing formation. So let me state my position clearly at the outset: in my judgment, ongoing formation is not an option but a necessity that comes with ordination to the priesthood. To meet the need, we must become more creative.

Historical Background

Prior to the Second Vatican Council (1962–65), the notion of ongoing formation or education of clergy was largely absent. Postordination education was rare except in instances when priests, destined for the chancery or seminary ministry, were sent for graduate studies in canon law or other subjects. The notion of inherent ongoing formation for clergy was largely unknown.

Even the council's principal teaching on ordained ministry did not address the theme in any detailed fashion. The main document on the priesthood, *Presbyterorum Ordinis*, the Decree on the Ministry and Life of Priests, only mentions it twice. In the context of urging bishops to be attentive to their priests as brothers, the council fathers wrote,

> For on their [the bishops'] shoulders particularly falls the burden of sanctifying their priests: therefore they are to exercise the greatest care in the progressive formation [*continua formatione*] of their diocesan body of priests. (7)

In another passage of the same document, the council fathers are more explicit:

> To facilitate study and the more effective learning of methods of evangelization and the apostolate, every attention is to be given to providing priests with suitable helps. Examples of these are the organization according to the conditions of each territory of courses or congresses, the setting up of centers designed for pastoral studies, the founding of libraries, and the proper direction of studies by suitable persons.
>
> In addition bishops . . . should consider more effective ways of arranging that their priests would be able to attend a course of study at certain times, especially for a few years after ordination. The aim of the course would be to give them an opportunity of increasing their knowledge of pastoral methods and theological science. (19)[1]

In *Christus Dominus*, the council's Decree on the Pastoral Office of Bishops in the Church, the notion of ongoing formation is also more explicit:

> A bishop should be solicitous for the welfare—spiritual, intellectual, and material—of his priests, so that they may live holy and pious lives, and exercise a faithful and fruitful ministry. With this end in view he should encourage courses and arrange for special conferences for his priests from time to time. These could take the form of extended retreats for the renewal of their spiritual lives or courses intended to deepen their knowledge of ecclesiastical studies, especially of sacred scripture and theology, of the more important social questions, or of new methods of pastoral activity. (16)

In general, Vatican II thus marks a shift in priestly formation in the sense of explicitly recognizing a role for ongoing formation and education of priests.

Thankfully, in fulfillment of this vision, many dioceses sponsor periodic meetings or convocations for their clergy, priests, and deacons to promote various types of ongoing formation. Note that the operative word is "formation" rather than "education," for the goal is not merely in the intellectual arena. Priestly formation also addresses human, spiritual, and pastoral dimensions of ministry, thus fostering a comprehensive approach to priestly formation as envisioned in the integration of the four pillars of *PDV*.

In the first three decades or so after the council, many programs of ongoing formation were developed and attracted sizable numbers of participants. In the United States, an organization was formed to promote such programs, with a somewhat cumbersome name, National Organization for Continuing Education of Roman Catholic Clergy (www.nocercc.org). Unfortunately, at the present time, many programs that held such promise and have fulfilled their mission faithfully for many years have diminished, owing to a lack of available participants and/or financial resources. One example is our own Sulpician-operated Vatican II Institute for Clergy Formation at St. Patrick's Seminary & University in Menlo Park, California. In its more than thirty years of ministry, the institute has had several thousand priests, and even a few bishops, go through its doors. Its signature program was always a three-month residential sabbatical, with an emphasis on holistic ongoing formation. Attention is given to all four pillars of formation—human, spiritual, intellectual, and pastoral. But in recent years the program has had to be cut back to one, rather than two, three-month sabbatical experience per year, owing to the lack of sufficient availability of participants. On the other hand, the institute has creatively designed many more short-term programs, varying from one to several weeks, which address various aspects of ongoing priestly formation. These include programs for newly ordained, new pastors, and those on the verge of retirement. The success of these newer, shorter programs has pointed out that needs are still present for ongoing formation experiences for priests. But there is also no real substitute for a three-month hiatus in ministry during which one can rest, recuperate, and reenergize. This will likely remain a challenge for many dioceses for years to come.

The Contribution of *Pastores Dabo Vobis*

With the publication of *PDV*, the initiative of ongoing formation got a big boost. This creative document, as noted in chapter 1 above, is notable for many reasons, but the most pertinent point to our topic is that it is the first time, to my knowledge, the church addressed the theme of ongoing formation of priests at length. The exhortation devotes an entire chapter (chap. 6, pars. 70–81) to the topic, which is worth summarizing here.

The chapter begins with a quotation from Scripture: "I remind you to rekindle the gift of God that is within you" (2 Tim 1:6). This quotation, Paul's advice to his younger colleague Timothy, sets the tone for the chapter. In a sense, it is the advice to be continually refreshed or renewed in ministry, precisely so that we can be more effective and grow in our capacity as servants of God's people.

The chapter also explains the process of ongoing formation as related to "continual conversion" (*PDV*, 70). This is an acknowledgment that we are never fully formed. There is always more to learn, more to explore, and more spiritual depth to gain. This is a profoundly biblical perspective. Ongoing formation is an invitation to delve deeper into the mystery of God. Jesus always called his disciples to conversion (*metanoia*), and Paul consistently reminded his colleagues to put into practice all that they had been taught.[2] For priests, the goal should ultimately be a harmonious maturity in the four pillars of priestly formation: human, spiritual, intellectual, and pastoral. As *PDV* says,

> The path toward maturity does not simply demand that the priest deepen the different aspects of his formation. It also demands above all that he be able to combine evermore harmoniously all these aspects, gradually achieving their inner unity. (72)

The document also notes an admirable practical goal:

> Ongoing formation helps the priest to overcome the temptation to reduce his ministry to an activism which becomes an end in itself, to the provision of impersonal services, even if these are spiritual or sacred, or to a businesslike function which he carries out for the Church. (72)

To flesh out this topic further, the final chapter of *PDV* speaks at length about many concrete aspects of ongoing formation, but I believe the most important points can be digested in the following list of eight:

- Ongoing formation is not a repeat of seminary content but should involve new and deeper insights into all aspects of pastoral ministry. (This is an important point easily overlooked by designing programs that mimic seminary formation; such programs generally "turn off" priests rather than stimulate them.)
- The recognition of and desire for ongoing formation should be instilled in seminarians during their years of seminary formation.
- All four principal areas—human, spiritual, intellectual, pastoral—should be addressed in ongoing formation; it is thus ideally a holistic process.
- Ongoing formation is an aid to staying fresh in pastoral ministry; it is another means of authentically serving the people of God.
- Ongoing formation with fellow presbyters can strengthen the bonds of communion that should exist in presbyterates.
- Where possible or practicable, ongoing formation of both religious and diocesan priests together is beneficial.
- Ongoing formation applies to all levels of priestly ministry: young priests, priests in middle age, and even those in retirement.
- Ongoing formation is a personal responsibility, but bishops and parishioners should do whatever is possible to permit and promote ongoing formation of priests.

One should also notice that *PDV* is not naive in proposing this vision. It cautions explicitly,

> The conditions in which the ministry of priests—often and in many places—has to be carried out nowadays do not make it easy to undertake a serious commitment to formation. The multiplication of responsibilities and services, the complexity of human life in general and the life of the Christian communities in particular, the activism and anxiety that are features of vast areas of society today often deprive priests of

> the time and energies they need to "take heed of themselves" (cf. 1 Tm. 4:16). (78)

Furthermore, the document does not endorse any one approach to the question. It acknowledges various models of ongoing formation, even though it recommends certain key elements, such as meeting regularly with a spiritual director.

In sum, *PDV* presents the church in great detail a clarion call to promote ongoing formation for its clergy. It is part and parcel of priesthood. But what about implementation?

Challenges and Obstacles

In 2001 the bishops of the United States took up the vision of *PDV* in the publication of their document The Basic Plan for the Ongoing Formation of Priests (often dubbed "the green book" for the color of its cover),[3] which set forth a comprehensive approach to implementing *PDV*. It is both an inspiring and practical document, with multiple suggestions of methods of ongoing formation at all levels of priestly ministry. Unfortunately, the sexual abuse crisis of 2002 hit just after its publication, and the document quickly receded into the background.

Several dioceses in the United States have nonetheless taken steps to implement this pastoral vision for priests, but I know of only a handful of dioceses that have taken ongoing formation seriously enough to *expect* it of clergy. At least one diocese actually *requires* verifiable evidence of attendance at sessions of ongoing formation, such as workshops, programs, an annual retreat, and conventions, in order to be eligible for a pastorate or a move to a more desirable assignment. That takes ongoing formation seriously!

The challenges of promoting ongoing formation among priests are well known. One needs time, money, temporary replacements for priests who will be absent from their assignments for a time, and practical and attractive programs. The latter item can certainly be found in many parts of the developed world, but time, money, and replacements are lacking, especially when other, more urgent, needs take precedence. Moreover, priests don't always perceive ongoing formation as important.

Multiple Contexts for Ongoing Formation

The Basic Plan itself places this question in ten distinct contexts (from a North American and US point of view, to be sure) that are important (pt. 1, H). They provide the broader motivation for and the situational factors that influence the importance of ongoing formation. I summarize them here:

(1) The first and most basic context is personal. Priests should recognize the need for ongoing formation for personal and professional reasons.

(2) The reality of divisions within presbyterates, which I believe mirror to some degree the divisions that exist in the post–Vatican II church today, makes ongoing formation in a communal dimension a necessity. We won't really find common ground without it.

(3) The priest shortage and the changing complexity of the lived experience of the priesthood that this diminishing resource entails could be, at least in part, addressed by ongoing formation and education efforts. Priests need help to understand what is happening around them today, and ongoing formation can provide multiple avenues for this process.

(4) The countercultural aspect of priesthood, and for that matter, the church itself, provides another important context. The church finds itself more and more at odds with many of the secular values of a society desperately searching for spirituality and answers to the complex questions of life but unable (or perhaps, to a degree, unwilling) to find it in our preaching and teaching. This context is made all the more complicated by the scandals that have rocked the priesthood. We cannot hope to address this complexity alone. Ongoing formation with other priests is essential.

(5) The multicultural reality that is so obvious in the church today provides another important context. The presence of many international priests who minister in the United States has entirely changed the practical lives of many presbyterates. Forging a common identity, surrounding a diocesan bishop and cooperating in ministry with him and fellow presbyters, is a major challenge today. Again, ongoing formation can play an essential role in surmounting the challenge that comes with this diversity, which is only going to increase in the years ahead.

(6) Economic and social shifts, both within the society at large and within the church, provide yet another context. Many dioceses have been turned practically upside down by the necessity to reorganize, some in the face of serious financial crunches, others more from the result of demographic shifts. Priests must cope with these realities.

(7) Engagement with the society at large on questions of justice, life, and reconciliation forms another context for ongoing formation. Recent years have seen serious discussion and even divisions or tensions among bishops, priests, and laity about how to handle such complex realities in the public forum. Again, the area is far too large for individuals to

manage. Ongoing formation can provide a format to make headway on such serious questions.

(8) The "new evangelization," which was a centerpiece of Blessed John Paul II's ecclesial strategy and which has been picked up and developed much further by his successor, Pope Benedict XVI, gives us the eighth context.[4] The Holy Father has made the unusual move to create a new dicastery in the Roman Curia, the Pontifical Council for the New Evangelization, to address this issue, highlighting its significance. Priests too need to join this effort, but we also should recognize that it is a message that we need to hear ourselves, as well as address to others.

(9) The fact that the church finds itself in a certain fluidity since the conclusion of the Second Vatican Council, and that polarization is still a reality on so many levels of church life, is another context. With the fiftieth anniversaries of both the opening (1962) and closing (1965) of Vatican II coming up, I believe this context will become even more important. It could provide clergy with a great opportunity to discuss in greater depth how the past fifty years have led us to this context in our history and how the next fifty years might impact priestly ministry.

(10) Finally, the Basic Plan points to the search for retrieving an authentic priestly identity in the midst of the need to recognize the multiplicity of diverse ministries within the church and necessity of collaboration with them. This is an ongoing question and one that holds much promise. But it requires that priests feel secure in their own identity, unthreatened by other legitimate and essential ministries within the church.

These ten contexts obviously present a broad, almost overwhelming, vision of what is at stake in ongoing priestly formation. If the list is not exhaustive, it is certainly comprehensive. It helps to explain also why the church would take so seriously the question of ongoing formation for its frontline ministers of Word and sacrament.

A Plan of Action

All of this poses a challenge for implementing ongoing formation. Although I do not have a solution to all the challenges that confront priests and dioceses for the implementation of a plan for ongoing formation, I would suggest that, in agreement with the DMLP and the Basic Plan, it is first and foremost the personal responsibility of every priest. It need not be an insurmountable obstacle, if we believe it is a necessity and not an option. I have also found that, if we truly make this a priority, ongoing formation can happen.

For example, where finances are lacking, some dioceses have developed a plan of shared expenses, in which the diocese, the parish, and the priest share the costs equally. Some have also found sponsors to subsidize priests taking time for ongoing formation. Dioceses should be encouraged to develop plans for ongoing formation and the means of implementing them. Priests, for their part, should take advantage of them. Even in cases where few opportunities are available, every priest could do at least some of the following:

- Get a spiritual director with whom you can meet on a regular basis.
- Take a personal day off each month for spiritual and intellectual renewal.
- Get at least one new commentary on the gospel of the liturgical year (whether Matthew, Mark, or Luke) and work your way through it as you prepare your homilies for the year. (John is covered each year, especially in Lent and Easter, so it is an option at any time.)
- Buy (or borrow) at least one new theological or serious religious book a year.[5]
- Subscribe to at least one theological, liturgical, or pastoral journal to try to keep abreast of developments.
- Attend whatever days of recollection, retreats, or workshops are sponsored by your diocese, religious community, or local church or university.
- Lobby your presbyteral council and diocesan bishop for ways to promote ongoing formation.
- Make your parishioners aware of your desire for ongoing formation and inform them of the opportunities you will take; let them know it is a priority that benefits you and them.
- For those who are computer savvy, take advantage of many resources on the internet. Although one has to be careful about the quality and accuracy of information on the World Wide Web, there is an incredible amount of fine resources available if you know how to find them. The Congregation for the Clergy itself has a web site worth visiting that can direct priests to other resources (http://www.clerus.org/english/00000041_Home_English.html).

A Renewed Biblical and Ecclesial Vision

To be a bit more focused, I propose that there are actually two main reasons why we should promote ongoing formation and education of priests. One is biblical, and one is ecclesiological.

First and foremost, ongoing formation should be seen as an essential ingredient of priesthood. It fulfills the biblical call to perpetual conversion and the recognition that we are, at least on this earth, never fully completed products. Ordination is not the end of a process but the beginning of a new one, by which we deepen our conformity to Christ the High Priest. We priests are also members of the pilgrim church. We too are called to be transformed by God's grace and to be renewed at every stage of our personal journey. As *PDV* proposes, ongoing formation really is a fulfillment of the call to "rekindle the gift of God" that we have received at ordination.

Even more important is the example of Jesus himself. Although the notion of ongoing formation or education is not a biblical category, as such, Jesus' practice of drawing apart from his ministry for times of prayer must be seen in an analogous light. In the face of the demands of ministry, it is both understandable and legitimate that ministers should take time away for themselves. Jesus periodically withdrew from active ministering to people for personal renewal and refreshment. The context is obviously a prayerful one, but it can be understood as a time for personal renewal, a type of holistic ongoing formation that could sustain him in ministry.

Matthew, for instance, records this one such occasion, recalling the biblical setting of the mountain as a place of revelation and a sacred site in which one could draw close to God: "And after he had dismissed the crowds, he went up the mountain by himself to pray" (Matt 14:23). Solitude, prayer, silence, being apart from frenetic activity, unavailable for a time to people's ceaseless pastoral needs—all these are part of what it means to be attentive to one's own ongoing formation. Luke likewise reports Jesus' activity, using the form of a verb that indicates it was a regular or habitual practice: "But he [Jesus] would withdraw to deserted places and pray" (Luke 5:16).[6] If Jesus himself could take time away from his ministry, surely we can do likewise; we have more need of holistic renewal than Jesus. For some priests, it means abandoning a kind of messiah complex in which they see themselves as indispensable. For all priests, it should be viewed as a normal part of ministry at every stage of priestly development.

The second reason for ongoing priestly formation and education is ecclesiological. The goal of such activity is ultimately pastoral and professional. If we are to meet the needs of our people in our day, then we must continually be renewed in the multiple aspects of our priesthood, especially the four pillars outlined in *PDV*. Attending to our human, spiritual, intellectual, and pastoral formation in an ongoing fashion not only benefits ourselves personally but it also makes us more effective and up-to-date ministers for our people. Implicitly, and in some instances explicitly, the church's recent multiple documents that call for ongoing formation of priests are an acknowledgment that there are professional dimensions of priesthood that should not be ignored.

The Curé of Ars as Model

During the Year for Priests (June 2009–June 2010), Pope Benedict proposed St. John Mary Vianney as a model for priests. The Curé of Ars's spiritual holiness was certainly the prime reason why the Holy Father invited priests to reflect again on the life of this remarkable pastor. His holiness was legendary and is certainly inspiring, and we priests need to be reminded on a regular basis of the need for personal holiness. But there was a strong pastoral aspect as well. The connection between ministry and holiness was evident in the Curé. We should not lose sight of the fact that, as the pope says in his letter that announced the Year for Priests, the Curé of Ars regularly "taught his parishioners primarily by the witness of his life." It was a life that essentially acknowledged the need to be reformed, renewed, and refreshed in God's grace. Father Vianney relied totally on God's grace but also worked hard to fulfill the mission his bishop entrusted to him.

This aspect of Father Vianney's ministry is obviously inspiring. Holiness is essential to priestly ministry. People want and need holy priests. But what sometimes is overlooked in this crucial perspective is another side to the Curé's ministry that remained in the shadows. Without question, he was certainly a holy priest. But he was not simplistic or naive when it came to pastoral ministry. Over time people wrongly developed the notion that he was not particularly intelligent but rather pious and simple. In reality, his main problem in the seminary was not a lack of intelligence. Rather, he could not master Latin! (He is hardly the only one to have endured this ignominy.) Although he was probably not the most academically inclined student, he did in fact possess a personal library that outnumbered those of most of his contemporary priests, amounting to some three hundred books. Moreover, from his experience and knowledge he gave people more than pious platitudes. They came to him to confess because he offered them sound spiritual advice that helped them cope with the challenges of their everyday lives. He also fed them with God's own message, not his own. Although he was personally ascetic, he went out of his way to host fellow priests with festive meals and to promote a common priestly bond. One might imagine him sharing thoughts on priestly ministry with brother priests in a fraternal setting, such as many priests do today by means of support groups.

My point is that the Curé was more than a model for holiness. He was also a good pastor who did everything he could to be effective in his ministry. In this he provides a model for ongoing priestly formation that is a multifaceted reality and that tries to promote integration in priestly ministry. His parish was troublesome, and he sometimes threatened to leave. He nearly gave up, but with God's grace and his own persistence he endured. Since I doubt that most of us priests today have the same spiritual depth as Father Vianney, I don't think we can rely only on our personal sanctity to make our priesthood bear the fruit of pastoral ministry. These days we need much more support and guidance. We also need to participate with fellow presbyters, joined with the bishop, to promote a common ministry. Ongoing formation is an essential means to foster this pastoral vision in our day.

In conclusion, the priestly vocation to which we are called is both gift and task. Priesthood is not a right but a privilege, a unique call to follow Jesus Christ as a disciple in a very specific way. It requires openness to God's grace, but it also demands certain knowledge, skills, and a willingness to grow in ministry. Ongoing formation is a kind of priestly way of cooperating with God's grace. It is an act of surrender to Jesus the High Priest, who can mold us more and more in his own image. If we take advantage of the resources that abound in our day and age, then I think we will fulfill our call to orders as well as anyone has the right to expect.

Chapter Twelve

The Graying of the Clergy: A Biblical-Pastoral Perspective

In the course of many priest convocations, retreats, and study days that I have had the privilege of attending, one fact is readily apparent—the graying of the clergy. Many dioceses not only face a priest shortage but the aging of the clergy has also become a major concern. Some dioceses do not have adequate resources, financial or otherwise, to accommodate a large number of elderly priests. Even more disconcerting is the threat to some priest retirement programs in the face of lawsuits that have stemmed from the sexual abuse crisis. Moreover, many priests are poor at planning for retirement and consequently face enormous challenges as retirement looms and practical questions of residence, health care, and the like arrive sooner than expected. So what can one say to this situation?

In this chapter, I propose to examine this question briefly through a biblical-pastoral perspective. After a brief contextual comment, we will take a look at a biblical perspective on aging, in general. Then we will examine a few pastoral aspects of the graying of the clergy.

The Context of Aging

Like so many other "baby boomers," in the past few years I have had to deal with aging parents. After the death of my father at the venerable age of ninety-two, my siblings and I decided that my mother, who had been diagnosed with Alzheimer's disease, would need to move to an assisted care facility.

Recently, that facility sponsored a special presentation on Alzheimer's. My mother dutifully attended and came back with a few interesting materials that she proceeded to describe to me. She pointed out that she was not sure if she was in the early stage, the middle stage, or the end stage of the disease. But then with a twinkle in her eye, she said to me, "It probably doesn't matter. Even if I did know, I wouldn't remember it anyway!" At least she has not lost her sense of humor.

We are privileged to live in a time when people are living longer, and generally healthier, lives. Reaching one hundred years of age is no longer a rare and special feat. Many countries have hundreds, even thousands, of centenarians. Supposedly, the verifiably oldest living human on the planet, a Texas woman, died in early 2011 at 115 years of age!

Seniors have become a special segment in our society. Businesses, politicians, and advertisers court seniors because they constitute such a powerful segment in society. The AARP has practically transformed representation of seniors' interests into an art form. Yet in a society that also touts youth, vitality, and sensuality—and uses these in all kinds of seductive advertising—one cannot help but wonder whether we really appreciate growing old the way we should. The Bible, I think, offers a useful perspective.

An Old Testament Perspective

In biblical times the average life span was really quite short. Most people could expect to live only perhaps into their forties, fifties, or sixties, if one survived infancy or childhood. Infant mortality was extremely high. Even the psalmist has to admit that the exceptions were, by our standards, not very remarkable: "Seventy is the sum of our years or, eighty if we are strong, and most of them are fruitless toil and they pass quickly and we drift away" (Ps 90:10, my translation).

Yet living a long life was a cherished goal. To live a long life meant that a person had received God's blessing. The book of Genesis, in particular, makes this point in almost comic fashion. Genesis 5 contains a long list of human ancestors, stretching from Adam to Noah. Note the remarkable ages attributed to them: Adam died at age 930, Seth at 912, Enosh at 905, Kenan at 910, Mahalalel at 895, and famous Methusaleh at 969! Not only that, but they are said to be fertile and have children at venerable ages as well. After his five-hundredth birthday, Noah was said to have fathered Shem, Ham, and Japheth (Gen 5:32). (What kind of vitamins did he use?)

These stories, of course, are not meant to be taken literally. The OT attributes long life to its heroes. The longer one lived, the more heroic, important, and honored the individual was considered. Living a long life also enabled people to fulfill their obligations to God honorably. The cry of the psalmist is instructive: "So even to old age and gray hairs, O God, do not forsake me, until I proclaim your might to all the generations to come" (Ps 71:18).

The OT also associates long life (and gray hair!) with wisdom. It is not the longevity itself that mattered as much as the experience that came with it. The book of Wisdom says, "For old age is not honored for length of time, or measured by number of years; but understanding is gray hair for anyone, and a blameless life is ripe old age" (Wis 4:8-9). Another wisdom figure, Ben Sirach, advises, "My child, from your youth choose discipline, and when you have gray hair you will still find wisdom" (Sir 6:18). And Job's young friend Elihu, out of respect, defers to the elders before speaking, when he offers his own interpretation of Job's calamities (Job 32:4).

If living a long life was an ideal, the OT is not naive about what often accompanies such length of days. The Bible's quintessential skeptic, Qoheleth (called in Greek, Ecclesiastes), was particularly blunt about growing old:

> Remember your creator in the days of your youth, before the days of trouble come, and the years draw near when you will say, "I have no pleasure in them"; before the sun and the light and the moon and the stars are darkened and the clouds return with the rain; in the day when the guards of the house tremble, and the strong men are bent, and the women who grind cease working because they are few, and those who look through the windows see dimly. (Eccl 12:1-3)

The authors of the OT knew well that old age often brought with it many physical ailments and vulnerability. One group is consistently singled out for special protection because they are so vulnerable—widows.

As in our day, women in biblical times generally lived longer than men. Little wonder that widows (along with orphans and strangers) became a focal point for Jewish acts of charity. As part of the reform God demanded of Jerusalem, the prophet Isaiah cried out, "learn to do good; seek justice, rescue the oppressed, defend the orphan, plead for the widow" (Isa 1:17), and the law itself commanded, "You shall not abuse any widow or orphan" (Exod 22:22).

The OT also narrates that old age can hold some real surprises. Through God's grace, some characters miraculously bear children in old age, like Abraham and Sarah, who are promised that they will bear a son, Isaac, in their old age (Gen 18:12-14). Indeed, this incredible life-giving act becomes symbolic of God's ability to achieve remarkable deeds beyond normal human expectations. Even in old age, one can become a special servant of God.

Finally, God includes older people in the restoration of Jerusalem after the Babylonian exile. The prophet Zechariah specifically promises,

> Thus says the Lord of hosts: Old men and old women shall again sit in the streets of Jerusalem, each with staff in hand because of their great age. And the streets of the city shall be full of boys and girls playing in its streets. (Zech 8:4-5)

In other words, the elderly will be part of the resurrection of the Holy City, along with the young.

A New Testament Perspective

Not surprisingly, the perspective of the NT on aging is similar to that of the OT. The early Christian community respected age as normally a sign of experience, wisdom, and prudence. The community purposefully sought out "elders" (Greek, *presbyteroi*) for leadership positions.[1] Such persons were also commended for their exceptional virtues and qualities achieved over time, such as integrity, wisdom, patience, tolerance, and the like (Titus 1:7-8).

Like the OT, the NT also affirms that surprising events can take place in old age. The conception of John the Baptist at the advanced age of his parents, Elizabeth and Zechariah, is another example of God's mysterious ability to foster life even at the most unexpected times (Luke 1:18).

Jesus himself, like his relative, the prophet John the Baptist, died at a fairly young age. Both were martyred before their time. Yet Jesus' teaching shows signs of traditional respect for elders. Although Luke's gospel portrays him as a precocious youngster of twelve, able to outshine the best teachers of the temple in Jerusalem, he nonetheless is said to be obedient to Mary and Joseph (Luke 2:41-51). The text goes on to emphasize his growth as he matured: "And Jesus increased in wisdom and in years, and in divine and human favor" (Luke 2:52). Thus, despite his special divine status, Jesus experienced growth in wisdom as he matured.

Jesus' teaching also acknowledged some sensitivity to the challenges of aging. He favorably contrasts the poor widow who gives of her poverty with the wealthy who give of their abundance (Luke 21:1-4). He also graciously raises to life a young man whose mother, a widow, would have otherwise been bereft of any support with the death of her only child (Luke 7:12-16).

In an even more tender scene that is filled with deep theological symbolism, Jesus entrusts the care of his mother to the Beloved Disciple (John 20:26-27), and vice versa, so that she will be properly taken care of when he is gone. This exchange symbolizes the birth of a new community—the church, the family of God—in which all will play a role, regardless of their age.[2]

In the teaching of Jesus, especially as phrased in John's gospel, "eternal life" is a promise made to those who believe in Jesus. Of course, this expression does not refer to human existence but to heavenly existence, life after death, or the resurrected life. But one should note that the meaning is not only length of days (eternity) but also quality of life (divine).

Interestingly, the NT exhibits evidence of a special role entrusted to widows in the early Christian community. In St. Paul's churches (among others), widows were entrusted with special ministerial duties in the community. One can almost speak of an "order" of widows. What is really noteworthy, though, is the advice that younger widows, still of marriageable age, should not be invited into these orders until they reach a distinguished status (age sixty or so). The reason is that they may well become distracted and desire to remarry and raise a family while they remain young! Thus the "order" of widows really was meant for older women who had already exercised good hospitality and care of the needy. (See the full description in 1 Tim 5:3-16.) So the NT shows a practical side to the issue of including the elderly in special ministries.

Summary of the Biblical Perspective on Aging

So what can we say about the Bible's view of aging? Let me pull it together by means of three summary statements.

First, the Bible sees long life as an ideal and a natural goal for human beings to seek. Long life is a gift from God that should be appreciated and honored. But neither is it an absolute value in itself. Living long does not guarantee the quality of the life lived; dying young does not mean one has failed.

Second, growing old is a normal part of life. It is one of life's seasons. It is also a double-edged sword. On the one hand, it brings experience, wisdom, and understanding. On the other, it is often accompanied by physical and/or mental decline, and vulnerability. All three are realities that often accompany aging.

Third, the community should honor its senior citizens and bring them into the center of community life. They should not be marginalized. The elderly still have much to contribute to the life of the community, whether formally (such as in organizations or specific ministries) or informally (such as sharing wisdom and life's experiences).

Senior Priests

Now we turn to the question of the aging clergy. I think the biblical perspective is helpful in evaluating our own experience of the increasing age of clergy today, especially in the northern hemisphere. The Basic Plan rightly states that senior priests are simply "part of the graying of America" (pt. 2, E). Aging is a reality that touches every aspect of American life today. Just as in ancient times, growing old can be both gift and struggle. The elderly bring a perspective that should never be cast aside, even though the young are the ones who will have to face the long-term future and create their own destinies. Priests are no different.

Our society has a tendency to hide the elderly away and to focus on being youthful. While we do not live in an age where families can necessarily take care of their elderly at home, we do have ways of keeping the elderly in the midst of our communities. Taking the time to visit the elderly, especially those in assisted care facilities and nursing homes, is still an important corporal work of mercy. Also, we should help seniors capitalize on what they can engage in productively. Most important is the ministry of prayer. Seniors often have lots of quiet time that could be used for prayer. But other possibilities come to mind: letter writing to other shut-ins or to troops overseas, tutoring school children, teaching people how to read, or collecting donations for the poor. Three other possible ministries include serving as spiritual directors for active clergy (as well as laity, of course); being special confessors for priests, seminarians, and others; or, for those who still have good eyesight, reading to people who are visually impaired.

Perhaps even more important is offering the elderly our assurance and comfort that aging is a natural part of life. It is not always easy. The late Pope John Paul II wrote eloquently in his 1999 Letter to the Elderly of the struggles of his own increasing frailty, which all the world witnessed for some years before his death. But he also emphasized the value of the elderly in society:

> Elderly people, help us to see human affairs with greater wisdom, because life's vicissitudes have brought them knowledge and maturity. They are the guardians of our collective memory and thus the privileged interpreters of that body of ideals and common values which support and guide life in society. (10)

Not everyone, of course, grows old in an equally gracious manner. Some of us fight it more than others. Some of us have greater struggles and health problems than others. Some of us are simply too stubborn to give in to the aging process. And some of us live under the illusion of the fountain of youth. (I liked a hat my father was given, which boasted: "I'm not old. I'm a recycled teenager.")

One of the more encouraging signs I find among senior priests is their willingness to engage in some form of ministry in accord with their "senior" status. Many priests continue to help out in parishes, often substituting in parishes so that pastors can get away once in awhile for vacation or some spiritual renewal. Of course, understandably, as we grow older we prefer to be out of the hectic pace of pastoral ministry, especially areas of administration that are so often energy-draining. But the motivation appears to be more than mere avoidance of administrative duties. For many priests, serving in parochial ministry as primarily sacramental ministers is a return to the reason they accepted their vocational call in the first place—namely, to serve the Lord and his people explicitly in priestly, and primarily sacramental, ministry. Whatever the exact circumstances of senior priests offering their services in this way, it is heartening to see their unwavering commitment. They also provide a great witness to younger priests and seminarians about the true nature of the priesthood as a lifelong commitment to selfless service.

Yet another striking aspect of the ongoing activity of some senior priests is their continued thirst for knowledge. I am sometimes amazed (and put to shame!) at how current some senior priests have remained, in theology in particular. Many senior priests enjoy the time they now have to read more at their leisure. Even for those who have failing eyesight, there are now many new technological aids, with the production of audiobooks, that make it easier to stay abreast of developments in many fields, including religion, Bible, and theology. Most impressive is that this informal updating encourages senior priests to ask questions and make observations about pertinent matters in the church's life, which sometimes indicates they have not lost their capacity to seek new ideas or new ways of understanding old truths. Surely such intellectual activity, coupled with a rich life of prayer in which one spends more quiet time with the Lord, has a way of helping seniors stay young at heart, if not in body.

This brings us to an easily overlooked aspect of the graying of the clergy, namely, the necessity to attend to some form of ongoing formation. As *PDV*, the DMLP, and the Basic Plan all mention, ongoing formation is something that belongs to the priesthood at every stage of one's priestly ministry, including as one reaches retirement.[3] The passage from *PDV* is worth quoting at length:

> Ongoing formation should also involve those priests who by their advanced years can be called elderly and who in some churches make up the greater part of the presbyterate. The presbyterate should show them gratitude for the faithful service they have performed on behalf of Christ and his Church, and also practical solidarity to help them in their condition. Ongoing formation for these priests will not be a matter so much of study, updating and educational renewal, but rather a calm and reassuring confirmation of the part which they are still called upon to play in the presbyterate, not only inasmuch as they continue—perhaps in different ways—their pastoral ministry, but also because of the possibilities they themselves have, thanks to their experience of life and apostolate, of becoming effective teachers and trainers of other priests.
>
> Also those priests who because of the burden of work or illness find themselves in a condition of physical weakness or moral fatigue can be helped by an on, going [sic] formation which will encourage them to keep up their service to the Church in a calm and sustained fashion, and not to isolate themselves either from the community or from the presbyterate. However, they should reduce their external activities and dedicate themselves to those pastoral contacts and that personal spirituality which can help them keep up their motivation and priestly joy. Ongoing formation will help such priests to keep alive the conviction—which they themselves have inculcated in the faithful—that they continue to be active members for the building up of the Church, especially by virtue of their union with the suffering Christ and with so many other brothers and sisters in the Church who are sharing in the Lord's passion, reliving Paul's spiritual experience when he said, "I rejoice in my sufferings for your sake, and in my flesh I complete what is lacking in Christ's afflictions for the sake of his body, that is, the Church" (Col. 1:24). (77)

I believe these words are an affirmation of priests even as we grow older. Even when we begin to have failing health, our priestly identity need not be diminished, although we will obviously have to restrict our duties and perhaps have serious physical limitations with which to contend. Priestly ministry does not end with the last assignment. Priesthood is an identity one "wears" for all of one's earthly existence. Although we cannot control our own destiny with regard to our physical and mental health as we grow older, we can sustain our spiritual path through prayer and ever more intense communion with the Lord. Each of us hopes to have done the best with the "talents" of our ministry as is humanly possible, and to hear the words of the heavenly Master when we are called to account, "Well done, my good and faithful servant. Since you were faithful in small matters, I will give you great responsibilities. Come, share your master's joy" (Matt 25:21, NABRE). Yet we should recall that the judgment we await is both a matter of how we *did* our ministry and how well we *were* faithful ministers.

Priestly Identity and Function in Senior Years

One of the perennial issues in priesthood is the relationship between identity and function. The DMLP, for example, strongly warns against functionality in priesthood (44). One elderly priest I know reminds priests in a humorous but truthful vein, "If you are what you do, and you don't, then you aren't!" Even senior priests face this challenge.

The Basic Plan speaks at length about priestly identity and function and the challenge we face neither to confuse the two nor fuse them into one and the same reality (pt. 1, E and F). Although what we *do* as priests is intimately related to who we *are*, there is a distinction. As we grow older, we have to be even more attentive to this distinction. The Basic Plan cautions against falling into a particular temptation for the elderly:

> Senior priests gather a lifetime of ministry and can be tempted to wonder whether their efforts made a difference, whether what they did was worthwhile, whether what remains undone eclipses the little that was accomplished. (pt. 2, E)

To fall into the trap of only looking backward and not looking forward can obviously lead one toward depression or, even worse, to despair. Priests are not immune to this temptation. If, however, one chooses even in old age to hold the two realities, being and doing, in tension, then there is a possibility of facing the future—short or long as it might be in literal terms—with hope. Growing old *graciously* and *gracefully* is what is needed, and fortunately there are many exemplary elderly priests in our midst who do this well.

As I write these words, I have just come from several weeks of visiting retired confreres in a few retirement homes in two of our three Sulpician provinces (France and Canada).[4] I was delighted to find that so many of our retired confreres, even those with some serious medical problems, have maintained a very positive, faith-filled, and hopeful attitude. As they look back, it is with gratitude. As they look forward, it is with faith. And in the meantime, they live in communities that clearly exhibit love for one another, as Jesus taught. Even more astonishing was the openness to ongoing formation that some of these elderly confreres modeled. Many of them (several in their eighties!) have managed the complexities of computers and the internet, for instance, while others asked my opinion about recent books or journal articles in theology they had read, or about developments on the ecclesial scene about which I was scarcely aware.[5] Such an attitude takes to heart the expressed desire of the Basic Plan to promote ongoing formation even among senior priests.[6] In short, some older priests can be wonderful models of growing old with grace.

Another example can be found in Blessed John Paul II. As the third Christian millennium approached, the late pope's own thoughts turned to the aging process. I think he did a great service to the whole church and to the world by helping us focus on this major turning point in Christian history. But he was already quite conscious of his own fragility as he grew older. The Holy Father's Letter to the Elderly, mentioned above, provides a profound reflection on the meaning of growing old, viewed quite obviously from a faith perspective. He addresses the elderly of all walks of life but also focuses some comments pertinent to our topic here. In two passages, in particular, he speaks to elderly priests and bishops:

> My thoughts turn in a special way to you, . . . dear brother priests and bishops, who, for reasons of age, no longer have direct responsibility for pastoral ministry. The Church still needs you. She appreciates the services which you may wish to provide in many areas of the apostolate; she counts on the support of your longer periods of prayer; she counts on your advice born of experience, and she is enriched by your daily witness to the Gospel. (13)

The Holy Father then quotes Psalm 16:11: "You show me the path of life, in your presence there is fullness of life." His words, in fact, reflect the reality. Retirement for priests is a different kind of experience than it is for the general public. The reason is not hard to discern. A passage from the Basic Plan explicitly names it well:

> A distinctive moment and experience for senior clergy is "retirement." If "retirement" in priesthood is seen as exactly parallel to the secular sense of retirement—for example, as a complete withdrawal from activities and responsibilities that had marked one's active work life—then this may be a misnomer. Priests are not simply functionaries, workers, or professionals. Who they are sacramentally, their way of being, is as crucial, if not more so, than their particular functioning. In retirement they do not cease *to be* priests, even if there is a shift in what they *do* as priests or in the specific responsibilities they *have* as priests. The event of retirement for priests, then, marks not a radical change of life or vocation but a realignment of activity and responsibility that can have significant human and spiritual impact. (pt. 2, E, emphases in the original)

This is a key insight into the experience of elderly priests. Most priests accept the notion, and live it well, that they are not mere employees or professionals. They have a vocation, and that vocation does not come to an abrupt end with retirement or old age. That is why so many senior priests still admirably fulfill their priestly ministry of Word and sacrament, often as "senior priests" without administrative responsibility but fully engaged in faithful priestly ministry to the end.

Elderly Priests and Sickness

This perspective is well and good if one basically has decent health in old age. It can be another matter, however, if health deteriorates significantly, and illness becomes the major tune in the symphony of life. Frankly, I don't know anyone who likes to be sick. Sometimes laypeople seem to think it must be easier for priests to cope with sickness because of our perspective of faith and presumed serene prayer life. But we know better. In my many conversations with senior priests, many of them have mentioned how difficult it is for them, as they grow older and their bodies begin to wear out, to accept illness graciously. It is easy simply to say to them, "Just pray, and it will help." It sounds like good advice, but sometimes it is just not practical.

I remember being present when in 1995 the late Cardinal Joseph Bernardin, then archbishop of Chicago, received the President's Medal from the Sulpician owned and operated St. Mary's Seminary & University in Baltimore, where he had once studied. He was already very sick with cancer and within a year or so would die of the dread disease. In his gracious acceptance of the award, he spoke about the experience of getting older and especially about his struggle with cancer. I was struck by a piece of advice he gave the audience, among whom were the seminarians. Although I don't recall his exact words, he said something very close to the following: "Learn to pray now, and make prayer a regular feature of your life. If you think you will pray more or better when you get older, or that you will have time when you are sick, forget it. I have often struggled to pray and stay focused in prayer during many days when I had absolutely no energy or was even too sick to get out of bed. I found it extremely difficult. Praying when you are sick is really not that easy."

Cardinal Bernardin's words struck home. Many elderly priests have made similar observations when they were sick. Prayer is really not easy when you are sick. One can be too exhausted or simply unable to focus or concentrate. That is why it is so important to have others praying for us during such trials, and to be conscious that they are accompanying us from a distance in our suffering. I have also been struck by how frequently elderly priests have spoken to me about their eventual deaths. Almost universally they say they don't mind dying. Their faith perspective is intact, and they witness to their belief that death is but a doorway to another life, sharing in the resurrection of Jesus Christ. But almost in the same breath, they add, "But I don't want to suffer. I don't like pain. I don't tolerate it well. I hope the Lord takes me quickly and with as little pain as possible."

I suspect this sentiment is what sometimes drives priests to work to excess as they grow older. They want to "die in their boots," so to speak. I have truly been edified by the energy and stalwart ministry that many elderly priests perform, even in their eighties and nineties. But so much depends on one's health. There are spry ninety-year-olds who neither look nor act their age. And then there are the ancient looking (and acting) sixty- or seventy-year-olds. The fact is, we are not in charge of our own destiny. I think of the words of the risen Jesus to Peter at the conclusion of John's gospel:

> "Very truly, I tell you, when you were younger, you used to fasten your own belt and to go wherever you wished. But when you grow old, you will stretch out your hands, and someone else will fasten a belt around you and take you where you do not wish to go." (He said this to indicate the kind of death by which he would glorify God.) (John 21:18-19)

Like Peter, we priests too must ultimately surrender to the will of the one who calls us and sustains us in life. But we should not be naive about this process. Don't put off a regular personal life of prayer, thinking that when you are older or when you are sick, you will have time for prayer. All too often sickness, especially a serious and life-threatening condition, is so all-encompassing that we won't find the energy or mental and spiritual stamina to sustain prayer, despite our best intentions.

I think the key to maintaining a balanced perspective as we grow older in our ministry is to remain grateful for all that we have received through the grace of ordination. The priesthood is not a right but a great gift. And gratitude is what we owe God for such a great gift to us and to the world. For this attitude, I return briefly to John Paul II's Letter to the Elderly. He eloquently spoke of his own personal desire as he confronted his own mortality. His words should strengthen our own priestly resolve as we face the ultimate challenge that every human being must confront—death.

> In this spirit, dear elderly brothers and sisters, as I encourage each of you to live with serenity the years that the Lord has granted you, I feel a spontaneous desire to share fully with you my own feelings at this point of my life, after more than twenty years of ministry on the throne of Peter and as we await the arrival, now imminent, of the Third Millennium. Despite the limitations brought on by age, I continue to enjoy life. For this I thank the Lord. It is wonderful to be able to give oneself to the very end for the sake of the kingdom of God!
>
> At the same time, I find great peace in thinking of the time when the Lord will call me: from life to life! And so I often find myself saying, with no trace of melancholy, a prayer recited by priests after the celebration of the Eucharist: *In hora mortis meae voca me, et iube me venire ad te*—at the hour of my death, call me and bid me come to you. This is the prayer of Christian hope, which in no way detracts from the joy of the present, while entrusting the future to God's gracious and loving care. (17)

As a priest, I find this attitude worthy of emulation, and I believe most priests would agree. It is a faith-filled and hopeful perspective worthy of our "golden" years.

Conclusion

So what can we say about growing old as priests? We partake of the same aging process with all human beings who share the privilege and the heartache of growing old. If anything, the Bible teaches us that growing old is a gift from God. It should be appreciated as the precious gift it is. Many years ago, I read a book by John R. Powers who expressed in fanciful fashion an image about growing old that has stuck with me. In the book the main character, Tim Conroy, writes letters to God seeking answers to life's mysteries. In one letter he asks, "Why do people grow old?" God's response is,

> Dear Conroy: Although I've created all of you, I often find the way you think quite puzzling. For me the most beautiful moment on earth is old people. They are my human sunsets. Signed: God.[7]

Just as sunsets provide some of God's most awesome artwork in nature, so can the elderly fill us with awe. The Bible affirms this perspective. I only hope that when my time comes to sink below the horizon, I might be as gracious about it as so many of the elderly laypeople, friends, and priests I have known, including my own parents and many of my senior brother Sulpicians.

Epilogue

As we conclude these reflections on various aspects of the priesthood, I would like to return briefly to an image I invoked in the introduction. I recalled Father Jean-Jacques Olier's devotion to Mary and the fact that an emblem of this devotion appears, somewhat surprisingly, in Charles Le Brun's painting of Pentecost.

There is Mary in the midst of the disciples. She too awaits the coming of the Holy Spirit to inspire, to embolden, to set them on fire with so much love of Christ and his teaching that they will go forth and fulfill the command to make disciples of all nations (Matt 28:19; Mark 16:20; Acts 1:8). She who had so willingly said yes to the Lord's mysterious will to bear a Son and Savior for the world patiently awaits the action of the Holy Spirit once more with those who will be charged with this sacred mission.

I like to think that her presence must have been a comfort to the frightened disciples in the Upper Room. She apparently did not judge them or cajole them. She awaited the movement of the Holy Spirit, a silent but reassuring presence. For us now, this image can evoke the relationship between Mary and priests, a special group of disciples of Jesus today, who can sometimes be frightened or discouraged by the challenges in ministry and who need to be bolstered in our commitment.

The church has frequently made a connection between Mary and the priesthood. The Second Vatican Council's teaching on the priesthood, for instance, emphasizes the connection between Mary and the priesthood. The Decree on the Ministry and Life of Priests says of priests,

> They always find a wonderful example of such docility in the Blessed Virgin Mary who under the guidance of the Holy Spirit made a total dedication of herself for the mystery of the redemption of [people]. Priests should always venerate and love her, with a filial devotion and

worship, as the Mother of the supreme and eternal Priest, as Queen of Apostles, and as protectress of their ministry. (*PO*, 18)

Another image is evoked in the Directory on the Ministry and Life of Priests. It recalls a Johannine image of Mary at the foot of the cross being entrusted to the unnamed Beloved Disciple:

> Like John at the foot of the Cross, every priest has been entrusted, in a special way, with Mary as Mother (cf. John 19:26-27).
>
> Priests, who are among the favored disciples of Jesus, crucified and risen, should welcome Mary as their Mother in their own life, bestowing her with constant attention and prayer. The Blessed Virgin then becomes the Mother who leads them to Christ, who makes them sincerely love the Church, who intercedes for them and who guides them toward the Kingdom of heaven.
>
> Every priest knows that Mary, as Mother, is also the most distinguished modeler of his priesthood, since it is she who molds the priestly soul, protects it from dangers, from routine and discouragement, and maternally safeguards it, so he may grow in wisdom, age and grace, before God and men (cf. Luke 2:40). (DMLP, 68)

Finally, one recalls that during the pontificate of the late Blessed John Paul II, invoking the model of the Blessed Virgin Mary, to whom he was particularly devoted, became a feature of many of his official documents, especially those on priesthood and religious life.[1] He deepened and expanded what was already in the church's teaching.

Priests, who are called by the church to be ministers of Word and sacrament, bearers of Good News to the world, thus imitate Mary and also work closely with her in the accomplishment of this mission. She has been entrusted to us, and we to her.

So we return to the Upper Room and the desire for the Holy Spirit once more. If we priests are to experience a rebirth in a new Pentecost, we have to overcome our fear. We have to remain open to receiving the strength that God promises to faithful disciples who are willing to take up the cross to follow Jesus. We cannot allow the crisis of the moment to be the defining mark of our ministry. Nor can we be paralyzed by fear that we will make a mistake or that we are not strong enough or that we will not be accepted or that we will be persecuted. Jesus warned his followers that the road would not be easy (e.g., Matt 10:16-25).

Ultimately, the desire for a new Pentecost is a call to faith. Only faith overcomes fear, and only fear is the true stumbling block to faith (Mark 5:36). The teaching of Jesus in the gospels testifies to this truth. Jesus regularly exhorts, "Do not be afraid!" (e.g., Matt 10:26; Mark 6:50; Luke 12:7). With Mary, we hear the words of the angel say, "Do not be afraid, Mary, for you have found favor with God" (Luke 1:30). It is also with Mary that we will find the courage to say in all humility, "Behold, I am the handmaid of the Lord. May it be done to me according to your word" (Luke 1:38, NABRE). This very Marian attitude is, in fact, the exact expression of priestly docility, obedience, and openness with which we are asked to respond to God's call.

When I was ordained a priest, I received a modest-sized, monochrome, plaster statue as a gift from the vocation director. It was the statue he always gave to newly ordained. I still have it, though it has been chipped a bit over the years. It is the statue of a young woman kneeling on her haunches, with hands outstretched, palms up. It is called the *Adsum*, Latin for "Here I am." It represents Mary at her most vulnerable yet open moment, when she accepted the Lord's will announced to her by the angel Gabriel and said, "May it be done to me." This simple statue still speaks volumes about why priesthood and Mary are so intimately related. She is the model disciple, and thus the model priest. In her, Word and sacrament come together in a unique way. She who bore the Word made flesh in her womb, who became a sacred vessel for this precious gift, also freely gave him to the world. We seek to follow her humble example in willingly and freely accepting the unique vocational call from the Lord. Her yes should become our yes to the will of God.

If we priests are to be made more durable by the testing through fire we have undergone in recent years, it is not an experience we endure alone. Mary is with us. Nor should we take an attitude of self-pity. We are not merely victims of the world's unjust persecution. We justly deserve criticism for our true failures. As Jesus says, "Much will be required of the person entrusted with much, and still more will be demanded of the person entrusted with more" (Luke 12:48, NABRE). And almost no one has been entrusted with more than priests, who daily are invited to bring Word and sacrament to the people of God and to make known to them the gracious love of Christ. Mary will help us be worthy ministers of her Son for this task.

In short, I find every reason to be hopeful for priests and the priesthood. Once tested in fire, we will be made more durable until the kingdom of

God comes in its full glory. I believe that the present testing in the priesthood is not a crisis so much as an opportunity, a new call to conversion, and a profound summons to a new Pentecost. It is an opportunity to be embraced, not shunned. If we priests have sometimes failed in our ministry, we should never lose hope. God grants us a chance to be remade day after day. We who bear the Word for the world, that is primarily the Word made flesh,[2] and who distribute the sacraments to the faithful, must always remember our own fragility and weakness. We must turn again to God and, with the intercession of a loving Mother who is at the same time our model, ask for the grace of a new creation.

As noted in the introduction, devotion to Mary and the close connection between Mary and the priesthood have been hallmark of the Sulpician tradition since our founding in the seventeenth century. In a letter to a newly ordained priest Father Olier explains reasons why priests should have a special devotion to Mary.[3] It amounts to love. He notes Jesus' love for her as his mother, her love for him as her Son, her "charming ability" to attract souls to Christ, and her motherhood or her fecund ability to "give birth" to faithful disciples of her Son. Olier exhorts the young priest in this way:

> The state of the priesthood, in which you presently find yourself, obliges you to have a precise and profound love for this divine princess. And it seems to me that every priest and every cleric has pressing reasons to engage in this devotion. . . . for Our Lord, who is pleased by the love anyone bears for his Mother and the services they render her, will justify your conduct in time.

Our priestly conduct, then, can be improved over time. Our devotion to Mary and imitation of her Son is the path we must take. As Mary bore the Word made flesh for the world, so we priests are now called to bear that Word with the same faithfulness.

In small homage to this historical and ecclesial perspective, I conclude with a special Marian prayer composed by Father Olier. It is known simply as the "Prayer of Father Olier"[4] and it is taught to all Sulpicians as a virtual summary of the priestly spiritual tradition to which Olier was devoted. Brief as it is, this prayer embodies a theological, christological, pneumatological, trinitarian, and Marian vision that is expansive. May these words comfort, strengthen, and sustain all priests, so that we might indeed be renewed by God's own grace, be emboldened by a new

Pentecost, and be transformed more and more into the image of Christ the High Priest, Son of Mary, from whom we have our presbyteral call and our priestly identity.

O Jesus, living in Mary,
Come and live in your servants,
In the spirit of your holiness,
In the fullness of your power,
In the perfection of your ways,
In the truth of your virtues,
In the communion of your mysteries:
Overcome every oppressing force
In your Spirit,
For the glory of the Father. Amen.

Notes

Introduction

1. Other biblical passages with a similar theme include Zech 13:8-9; Prov 17:3; 27:21; Wis 3:5-7; Mal 3:2-3; Rev 3:18.

2. Address of His Holiness Benedict XVI On the Occasion of Christmas Greetings to the Roman Curia (Vatican City: Libreria Editrice Vaticana, 2010). The following quotations are taken from this source. The reference to Hildegard's vision given in the papal text is Letter to Werner von Kirchheim and his Priestly Community: PL 197, 269ff.

3. One factor that mars the church's otherwise admirable attempts to address sexual abuse with proper controls is the lack of public accountability for bishops who knowingly shuffled pedophile priests around in ministry. Unfortunately, in the public eye, this overshadows other positive gains that have been made since the mid-1980s. One positive sign of progress on the international level is the announcement of a meeting called for by the Gregorian University in Rome, with the support of the Holy See, to be held February 6–9, 2012, to address the issue of sexual abuse of minors by clergy. Titled "Toward Healing and Renewal," the meeting will assemble experts from various parts of the world, along with bishops and religious superiors, to search for ways to change the culture of the Catholic Church's response to sexual abuse. One hopes this will be a major step forward.

4. This assertion is based upon the John Jay study conducted at the request of the US bishops to examine cases of priest pedophilia from 1950 to 2002. It is the only study of its kind that has been done anywhere in the world. Although even one case of pedophilia among priests is intolerable, the evidence of the study suggests that priests are no more susceptible to this aberration than any male in the general public. See The Nature and Scope of the Problem of Sexual Abuse of Minors by Catholic Priests and Deacons in the United States (John Jay College of Criminal Justice, 2004), available online at http://www.usccb.org/nrb/johnjaystudy/. A follow-up study of the causes of the sexual abuse crisis was published in mid-2011 and confirms this judgment. See The Causes and Context of Sexual Abuse of Minors by Catholic Priests in the United States, 1950–2010 (John Jay College of Criminal Justice, 2011), also available online at http://www.usccb.org/mr/causes-and-context.shtml. Critics of both studies have raised

questions about some of the assertions, methodology, and conclusions of both of these studies, yet with virtually no other studies available for comparison, these studies remain the most authoritative information to date.

5. A common misunderstanding about conversion in the biblical sense is that it is a once-for-all-time occurrence. This is not the case. See Ronald D. Witherup, *Conversion in the New Testament* (Collegeville, MN: Liturgical Press, 1994).

Chapter One

1. Throughout this book, I use the standard convention of referring to official church documents, which exist in various formats, by paragraph number, not page number.

2. See also *PO*, 12. Quotations from *PDV* are taken from the Vatican's web site: *Pastores Dabo Vobis* (Vatican City: Libreria Editrice Vaticana, 1992), http://www.vatican.va/holy_father/john_paul_ii/apost_exhortations/documents/hf_jp-ii_exh_25031992_pastores-dabo-vobis_en.html.

3. For a good overview of religious priesthood, see Paul K. Hennessy, ed., *A Concert of Charisms: Ordained Ministry in Religious Life* (New York/Mahwah: Paulist Press, 1997).

4. I speak of "ordained" priests to acknowledge the reality of "the priesthood of the faithful," in which all the baptized people of God participate (1 Pet 2:9). Lay ministry is an important reality in the church, especially since the Second Vatican Council. Two helpful books on this topic are Kenan B. Osborne, *Ministry, Lay Ministry in the Roman Catholic Church: Its History and Theology* (New York/Mahwah: Paulist Press, 1993); and Paul J. Philibert, *The Priesthood of the Faithful* (Collegeville, MN: Liturgical Press, 2005). See also the US bishops' document Co-Workers in the Vineyard of the Lord: A Resource for Guiding the Development of Lay Ecclesial Ministry (Washington, DC: USCCB, 2005).

5. The quotation in the passage is from *PO*, 5.

6. One should note that the preferred word for "priest" in the early Christian tradition was presbyter (elder), something that was also emphasized in Vatican II and later in *PDV*. Over time the word "priest" (Latin, *sacerdos*) became predominant. In NT terms, the only "priest" is Jesus Christ, but in the Catholic tradition "priest" and "elder" have merged somewhat into one concept. Yet it is interesting to note that Vatican II generally preferred "presbyter," as in the case of the title of the decree on the priesthood, *Presbyterorum Ordinis*. For more on this from the perspective of Paul's letters, see below in chapter 4. For a study of *PO* and *Optatam Totius*, see Maryanne Confoy, *Religious Life and Priesthood:* Perfectae Caritatis, Presbyterorum Ordinis, Optatam Totius (New York/Mahwah: Paulist Press, 2008).

7. At least in the United States, the model of the four pillars has been adopted, not only for priestly formation (as in the fifth edition of the US bishops' Program of Priestly Formation [2006]), but also for the formation of lay ministers and permanent deacons.

8. The Holy See addressed the use of psychology in seminary formation in a 2008 document titled Guidelines for the Use of Psychology in the Admission and Formation of Candidates for the Priesthood, available on the internet. Although some countries lack resources and experience for psychological testing, the priesthood requires attention to this aspect of formation and training to ensure sound candidates for the priesthood.

9. Although *PDV* has a lengthy treatment on celibacy (49), I treat this theme separately at greater length in chapters 5 and 6 below.

10. This is one of the repeated observations made in a recent sociological study of priests and affirmed in earlier research. See Stephen J. Rossetti, *Why Priests Are Happy: A Study of the Psychological and Spiritual Health of Priests* (Notre Dame, IN: Ave Maria, 2011).

Chapter Two

1. This chapter was originally a lecture given in French for the Canadian Province of Sulpicians as part of a series during the Year for Priests (2009–10). I am grateful to Father Jacques D'Arcy, PSS, provincial, and his planning committee for their invitation to address this topic.

2. For an analysis of the contribution of Hebrews to the church's theology of the priesthood, see below, chapter 4.

3. Eusebius, *Ecclesiastical History*, 6.24, 11–14.

4. In an earlier period, it was quite acceptable to refer to Paul literally as a priest. For example, Dom C. Marmion does not hesitate to call Paul a priest. See his celebrated book, *Le Christ— idéal du prêtre* (Maredsous, 1949), 57–59. Despite the hyperbolic language, Marmion is correct in his basic understanding of Paul as a priest. See also E. Cardinal Suhard's well-known pastoral letter, *Le Prêtre dans la Cité* (Paris: A. Lahure, 1949).

5. The vocabulary evokes an act of commissioning for ministry. The language of ordination, however, is anachronistic to the NT. The ancient pre-Christian tradition of the "laying on of hands" is an antecedent to what became central to later ordination rituals. For a recent study of this ancient practice, see J. F. Tipei, *The Laying on of Hands in the New Testament: Its Significance, Techniques, and Effects* (Lanham, MD: University Press of America, 2009). Note that the *Catechism of the Catholic Church*, 2nd ed. (Vatican City: Libreria Editrice Vaticana, 1997), relates "the laying on of hands" (Acts 13:3 and elsewhere) to the gift of the Holy Spirit upon the apostles; it does not explicitly speak of ordination but notes the gesture as a "sacramental epiclesis" (*CCC*, 699), although the gesture is an essential part of all later ordination rituals (*CCC*, 1573). We should keep in mind that the same gesture is also associated with healing (Mark 6:5; 16:18; Acts 5:12; 9:12 and 17; *CCC*, 699).

6. Note also that, since Paul's undisputed letters all date prior to the destruction of the temple and Jerusalem in AD 70, the language of "priesthood" for the early (Jewish) Christians would refer to the priests associated with the temple.

7. By this statement I do not mean to assert that there is no possible connection between Hebrews and the Pauline corpus. To the contrary, there are some intriguing Pauline allusions found in Hebrews that raise questions about the relationship between it and the Pauline corpus (e.g., Heb 5:12-14; 6:12; 11:1, 16). However, assuming that Hebrews is written considerably later than Paul's letters, the allusions are more than likely evidence of the unknown author of Hebrews introducing into his material some Pauline teachings with which he was familiar.

8. A broad outline of my basic approach in popular format can be found in R. D. Witherup, "Paul the Pastor," *The Priest* 65:3 (2009): 12–14, 23.

9. See Acts 9; 22; and 26. For a narrative analysis of the three versions of the same event, see R. D. Witherup, "'Functional Redundancy' in the Acts of the Apostles: A Case Study," *Journal for the Study of the New Testament* 48 (1992): 67–86.

10. Note that the word used for "set apart" in Gal 1:15 (Greek, *aphorizō*) is the same word used in Acts 13:2 (also Rom 1:1). It is language typical of a prophetic "call."

11. See, for example, Rom 1:2; 4:3; 9:17; 10:11; 11:2; 15:4; 1 Cor 15:3-4; 2 Cor 4:13; Gal 3:8, 22; 4:30; 1 Tim 4:13; 5:18; 2 Tim 3:16. Scholars sometimes have difficulty identifying the exact form of the LXX used by Paul, as the citations occasionally do not provide an exact match to the existing LXX text.

12. It is not unreasonable to apply the title "rabbi" to Paul (as also to Jesus). See, for example, Bruce Chilton, *Rabbi Paul: An Intellectual Biography* (New York: Doubleday, 2004).

13. See the Pontifical Biblical Commission's document The Interpretation of the Bible in the Church (Vatican City: Libreria Editrice Vaticana, 1993), §IV.

14. Note that the Greek text (εἰς τὸ εἶναί με λειτουργὸν Χριστοῦ Ἰησοῦ εἰς τὰ ἔθνη, ἱερουργοῦντα τὸ εὐαγγέλιον τοῦ θεοῦ [Rom 15:16]) refers to ministerial service before God; the NRSV translates the expression as "to be a minister of Christ Jesus to the Gentiles in the priestly service of the gospel of God" (Rom 15:16; cf. 12:1 for the cultic and sacrificial nature of Christian life in general). The Greek participle refers to performing a holy service as a priest does.

15. In order to be concise I have not made distinctions here about this ministry of Word that can properly be made, such as the difference between preaching, teaching, catechizing, and evangelizing, all of which I believe were part of Paul's ministry.

16. Vestiges of liturgical influence in Paul's letters are found in the Aramaic expressions *Abba* (Rom 8:15; Gal 4:7) and *Maranatha* (1 Cor 16:22, meaning "O Lord, come!"), the Hebrew word *Amen* (Rom 1:25; 11:36; Phil 4:20), greetings (Phil 4:23), eucharistic practices (1 Cor 11:24-26), and the trinitarian formula (2 Cor 13:13).

17. The root idea of the Greek word *baptizō* means "to immerse in water"; immersion was likely the customary practice in the early church.

18. A recent article has proposed Paul as a model for priests with regard to the ministry of reconciliation. See Thomas Stegman, "New Testament Images of Priesthood," *Pastoral Review* 6:2 (2010): 12–18.

19. The *Didache* (14), again, is another early witness to the development of reconciliation, the forgiveness of sins.

20. The threefold ministry emerged from three Greek expressions: *episkopos*, *presbyteros*, and *diakonos*. The word *presbyteros* ("elder") eventually came to signify "priest" in later tradition. Interestingly, Paul's undisputed letters never use the word, though the other two are mentioned in Philippians and the Pastorals. (Note, however, that the related word *presbytēs* ["old man"] is used in Phlm 9.) Paul does use the word "minister" (Greek, *leitourgos*) of himself once (Rom 15:16; cf. 2 Cor 9:12; Phil 2:17 and 25) in a cultic context, referring to priestly service for the Lord. The notion of ministry or service (Greek root, *diak-*) is also frequent in Paul. See Francis A. Sullivan, *From Apostles to Bishops: The Development of the Episcopacy in the Early Church* (New York: Newman/Paulist, 2001), who relies for his biblical analysis on the classic study by Raymond E. Brown, *Priest and Bishop* (Eugene, OR: Wipf & Stock, 1998, orig. 1970).

21. Paul uses this priestly language figuratively, not literally. See Horst Balz and Gerhard Schneider, eds., *Exegetical Dictionary of the New Testament*, 3 vols. (Grand Rapids: Eerdmans, 1991), 2.348–49.

22. For example, Rom 15:30; 2 Cor 1:11; 1 Thess 5:25; Eph 6:19; Phlm 22.

23. Paul is quite strong on this point, for he says, "I thank God that I speak in tongues more than all of you; nevertheless, in church I would rather speak five words with my mind, in order to instruct others also, than ten thousand words in a tongue" (1 Cor 14:18-19).

24. Of all the NT documents, Paul's letters give special emphasis to *koinōnia* and related words. See *Exegetical Dictionary of the New Testament*, 2.303–5.

25. Paul's use of the vocabulary of "love" is quite extensive, totaling more than 135 references in all thirteen letters.

26. While the Greek word for the collection (*logeia*) occurs only once in Paul (1 Cor 16:1), the concept of concern for the poor of Jerusalem is frequently mentioned, most visibly in the extended passage on generosity (2 Cor 8:1–9:15).

27. By definition, anyone who was "a dealer in purple cloth" (Acts 16:14) was wealthy. See Richard S. Ascough, *Lydia: Paul's Cosmopolitan Hostess* (Collegeville, MN: Liturgical Press, 2009), 50–52. Numerous members of Paul's communities were wealthy, especially if they were heads of households. We must remember that the early Christians met for their religious services in personal houses (villas), not in churches.

28. Many scholars today note Paul's metaphorical use of family language for the Christian community. See, for instance, Raymond F. Collins, *The Power of Images in Paul* (Collegeville, MN: Liturgical Press, 2008), 78–85. Collins rightly calls Paul the "master of metaphor" in the early Christian church (p. 262).

29. The text reads, "I became your father in Christ Jesus through the gospel." Cf. 1 Cor 4:14; 2 Cor 6:13; Phil 2:22; Phlm 10; 1 Tim 5:1; 2 Tim 1:2; 2:1. Some fundamentalists who object to the Catholic practice of addressing priests as "father" overlook Paul's practice. Modern Catholic custom is merely an extension of Paul's pastoral understanding.

30. For a groundbreaking study of feminine imagery in Paul, see Beverly R. Gaventa, *Our Mother Saint Paul* (Louisville: Westminster John Knox, 2007); as well as Susan Eastman, *Recovering Paul's Mother Tongue: Language and Theology in Galatians* (Grand Rapids: Eerdmans, 2007).

31. See also Gal 4:19; 1 Cor 3:1-2.

32. In fact, the Greek verb *parakaleō* (and the related noun, *paraklēsis*) means both "urge, exhort" and "comfort, encourage"! Paul uses this vocabulary frequently, with diverse meanings, depending on context. E.g., 1 Thess 2:12; 5:11; 1 Cor 4:16.

33. Interestingly, Prisca is always named first. One wonders if this means she may have been the dominant partner in the team.

34. Despite the mixed evidence of the name "Junia/Junias" in the manuscript traditions, it seems more likely that the feminine form (Junia) was original. See the convincing study of Eeldon J. Epp, *Junia: The First Woman Apostle* (Minneapolis: Fortress, 2005).

35. An excellent series of small books on Paul's colleagues in ministry, studied from the viewpoint of sociological methods, has been published by Liturgical Press in Collegeville, Minnesota. The series is titled "Paul's Social Network." So far, books have appeared on Timothy, Titus, Epaphras, Apollos, Stephen, Lydia, Phoebe, Priscilla and Aquila, and Luke, with several more to follow.

36. See, for example, Édouard Cothenet, "Le sacerdoce commun et le sacerdoce ministèriel," *Esprit et Vie* 223 (2010): 12–17.

37. The story of Paul's speech on the Areopagus is an example of Paul's quick-witted adaptation to immediate circumstances (Acts 17:1-31).

38. The document also refers frequently to Vatican II's Decree on the Ministry and Life of Priests (*PO* [1965]), but I will not include citations here, in the interest of time and space. Suffice it to say that the main ideas of *PDV* are rooted in this important conciliar teaching.

39. Although it would take us far afield, one should note the shift in emphasis in *PDV* in the language of the threefold priestly ministry, as noted in the previous chapter. The ministry of administration or governance (king) is expressed in terms of "pastoral charity" (par. 26). The nuance is striking, for it moves the emphasis from the "ruling" dimension of the role of the king to pastoral care of the flock.

Chapter Three

1. This chapter grew out of a talk to the priests of the Diocese of Green Bay in 2004 during a diocesan convocation on the priesthood. I am grateful to Bishop David A. Zubik, now bishop of Pittsburgh, for the invitation to address this theme.

2. The topic of integrity in the priesthood could provide a lengthy detour in the topic of leadership, but I am not able to address it here. A perceptive study of this theme, viewed from a broad and secular perspective, is Stephen L. Carter, *Integrity* (New York: HarperCollins, 1996).

3. James MacGregor Burns, *Leadership* (New York: Harper & Row, 1978), 2. For an analysis of priests as leaders, see Bartholomew Winters, *The Priest as Leader: The Process of the Inculturation of a Spiritual-Theological Theme of Priesthood in a United States Context*, Tesi Gregoriani Serie Spiritualità, 3 (Rome: Gregorian University, 1997).

4. Of course, the image is still used today, as indicated by chapter 1 above. John Paul II used it to great effect in two of his apostolic exhortations, *Pastores Dabo Vobis* (1992), on the formation of priests, and *Pastores Gregis* (2003), on the ministry of bishops.

5. On this topic, see Robert M. Schwartz, *Servant Leaders of the People of God: An Ecclesial Spirituality for American Priests* (New York/Mahwah: Paulist Press, 1989).

6. For example, the present participle of the verb *hēgeomai* ("to lead") is used in Heb 13:7, 17, 24 and elsewhere in the NT and in early Christian literature in the sense of leadership in general.

7. See also Mark 10:42-46; Luke 22:25-26; and 1 Pet 5:3.

8. See Andrew D. Clarke, *Serve the Community of the Church: Christians as Leaders and Ministers* (Grand Rapids: Eerdmans, 2000), for a summary of leadership in the Pauline churches, especially pp. 209–47.

9. I am assuming here the generally accepted dating of the NT books, with 1 Thessalonians being the earliest book (ca. AD 51) and 2 Peter being the latest (ca. AD 120). Between these dates there was increasing institutionalization of ministries within the church. The NT books exhibit both charismatic and institutionalized elements that may reflect diverse time periods.

10. Paul uses the self-designation "apostle" to defend his authority and to confirm that his status is no less than that of the premier apostles, such as the Twelve, appointed by Jesus prior to his death and resurrection. See 1 Cor 1:1; 2 Cor 1:1; 11; Gal 1:1.

11. It is also worth noting that the Acts of the Apostles portrays Paul addressing the "elders" (*presbyteros*) at Ephesus, indicating that they are local leaders who may act in Paul's stead (Acts 20:17). Paul uses the related word *presbytēs* of himself once, but in context it means an "old man" rather than presbyter (Phlm 9).

12. The story of Medad and Eldad in the OT (Num 11:25-29) and the instruction of Jesus to the disciples not to denigrate others apart from them who have received special gifts (Luke 9:49-50) are reminders that we should not overly constrain the work of the Holy Spirit.

13. Another way of approaching these divisions is to note that ministry, especially the ordained priesthood, is rooted in and takes its identity from the Trinity. Priesthood is thus deeply trinitarian in nature because it is essentially relational. There are theological, christological, and pneumatological dimensions of ministry. In this presentation, however, I am emphasizing broadly the "both/and" aspects of the ministry of leadership and not restricting myself to the ordained ministry.

14. In a contemporary theology of the priesthood, note that the threefold *munera* (authoritative functions) attributed to ordained ministers in the church (priest, prophet, and king) all derive from OT concepts fulfilled perfectly in Jesus Christ, from whom the ordained take their vicarious ministerial identity. The ability of the priest to act *in persona Christi capitis* (in the person of Christ, the head [of the church]) comes from this configuration to Christ himself by the sacrament of holy orders.

15. See Co-Workers in the Vineyard of the Lord (Washington, DC: USCCB, 2005). The document rightly defends the use of the term "lay ecclesial ministry" for the many different kinds of ministerial leadership exercised in the church today.

16. See *PDV*, 43.

17. Quoted in Francis A. Sullivan, *From Apostles to Bishops: The Development of the Episcopacy in the Early Church* (New York/Mahwah: Newman, 2001), 120.

18. Sermon 340, 1, quoted in *Lumen Gentium*, 32.

19. Sermon 46, 6–7, quoted in the Breviary, Vol. 4, Wednesday of the 24th Week, Office of Readings.

20. Some ministries of leadership apparently fell by the wayside (e.g., widows, prophets, sages) or were greatly transformed (e.g., religious life took on a prophetic dimension). The development of the ordained ministry is far more complex than I can address here. For a historical overview, see Raymond E. Brown, *Priest and Bishop: Biblical Reflections* (Eugene, OR: Wipf & Stock, 1998; orig. 1970); and *The Churches the Apostles Left Behind* (New York/Ramsey: Paulist, 1984); Kenan B. Osborne, *Priesthood: A History of the Ordained Ministry in the Roman Catholic Church* (New York/Mahwah, 1988); and more recently, Sullivan, *From Apostles to Bishops*, noted above.

21. Quoted in Edward L. Heston, *The Priest of the Fathers* (Milwaukee: Bruce, 1945), 105. The patristic quotations that follow are from this source, which remains an old but venerable treatise on the topic.

22. See chapter 11 below for a perspective on ongoing formation of priests.

23. Heston, *Priest of the Fathers*, 104–5.

24. Ibid., 49–50.

25. Ibid., 84.

26. Letter #49 to Pammachius, ibid., 157, emphasis in the original.
27. Ibid., 85.
28. Ibid.
29. Ibid., 81.
30. *The Rites of the Catholic Church as Revised by the Second Vatican Ecumenical Council*, vol. 2 (Collegeville, MN: Liturgical Press, 2002), no. 210.
31. Heston, *Priest of the Fathers*, 160.

Chapter Four

1. This chapter was originally a lecture at a symposium on the priesthood at The Catholic University of America in Washington, DC, in October 2009. I extend sincere gratitude to Most Rev. David M. O'Connell, CM, former president of the university and now bishop of Trenton, and to Rev. Melvin C. Blanchette, SS, former rector of Theological College, for their gracious invitation to participate in this symposium. I also thank Rev. Msgr. Paul J. Langsfeld for several helpful comments on an earlier version of this material. This essay first appeared in *Ministerial Priesthood in the Third Millennium: Faithfulness of Christ, Faithfulness of Priests* (Collegeville, MN: Liturgical Press, 2009), which also includes the other four major presentations of the symposium. I am grateful to Liturgical Press for allowing me to use this essay here in a slightly modified format.
2. A superb guide to the contemporary scholarship on Hebrews is Daniel J. Harrington, *What Are They Saying about the Letter to the Hebrews?* (New York/ Mahwah: Paulist, 2005). See also Richard Ounsworth, "What are They Saying about the Letter to the Hebrews?," *Scripture Bulletin* 39:2 (2009): 76–90. Important recent commentaries include Harold W. Attridge, *Hebrews*, Hermeneia Series (Philadelphia: Fortress, 1989); Craig R. Koester, *Hebrews*, AB 36 (New York: Doubleday, 2001); Alan C. Mitchell, *Hebrews*, ed. Daniel J. Harrington, Sacra Pagina Series (Collegeville, MN: Liturgical Press, 2007); Thomas G. Long, *Hebrews*, Interpretation Series (Louisville: Westminster John Knox, 1997); and James W. Thompson, *Hebrews*, Paideia Series (Grand Rapids: Baker Academic, 2008). Two fine introductions to the theology of Hebrews are Donald A. Hagner, *Encountering the Book of Hebrews: An Exposition* (Grand Rapids: Baker Academic, 2002); and Barnabas Lindars, *The Theology of the Letter to the Hebrews*, New Testament Theology Series (Cambridge: Cambridge University, 1991). See also Richard Bauckham et al., eds., *A Cloud of Witnesses: The Theology of Hebrews in Its Ancient Contexts*, Library of New Testament Studies 387 (London: T&T Clark, 2008).
3. Some scholars rightly emphasize that Hebrews was intended to be *heard* rather than read. One could thus properly speak of "hearers" rather than "readers." Centuries later, however, we read this document and call it a "letter." I stick with convention and refer to the author (rather than the "preacher") and designate it a letter rather than a sermon or a treatise.

4. See, for example, the expression "someone has testified somewhere" (2:6; cf. 4:4).

5. Although the Christology of Hebrews overshadows the trinitarian underpinnings, they are nonetheless present. God as "Father" is mentioned only three times, yet the very concept of Jesus as God's Son, which is omnipresent in Hebrews, implies the fatherhood of God. The Holy Spirit is mentioned only seven times in the letter yet functions in accord with both Christian theology in the NT and its OT antecedents. A key verse where all three persons of the Trinity are referenced is Hebrews 9:14. For a good exposition of the importance of trinitarian thought for ministry, see Peter Drilling, *Trinity and Ministry* (Minneapolis: Fortress, 1991).

6. Frank J. Matera, *New Testament Theology: Exploring Diversity and Unity* (Louisville: Westminster John Knox, 2007), 336, 349. Similarly, another scholar calls the author of Hebrews "one of the great pastoral theologians of the apostolic period" and describes the letter as "a pastoral theologian's rhetorical effort to shore up the faith" of his community. See John C. Laansma, "Hebrews, Book of," in *Dictionary for Theological Interpretation of the Bible*, ed. Kevin J. Vanhoozer (Grand Rapids: Baker Academic, 2005), 274, 276.

7. The Greek verb *teleioō* ("to complete, be perfect, reach a goal") features prominently in the theology of Hebrews, orienting the hearers/readers to the heavenly Jerusalem where God's salvation will be fully accomplished. The same verb is used of Jesus as "having been made perfect" through his obedience and suffering (Heb 5:9). See John M. Scholer, *Proleptic Priests: Priesthood in the Epistle to the Hebrews*, Journal for the Study of the New Testament Supplement Series 49 (Sheffield: Sheffield Academic, 1991), 201–2.

8. The Holy Father uses Hebrews throughout the encyclical, but one of his most striking observations is the strong connection in Hebrews between faith and hope. See *Spe Salvi*, 2.

9. There may be a connection with Christians from or in Rome, but no certain judgment can be made (the greetings of "those from Italy," 13:24).

10. Important studies include four works by (now Cardinal) Albert Vanhoye, *A Different Priest: The Epistle to the Hebrews* (Miami: Convivium, 2011); *Our Priest is Christ: The Doctrine of the Epistle to the Hebrews* (Rome: Pontifical Biblical Institute, 1977); *Old Testament Priests and the New Priest, according to the New Testament* (Petersham, MA: St. Bede's, 1980); *Structure and Message of the Epistle to the Hebrews, Subsista Biblica* 12 (Rome: Pontifical Biblical Institute, 1989); and Scholer's *Proleptic Priests*, mentioned above in n. 7.

11. Actually, Hebrews contains one of only three passages in the NT (Heb 1:8-9; John 1:1; 20:28) that explicitly acclaim Jesus as "God," supporting the notion of the letter's high Christology. See Raymond E. Brown, *Jesus: God and Man* (Milwaukee: Bruce, 1967), 23–25.

12. On the nature of Jesus' priesthood as royal, see Deborah W. Rooke, "Jesus as Royal Priest: Reflections on the Interpretation of the Melchizedek Tradition

in Heb 7," *Biblica* 81 (2000): 81–94. Although I am largely persuaded by Rooke's main thesis that there is a connection between the royal and cultic identity of Jesus the High Priest, whether it is wise to use the word "ontological" (p. 82) is less certain from a strictly biblical viewpoint. However, it would be fair to say that Jesus' High Priesthood is not merely *functional* but is bound up with his identity as God's Son.

13. For the Jewish antecedents of Hebrews' understanding of priesthood, see Attridge, *Hebrews*, 97–103.

14. For background on the biblical vocabulary of priesthood (Hebrew, *kōhēn*; Greek, *hiereus* and *archeireus*), see G. Johannes Botterweck, Helmer Ringgren, and Heinz-Josef Fabry, eds., *Theological Dictionary of the Old Testament*, 15 vols. (Grand Rapids: Eerdmans, 1995), VII.60–75; Gerhard Kittel, ed., *Theological Dictionary of the New Testament*, 10 vols. (Grand Rapids: Eerdmans, 1965), III.257–83; Horst Balz and Gerhard Schneider, eds., *Exegetical Dictionary of the New Testament*, 3 vols. (Grand Rapids: Eerdmans, 1991), 2.174. A good overview of the OT priesthood can be found in Merlin D. Rehm, "Levites and Priests," *Anchor Bible Dictionary*, ed. David Noel Freedman, 6 vols. (New York: Doubleday, 1992), 4.297–310.

15. Sitting at God's right hand (1:3, 13; 8:1; 10:12; 12:2) is not meant to indicate a mode of rest but a position of power and authority; it constitutes a location whence Jesus still acts as High Priest. See David R. Anderson, *The King-Priest of Psalm 110 in Hebrews*, Society of Biblical Literature 21 (New York: Peter Lang, 2001), 174.

16. Covenant theology is prominent in Hebrews. At times, however, there is a play on the word covenant (Greek, *diathēkē*), which can also mean "last will and testament" (9:17; cf. 9:15).

17. In an extensive study of Ps 110 in Hebrews, one scholar suggests that Heb 5:1-10, in particular, makes a unique contribution to the theology of the High Priesthood of Jesus Christ by explicitly connecting Ps 2:7 and Ps 110:4. See Anderson, *The King-Priest*, 288. With many commentators, Anderson also points to the chiastic parallel in 5:1-10 in which vv. 5-6, the OT quotations, are central. See also Lindars, *Theology of the Letter to the Hebrews*, 61; and Scholer, *Proleptic Priests*, 87.

18. Hebrews is perhaps the most obvious NT document that could, if not carefully interpreted, lead to supersessionism (negating the value of the OT and its religion in favor of the NT). This is a danger to be avoided. Hebrews is not really supersessionist, in part because of this dual tendency to accept "both/and" tensions, and because the OT foundations are critically necessary to understand the letter's unique theological perspective. All the major details associated with the High Priesthood of Jesus are from the OT. The author is more in line with the Matthean Jesus, who speaks of fulfilling, not abolishing, the law (Matt 5:17). More cautiously, Andrew Lincoln warns against jettisoning the notion of supersessionism altogether, as both Judaism and Christianity have succumbed to it at one time or another (e.g., the sacrificial system of the temple). See his *Hebrews: A Guide* (London: T&T Clark, 2006), 118.

19. Lindars, *Theology of the Letter to the Hebrews*, 139. He adds, however, that the understanding of the Eucharist as sacrifice did not arise until after the NT period, beginning with the *Didache*.

20. *CCC*, 1592; *PDV*, 26. The royal dimension can be seen in the figure of Melchizedek himself, a king, and the prophetic or teaching dimension is seen both in Jesus' connection to the Word of God (Heb 1:2-3; 6:5) and the mention of the leaders' faithful rendering of it (Heb 13:7).

21. In my own Sulpician spiritual tradition, which is rooted in the seventeenth-century French school of spirituality, Hebrews was the main source for a high theology of the priesthood. One author goes so far as to say that Hebrews contains the entire doctrinal content of the French school's teaching. So, Eugene A. Walsh, *The Priesthood in the Writings of the French School: Bérulle, De Condren, Olier*, STD thesis (Washington, DC: Catholic University of America, 1949), 24.

22. Hebrews also twice labels Jesus a "leader" (NABRE) but with a different word (Greek, *archēgos* [2:10; 12:2]), which has the nuance of an innovative leader or "pioneer," the translation used in the NRSV.

23. Vanhoye, *Old Testament Priests*, 312–13. Note how the very title of his book makes his point clear.

24. Vanhoye, *Our Priest is Christ*, 42.

25. It is also worth noting that Hebrews does not apply priestly terminology to the people of God. We must look elsewhere in the NT for an understanding of "the priesthood of the faithful" (1 Pet 2:5; Rev 1:6; 5:10; 20:6). This concept, though, is also properly rooted in an OT tradition of a priestly people, the holy nation of Israel (Exod 19:6). See *Lumen Gentium*, 10.

26. Vatican II's Dogmatic Constitution on the Church (*Lumen Gentium*) also contains a section on the priesthood (28) that dovetails with *PO*. Another official document that incorporates some insights from these works was issued by the Congregation for the Clergy, Directory on the Ministry and Life of Priests (Vatican City: Libreria Editrice Vaticana, 1994). Interestingly, Vatican II's Decree on the Training of Priests (*Optatam Totius*, 1965) does not mention Hebrews at all. *PDV* makes up for this lacuna.

27. *PDV*, 1. The opening quotation from Jeremiah (in the Latin Vulgate) provides the document's title, "I will give you shepherds." Most theologians consider *PDV* to be the most important official teaching on the priesthood since Vatican II. It was the result of the 1990 synod of bishops on priestly formation, and its teaching has directed the model of priestly formation adopted in many countries, especially in the United States. See the US bishops' Program of Priestly Formation, 5th ed. (Washington, DC: USCCB, 2006).

28. *PDV*, 43, which cites Heb 5:1 a second time. The other three pillars are spiritual, intellectual, and pastoral formation.

29. See also *PDV*, 47 and 72, where Hebrews (2:17; 4:15) is referred to twice more in the context of the human qualities necessary for priests.

30. A succinct summation of these teachings, as well as many others from church history, can be found in *CCC*, 1539–53).

31. *CCC*, 1548.
32. *Summa Theologiae* III, 22, 4c, quoted in *CCC*, 1548.
33. *CCC*, 1538.
34. *Lumen Gentium*, 10; *CCC*, 1539.
35. *PDV*, 36, which draws attention to Jesus' words in John 15:16.
36. *PDV* (17) is quite explicit about this point.
37. *CCC*, 1545.
38. The apt description in quotation marks comes from Laansma, "Hebrews," 280.
39. Vanhoye, *Structure and Message*, 73.
40. *CCC*, 1539.

Chapter Five

1. This chapter was first given as a lecture at a conference for major superiors of men in Jacksonville, Florida, in January 2003. It originally appeared in print in *Seminary Journal* 9:2 (2003): 43–49; and *InFormation* 11:5 (2003): 1–7. I am grateful to the Conference of Major Superiors of Men (CMSM) for the invitation to participate in the conference.
2. David Noel Freedman et al., eds., *The Anchor Bible Dictionary*, 6 vols. (New York: Doubleday, 1992), 1.879.
3. For further treatment of this topic, see Ronald D. Witherup, *Biblical Fundamentalism: What Every Catholic Should Know* (Collegeville, MN: Liturgical Press, 2001).
4. This is scarcely a new insight. See, for example, the conclusions of Ignatius Hunt, "Celibacy in Scripture," in *Celibacy: The Necessary Option*, ed. George H. Frein, 123–37 (New York: Herder and Herder, 1968).
5. For a brief but helpful overview of this historical development, see John W. O'Malley, "Some Basics About Celibacy," *America* 187:13 (Oct. 28, 2002): 7–10 and Joseph T. Lienhard, "Continence and Celibacy in the Early Church," *Dunwoodie Review* 33 (2010): 127–39.
6. See, for example, Sandra Schneiders, *New Wineskins: Re-imagining Religious Life Today* (Mahwah: Paulist, 1986), 114–36.
7. Scripture quotations in this chapter are taken from the NABRE.
8. See Ronald D. Witherup, *101 Questions & Answers on Paul* (New York/Mahwah: Paulist Press, 2003).
9. What is nonetheless remarkable about the passage is that already by the time of Matthew (ca. AD 80–90), his community was struggling to be faithful to Jesus' prohibition of divorce. The exception clause most likely stems from his own community's experience. It is not part of Jesus' original teaching.
10. For a fuller examination of the strange image of the eunuch, see chapter 6 below.
11. See Witherup, *101 Questions*, 42–44.

12. It should be noted that using the term *alter Christus* for celibates in no way diminishes the importance of this identification for *all* baptized Christians. Unfortunately, this expression today connotes for some a new kind of clericalism, a kind of special "club" to which priests belong apart from the laity. That is not its original meaning, for baptism makes of all Christians "another Christ." Yet if one keeps this reality in mind, I see no problem in also using it of priests in their ministry, which theologically is a special conforming to the image of Christ in a unique priestly fashion.

13. The expression in quotation marks was used by Father Paul J. Philibert, OP, during his talk at the same conference at which I gave this address.

14. For an overview, see the treatment of this topic in Thomas McGovern, *Priestly Celibacy Today* (Princeton, NJ: Scepter Publishers; Chicago: Midwest Theological Forum, 1998).

15. See, for example, *PDV*, 22.

Chapter Six

1. For a recent interpretation of this passage, see Charles H. Talbert, *Matthew*, Paideia (Grand Rapids: Baker, 2010), 232–34. As noted in the previous chapter, scholars debate the exact meaning of *porneia*, and various interpretations are possible. In any case, the saying indicates that Matthew's community knew of one exception to the "no-divorce" rule of Jesus. See also Paul's teaching in First Corinthians (1 Cor 7:12-15).

2. In addition to the standard Matthean commentaries, important studies in English include Jerome Kodell, "The Celibacy Logion in Matthew 19:12," *Biblical Theology Bulletin* (1978): 19–23; Francis J. Moloney, "Matthew 19, 3-12 and Celibacy. A Redactional and Form-Critical Study," *Journal for the Study of the New Testament* 2 (1979): 42–60; and Sandra Schneiders, *New Wineskins: Re-imagining Religious Life Today* (New York/Mahwah: Paulist, 1986), 119–26.

3. John P. Meier, *A Marginal Jew*, 4 vols., Anchor Bible Reference Library (New York: Doubleday, 1991–2009), 1.332–45; 3.503–6. This is also the judgment of W. D. Davies and Dale C. Allison, *The Gospel According to Saint Matthew*, 3 vols. (Edinburgh: T&T Clark, 1988–97), 3.22–25; Ulrich Luz, *Matthew 8-20*, Hermeneia (Minneapolis: Augsburg Fortress, 2001), 501; and Moloney, "Matthew 19, 3-12," 52.

4. Meier, *A Marginal Jew*, 1.342.

5. St. Paul's own view and practice of celibacy in 1 Corinthians 7 is consistent with that of Jesus, as I indicate in chapter 5 above.

6. One should note that, from a physical standpoint, eunuchs could often still engage in sexual relations (give and receive pleasure) if only the testicles had been removed, but there was no danger of impregnating a woman. This is a primary reason that eunuchs in the Orient were entrusted with the care of royal harems.

7. Although the church fathers rarely cite Matthew 19:12 in their writings, the fathers nevertheless sometimes made the distinction of eunuchs "of necessity" and eunuchs "of free will." See Davies-Allison, *Matthew*, 3.23, where a citation from St. Jerome is given as one example.

8. A helpful illustration of this distinction, shared in a private email communication from Abbot Jerome Kodell, OSB, is found in Matthew's parables of treasure in the field and the exceedingly valuable pearl (Matt 13:44-46). In the first instance, the person sells all "because of" the treasure he has found and hidden again; in the second, the person sells all "for the sake of" the pearl of great price. The participle *dia* is rarely used in Matthew or in the NT in the final sense. See Kodell, "Celibacy Logion," 21.

9. A thorough treatment of celibacy in the ancient world is found in Dale Launderville, *Celibacy in the Ancient World: Its Ideal and Practice in Pre-Hellenistic Israel, Mesopotamia, and Greece* (Collegeville, MN: Liturgical Press, 2010).

10. It is perhaps ironic that the Greeks, who also highly prized and idealized the unblemished human body, thought of the Jewish practice of circumcision as a barbaric defilement of the body. For the Jews, however, circumcision became an identity marker (probably in later Jewish periods of history), designating them as members of the covenant of God with Abraham (Gen 17:10-12). See David A. Bernat, *Sign of the Covenant: Circumcision in the Priestly Tradition*, SBL Ancient Israel and Its Literature 3 (Atlanta: Society of Biblical Literature, 2009).

11. See B. Kedar-Kopfstein, *Theological Dictionary of the Old Testament*, 10:344–50.

12. Ibid. See also J. Schneider, *Theological Dictionary of the New Testament*, 2:765–68.

13. See Janet S. Everhart, "Jezebel: Framed by Eunuchs?," *Catholic Biblical Quarterly* 72:4 (2010): 688–98, from whom I summarize the data that follow.

14. The notion of liminality is crucial to this discussion. The precise origin of the word is disputed but it comes from a word meaning "threshold" or "margin." The *Oxford English Dictionary Online* (http://www.oed.com/) identifies it as a word primarily used in the context of cultural anthropology, but it has become quite familiar in theological circles as well.

15. Everhart, "Jezebel," 697–98.

16. See Lev 21:20. Men with "crushed testicles" were excluded from the Aaronic priesthood.

17. According to this notion, priests must be able to view themselves as proper spouses. This is ostensibly one reason given for the exclusion of homosexuals from the priesthood, since heterosexual marriage is obviously not an option for them. Priests must be open to marriage but voluntarily renounce it for the kingdom of God. This became a critical aspect of the teaching of the late John Paul II on the priesthood. See *PDV*, 22; and John Paul II, *The Theology of Marriage and Celibacy* (Boston: St. Paul, 1986). The notion is derived primarily from the Letter to the Ephesians, drawing on the analogy of Christ's love for the church and the use of marriage as the model for this love. One limitation of this viewpoint,

however, is that it does not take into account that Jesus' word about "eunuchs" is not simply addressed to men nor is it tied to priesthood. Analogies or metaphors work well insofar as they communicate a basic truth, but one must be cautious to recognize their limitations.

18. The very title of John Meier's magnum opus, *A Marginal Jew*, evinces this fact.

19. Jeremiah (Jer 16:1-2) is not the only exception in Judaism, though he is the most famous. Both Josephus and Philo of Alexandria speak of certain groups of Jews who espoused celibacy at Elephantine or Qumran.

20. One might also say that priests should, by their very nature, be seen as "safe" individuals, not on the prowl for intimacy or a relationship. Sometimes this makes priests attractive to certain women. Professionally, priests must be aware of such complex psychological dynamics to ensure that we do not cross appropriate professional boundaries. Sadly, part of the lasting damage done by priests who have abused others, whether sexually, psychologically, or physically, is that some people now view most priests as predators. For moving testimony on some of the implications of the sexual abuse crisis, see Patrick Fleming, Sue Lauber-Fleming, and Mark T. Matousek, *Broken Trust: Stories of Pain, Hope, and Healing from Clerical Abuse Survivors and Abusers* (New York: Crossroad, 2007); and Christopher Ruddy, *Tested in Every Way: The Catholic Priesthood in Today's Church* (New York: Crossroad, 2006).

21. This useful distinction is emphasized by Sandra M. Schneiders, *Selling All: Commitment, Consecrated Celibacy, and Community in Catholic Religious Life* (New York/Mahwah: Paulist, 2001), 129.

22. See, for example, Michael H. Crosby, *Celibacy: Means of Control or Mandate of the Heart?* (Notre Dame, IN: Ave Maria, 1996), 159–80. Crosby speaks of fasting *from*, fasting *for*, and fasting *with* as three primary aspects of celibacy.

23. See *Vita Consecrata*, 88.

24. If one can make a comparison to celibate priests today, the fact that some have proven to be unfaithful in their promises should not tarnish the whole group.

25. This is true even if the Roman Catholic Church requires celibacy of its priests. Priests still make a choice, knowing that celibacy is part of the package.

26. I need not reference such studies here. A glance at some of the sociological studies listed in the reading list at the end of this book verifies this assertion. Most recently, see Stephen J. Rossetti, *Why Priests Are Happy: A Study of the Psychological and Spiritual Health of Priests* (Notre Dame, IN: Ave Maria, 2011).

27. Moloney, "Matthew 19, 3-12," 53.

Chapter Seven

1. *Theological Investigations* 3 (Baltimore: Helicon, 1967), 294–317. Bishop Robert Morneau, auxiliary bishop of Green Bay and author of numerous spiritual books,

is one cleric who has taken seriously the vocation of poet in his own priestly and episcopal ministry. See, for example, his *The Color of Gratitude and Other Spiritual Surprises* (Maryknoll: Orbis, 2009); *A New Heart: Eleven Qualities of Holiness* (Maryknoll: Orbis, 2008); and *Songs Out of Silence: 99 Sayings by Jessica Powers* (Hyde Park, NY: New City, 2010). He often uses poetry to great effect in his homilies, spiritual conferences, and writings. See also his informative essay, "Spiritual Direction: Guidelines for Some Poets," in *Handbook of Spirituality for Ministers*, ed. Robert J. Wicks, 141–52 (New York/Mahwah: Paulist Press, 1995).

2. *The American Heritage Dictionary*, 2nd College Ed. (Boston: Houghton & Mifflin, 1991), 957.

3. Quoted by the character Imlac in Johnson's novel *The History of Rasselas, Prince of Abyssinia* (1759). The words are usually taken as Johnson's own observations.

4. Flannery O'Connor, *Mystery and Manners*, ed. Sally and Robert Fitzgerald (New York: Farrar, Straus & Giroux, 1969), 184.

5. John Ruskin, *Modern Painters* (London: Smith, Elder and Co., 1856), vol. 3:253.

6. Quoted in O'Connor, *Mystery and Manners*, 80.

7. See Angela O'Donnell, review of *Swan: Poems and Prose Poems* by Mary Oliver, *America* 203:12 (Nov. 1, 2010): 23.

8. "God's Grandeur" (1918).

9. *Theological Investigations* 4 (Baltimore: Helicon, 1966), 363.

10. Rahner, *Theological Investigations* 4.362.

11. The recognition of the value of poetry for prayer is subtly symbolized by the presence of poems in the appendixes of the volumes on the Liturgy of the Hours.

12. An accessible edition of Athanasius's "Letter to Marcellinus on the Interpretation of the Psalms" is found in R. C. Gregg, *Athanasius*, Classics of Western Spirituality (New York: Paulist, 1980).

13. For example, *The Revised Grail Psalms: A Liturgical Psalter* by the monks of Conception Abbey (Chicago: GIA Publications, 2010), *The Revised Psalms of the New American Bible* (New York: Catholic Book Publishing, 1991), and *The Psalter* (Chicago: Liturgy Training Publications, 1995).

14. Walter Brueggemann, *Finally Comes the Poet: Daring Speech for Proclamation* (Minneapolis: Fortress, 1989), 109.

15. George H. Niederauer, "Ordained Priesthood at the Millennium: Problems and Opportunities," *The Charism of the Priesthood, II* (Washington, DC: National Catholic Educational Association, 1997), 13, quoting Father Donald Cozzens.

16. Congregation for the Clergy, Directory on the Ministry and Life of Priests (Vatican City: Libreria Editrice Vaticana, 1994).

17. Fulfilled in Your Hearing: The Homily in the Sunday Assembly (Washington, DC: USCCB, 1982). Another older document of the US bishops is still useful in the arena of spirituality, and it touches briefly the poetic dimension of a priest's spiritual life. See Ernest E. Larkin and Gerard T. Broccolo, eds., The Spiritual

Renewal of the American Priesthood (Washington, DC: United States Catholic Conference, 1973, reprinted 1983).

18. Fulfilled in Your Hearing, 13.

19. *Mystery and Manners*, 146.

20. I have tried to illustrate this principle somewhat in chapter 10 below and in "The Liturgical Context as an Aid to Interpretation," *The Priest* 51:12 (1995): 10–16.

21. For an overview of this document, see Ronald D. Witherup, "*Deo Gratias* for *Verbum Domini*: Pope Benedict XVI's Teaching on the Word of God," *Pastoral Review* 7:1 (2011): 12–17.

Chapter Eight

1. Quoted from Norman P. Tanner, *Decrees of the Ecumenical Councils*, 2 vols. (Washington, DC: Georgetown University Press, 1990), 2:1077.

2. See Avery Dulles, *Models of the Church* (New York: Doubleday, 2002; orig. 1978).

3. One should not exaggerate this point, however, as even *PO* begins with the ministry of the Word, continues with the ministry of the sacraments, and then rounds out the threefold priestly ministry with the ruling dimension. See also *DMLP*, where the threefold model of priesthood is not emphasized excessively, and the Congregation for the Clergy's Priest and the Third Christian Millennium (1999), which outlines this threefold ministry and provides some discussion questions that could be useful to priests to reflect on their ministry.

4. For a very good introduction to the wisdom literature, see Roland E. Murphy, *The Tree of Life: An Exploration of Biblical Wisdom Literature*, 3rd ed. (New York: Doubleday, 2002).

5. Scholars have shown that many of these biblical traditions, in fact, stem from more ancient prebiblical sources, especially some very old Egyptian traditions. The generic human quality of these values, however, receives a certain religious character when preserved and transmitted through the Bible. The ancient Hebrews believed all wisdom came from God and is not merely human invention.

6. Unlike the prophets, such as Deborah (Judg 4:4) or Huldah (2 Kgs 22:14-20), we do not have in the Bible names of sages who were women, although the wise behavior of many women is commended.

7. Walter Brueggemann, *In Man We Trust* (Richmond, VA: John Knox, 1972), 104–14.

8. There is an obvious connection in this image with the notion of the poet, treated in the previous chapter. Both the poet and the sage have extra sensitivities to the human experience that allow for deeper perceptions and better comprehension of how God is at work in the world.

9. Paul picks up on this perspective in reminding his beloved Corinthians that the kind of wisdom he brought them was not merely human but divine (1 Cor 2:2-8).

10. Quoted in *L'Osservatore Romano* 42 (October 15, 1990), 3.

Chapter Nine

1. An earlier version of this chapter was originally a talk given to the annual convention of the National Organization for the Continuing Education of Roman Catholic Clergy (NOCERCC) in 2006 in Florida. It was only one part of a program that treated all three priestly *munera*; I was asked to address only the *munus docendi*. I am grateful to the Board of NOCERCC, and especially to Rev. Patrick Carrion of the Archdiocese of Baltimore, for the invitation to explore this theme.

2. During the Year for Priests (2009–10) Pope Benedict XVI gave very informative general audiences on these three *munera* (April 14, 2010, on the *munus docendi*; May 5, 2010, on *munus sanctificandi*; and May 26, 2010, on *munus regendi*). His teaching explains how each of these work in the ministry of priests who are called to act *in persona Christi Capitis* (in the person of Christ, the head [of the church]). It is important to note that he begins with the *munus docendi*, the topic of this chapter. I also point out that the Congregation for the Clergy's practical document The Priest and the Third Christian Millennium (abbreviated as PTCM in this chapter) bears the subtitle "The Teacher of the Word, Minister of Sacraments, and Leader of the Community." These are treated as the primary categories of the priest's tripartite ministry. It is significant that the word "teacher" characterizes the priest as minister of the Word, which is accomplished "in nomine Christi et nomine Ecclesiae" (in the name of Christ and in the name of the church); see PTCM 14–21.

3. See John L. McKenzie, "Teach, teaching," *Dictionary of the Bible* (New York: Macmillan, 1965), 869–71.

4. McKenzie, *Dictionary of the Bible*, 870.

5. See the five discourses, Matt 5–7; 10; 13; 18; and 24–25; and the summary passages in 4:23-25 and 9:35. For Matthew, the order of the words "teaching, proclaiming, and healing" is significant; Jesus' first and foremost activity in ministry is teaching God's will. Moreover, although he gives his disciples a share in the ministry of preaching and healing (10:1), they are never instructed to "teach" until the great commission is given them by the risen Jesus at the conclusion of the gospel (28:16-20).

6. Ephesians 4:11-12 gives a similar listing in which teaching falls later in the list: "The gifts he [Christ] gave were that some would be apostles, some prophets, some evangelists, some pastors and teachers, to equip the saints for the work of ministry, for building up the body of Christ."

7. This is also the order dictated by the Program of Priestly Formation, 16, 23, and 24; Basic Plan, 109; *CCC*, 1592; and PTCM.

8. Unfortunately, I have seen instances in which this order is reversed, including in official church documents, e.g., *PDV*, 20.

9. Curiously, the cover of the physically printed document reverses the order and reads "Directory for the Life and Ministry of Priests," but it is clear from the Latin title (and English title in the inside cover) that the correct order follows *PO*.

10. Although this applies to all priests in performance of their ministry, it is especially a distinguishing characteristic of diocesan priesthood. The spirituality of religious priests is bound to their community life and the spiritual charism of their particular religious family (see *Vita Consecrata*, 30).

11. See *Rites of Ordination*, Second Typical Edition (Washington, DC: USCCB, 2003), 151. This is the order and wording of the 1968 revised rite of Vatican II as well. See *The Rites of the Catholic Church as Revised by the Second Vatican Ecumenical Council*, vol. 2 (Collegeville, MN: Liturgical Press, 1991), 40–41.

12. For an analysis of the Constitution on Divine Revelation (*Dei Verbum*) and its role in this development, see Ronald D. Witherup, *Scripture:* Dei Verbum (New York: Paulist, 2006).

13. See Program of Priestly Formation above in note 7. It should be noted that originally the Holy See granted a *recognitio* of this document for five years; that has now been extended another five years.

14. Asserting this in no way diminishes the sacramental ministry of priests. In fact, as Vatican II points out, Word and sacrament belong intimately together. Celebrating the sacraments often allows priests opportunities for "teachable moments" as well, which can be viewed as a participation in the teaching ministry.

15. The first part of *CIC* focuses on the "Ministry of the Divine Word."

16. For an elegant description of the bishops' ministry of the Word, see John Paul II's post-synodal apostolic exhortation *Pastores Gregis*, 26–31.

17. One is mindful of St. Francis of Assisi's advice: "Teach always; when necessary, use words."

18. PTCM, chap. 2, "Teachers of the Word," 14–21.

19. *Rites of Ordination*, 151.

20. For an example, see my article, "The Liturgical Context as an Aid to Interpretation," *The Priest* 51:12 (1995): 10–16.

21. This has been a rather consistent position of the Roman Catholic Church since the mid-twentieth century. Most recently, see Pope Benedict XVI, *Verbum Domini*, 44.

22. This point is made in the still-useful US bishops' document on preaching, Fulfilled in Your Hearing: The Homily in the Sunday Assembly (Washington, DC: USCCB, 1982), 13–14. For an application of this aspect of priests' preaching, see chapter 7 above.

Chapter Ten

1. See the comments of Joseph M. White, *The Diocesan Seminary in the United States: A History from the 1780s to the Present* (Notre Dame, IN: University of Notre Dame, 1989), 399.

2. For a survey of these developments, see Alexa Suelzer and John S. Kselman, "Modern Old Testament Criticism," and John S. Kselman and Ronald D. Witherup, "Modern New Testament Criticism," in *The New Jerome Biblical Commentary* (Englewood Cliffs, NJ: Prentice-Hall, 1990), 1113–29 and 1130–45.

3. See White, *The Diocesan Seminary in the United States*, 365-67, 375-78. A full account of the gradual, intriguing development of new exegetical methods is found in Gerald P. Fogarty, *American Catholic Biblical Scholarship: A History from the Early Republic to Vatican II* (San Francisco: Harper & Row, 1989). It is gratifying to see the influential role Sulpician biblical scholars played in developing the historical-critical study of Scripture in the United States, sometimes in the face of devious persecution.

4. John Baptist Hogan, *Clerical Studies* (Boston: Marlier, Callanan & Co., 1898). For a brief overview of the reception of this book, see Christopher J. Kauffman, *Tradition and Transformation in Catholic Culture* (New York: Macmillan, 1988), 174–76. More recently, for a study of the influence of Hogan's work abroad as well as in the United States, see C. J. T. Talar, "Seminary Reform and Theological Method on the Eve of the Modernist Crisis: Transatlantic Reception of J. B. Hogan's *Clerical Studies* (1898)," *U.S. Catholic Historian* 28:3 (2010): 1–17.

5. Hubert S. Box, *The Priest as Student* (New York: Macmillan, 1939). The book is not limited to the British scene. In fact, the first page (v) mentions "an American Report" that surveyed Anglican priests on the question, "How do pastors spend their time?"

6. See also similar advice from Pope Benedict XVI, *Verbum Domini*, 80 and 121.

7. Norman P. Tanner, ed., *Decrees of the Ecumenical Councils*, vol. 2 (London: Sheed & Ward; Washington, DC: Georgetown University, 1990).

8. Ibid.

9. An early document that drew attention to this fact and its influence on priestly spirituality was The Spiritual Renewal of the American Priesthood, ed. Ernest E. Larkin and Gerard T. Broccolo (Washington, DC: United States Catholic Conference, 1973), 51. The text cites the National Opinion Research Center sociological study of priests (1972) as evidence of priests' increasing thirst for scriptural knowledge.

10. Eugene F. Hemrick and Dean R. Hoge, *A Survey of Priests Ordained Five to Nine Years* (Washington, DC: National Catholic Educational Association, 1991).

11. For an overview of this exhortation, see Ronald D. Witherup, "*Deo Gratias* for *Verbum Domini*: Pope Benedict XVI's Teaching on the Word of God," *Pastoral Review* (2011): 12–17.

12. See Katarina Schuth, *Reason for the Hope: The Futures of Roman Catholic Theologates* (Wilmington: Michael Glazier, 1989), 121–24.

13. Donald Senior, "Scripture and Homiletics: What the Bible Can Teach the Preacher," *Worship* 65 (1991): 386–98.

14. Ibid., 394. See also the warnings in Priest and the Third Christian Millennium, 16–20.

15. Two popular early examples of ecumenical publishing are *Peter in the New Testament*, ed. Raymond E. Brown et al. (Minneapolis: Augsburg, 1973); and *Mary in the New Testament*, ed. Raymond E. Brown et al. (Philadelphia: Fortress, 1978).

16. See Benedict T. Viviano, *Study as Worship: Aboth and the New Testament*, Studies in Judaism and Late Antiquity 26 (Leiden: Brill, 1978).

17. *Clerical Studies*, 453.

18. *Reason for the Hope*, 164.

19. *Priest as Student*, 61.

Chapter Eleven

1. *Optatam Totius*, the council's Decree on Priestly Training (1965), never mentions ongoing formation.

2. See Ronald D. Witherup, *Conversion in the New Testament* (Collegeville, MN: Liturgical Press, 1994).

3. This short book is available through the USCCB, Washington, DC, and also on their web site at http://www.usccb.org/plm/ongoing.shtml. Another resource, published by the Congregation for the Clergy in Rome, contains some practical suggestions. See DMLP, 75–98.

3. Several dioceses have also engaged in creative projects to promote evangelization. Two fine examples are the Archdiocese of Washington and the Archdiocese of San Antonio. Cardinal Donald Wuerl has written an insightful instruction on the theme. See his pastoral letter, Disciples of the Lord: Sharing the Vision. A Pastoral Letter on the New Evangelization (2010), available at www.adw.org. Archbishop José Gomez, formerly archbishop of San Antonio and now archbishop of Los Angeles, wrote a pastoral letter on a similar theme, You Will Be My Witnesses: A Pastoral Letter to the People of God of San Antonio on the Christian Mission to Evangelize and Proclaim Jesus Christ (2010), available at www.archsa.org.

4. For some practical suggestions of resources, in print and electronically, see my article, "A Pastor's Bookshelf," *Priest* 65:11 (2009): 37–45.

5. The NET Bible translates the verb as "frequently withdrew" but also cautions that the form could mean he "began to withdraw." I think the habitual idea is more likely, however, as the NRSV, NABRE, NIV, and NJB all indicate.

Chapter Twelve

1. Note the NT word *presbyteros* does not mean "priest." At a later time, however, the word became associated with the priestly ministry. Thus today we speak

of priests as *presbyters* and a group of diocesan priests, united with and cooperating in ministry with a bishop, as a *presbyterate*. This is an extension of the NT usage.

2. Naturally, this is not the only meaning of the passage. Other aspects of the passage pertinent to priesthood are more deeply explored in DMLP, 68.

3. See *PDV*, 77; DMLP, 95; and Basic Plan, pt. 2, E, "Priests Growing in Wisdom and Grace: Ongoing Formation and Senior Clergy."

4. I will do the same for the third province, the United States, at a later date.

5. For a view of the role computers and the World Wide Web can play in priests' lives, see Ronald D. Witherup, "Priests and the Internet: The Peril and the Promise," *Pastoral Review* 7:3 (2011): 12–17.

6. Basic Plan, pt. 2, E. See chapter 11 above on ongoing formation of priests.

7. John R. Powers, *The Unoriginal Sinner and the Ice-Cream God* (New York: Warner, 1978; reprint Chicago: Loyola, 2006), 189.

Epilogue

1. See especially *PDV*, 82; *Vita Consecrata*, 112; *Christifidelis Laici*, 64; cf. DMLP, 68.

2. Pope Benedict XVI has recently emphasized the notion of the Word being first and foremost the Word made flesh, Jesus Christ, in his post-synodal apostolic exhortation *Verbum Domini* (2010). In addition, it is noteworthy that he concludes the exhortation by recalling the close connection between Mary and the Word (124). For a summary of this document's principal teachings, see Ronald D. Witherup, "*Deo Gratias* for *Verbum Domini*: Benedict XVI's Teaching on the Word of God," *Pastoral Review* 7:1 (2011): 12–17.

3. Jean-Jacques Olier, *Lettre CCCXVI* (Sulpician Archives, Paris); privately published in *Texts from the French School of Spirituality*, trans. David D. Thayer (Baltimore: Sulpician Provincial House, 2003), 56. A definitive edition of the letters of Father Olier is in process and will be published in French in the near future.

4. Several versions of this prayer exist in Olier's writings. It was an adaptation of the sentiments of a French mystic of the same period, Father Charles de Condren, but it has come down in the tradition as the prayer of Father Olier. See Bernard Pitaud, *Petite vie de Jean-Jacques Olier* (Paris: Desclée de Brouwer, 1996), 128–29; and ibid., *Prier 15 Jours avec Monsieur Olier* (Bruyères-le-Châtel: Nouvelle Cité, 2007), 49–54.

Selected Resources on Catholic Priesthood

Aschenbrenner, George A. *Quickening the Fire in Our Midst: The Challenge of Diocesan Priestly Spirituality*. Chicago: Loyola, 2002.

Bernanos, Georges. *The Diary of a Country Priest*. New York: Carroll & Graf, 2002; orig. 1937.

Bleichner, Howard P. *View from the Altar: An Insider's Look at the Changing Catholic Priesthood*. New York: Crossroad, 2004.

Boadt, Lawrence, and Michael J. Hunt, eds. *Why I am a Priest: Thirty Success Stories*. New York/Mahwah: Paulist, 1999.

Bohr, David. *The Diocesan Priest: Consecrated and Sent*. Collegeville, MN: Liturgical Press, 2009.

Brinkley, Douglas, and Julie M. Fenster. *Parish Priest: Father Michael McGivney and American Catholicism*. New York: William Morrow, 2006.

Coleman, Gerald D. *Catholic Priesthood: Formation and Human Development*. Liguori, MO: Liguori, 2003.

Congregation for the Clergy. Directory on the Ministry and Life of Priests. Vatican City: Libreria Editrice Vaticana, 1994.

Congregation for the Clergy. The Priest and the Third Christian Millennium: Teacher of the Word, Minister of the Sacraments, and Leader of the Community. Vatican City: Libreria Editrice Vaticana, 1999.

Congregation for the Doctrine of the Faith. From "Inter Signiores" to "Ordinatio Sacerdotalis": Documents and Commentaries. Washington, DC: United States Catholic Conference, 1997.

Cozzens, Donald B., ed. *The Spirituality of the Diocesan Priest*. Collegeville, MN: Liturgical Press, 1992.

———. *The Changing Face of Priesthood*. Collegeville, MN: Liturgical Press, 2000.

Dolan, Timothy M. *Priests for the Third Millennium*. Huntington, IN: Our Sunday Visitor, 2000.

Donovan, Daniel. *What Are They Saying about the Ministerial Priesthood?* New York/Mahwah: Paulist Press, 1992.

Dulles, Avery. *The Priestly Office: A Theological Reflection*. New York/Mahwah: Paulist Press, 1997.

Galot, Jean. *Theology of the Priesthood*. San Francisco: Ignatius, 1985.

Gautier, Mary L., Paul M. Perl, and Stephen J. Fichter. *Same Call, Different Men: The Evolution of the Priesthood since Vatican II*. Collegeville, MN: Liturgical Press, 2012.

George, Francis. "Receiving Identity from the Risen Christ: Ordained Priesthood and Leadership in the Catholic Church." In *The Difference God Makes: A Catholic Vision of Faith, Communion, and Culture*, 185–206. New York: Crossroad, 2009.

Goergen, Donald J., ed. *Being a Priest Today*. Collegeville, MN: Liturgical Press, 1992.

Goergen, Donald J., and Ann Garrido, eds. *The Theology of Priesthood*. Collegeville, MN: Liturgical Press, 2000.

Greeley, Andrew M. *Priests in the United States: Reflections on a Survey*. Garden City, NY: Doubleday, 1972.

———. *Priests: A Calling in Crisis*. Chicago/London: University of Chicago, 2004.

Heher, Michael. *The Lost Art of Walking on Water: Re-Imaging the Priesthood*. New York/Mahwah: Paulist Press, 2004.

Hoge, Dean R. *The First Five Years of Priesthood: A Study of Newly Ordained Catholic Priests*. Collegeville, MN: Liturgical Press, 2002.

———. *Experiences of Priests Ordained Five to Nine Years*. Washington, DC: National Catholic Educational Association, 2006.

Hoge, Dean R., and Jacqueline E. Wenger. *Evolving Visions of Priesthood*. Collegeville, MN: Liturgical Press, 2003.

Knott, J. Ronald. *Intentional Presbyterates: Reclaiming Our Common Sense of Purpose as Diocesan Priests*. Louisville: Sophronismos, 2003.

Levering, Matthew, ed. *On the Priesthood: Classic and Contemporary Texts*. Lanham, MD: Rowman & Littlefield, 2003.

McBride, Alfred. *A Priest Forever: Nine Signs of Renewal and Hope*. Cincinnati: Saint Anthony Messenger, 2010.

McGovern, Thomas. *Priestly Celibacy Today*. Princeton: Scepter, 1998.

Mitchell, Patricia, ed. *A Priest's Life: The Challenge, the Cost, the Joy*. Ijamsville, MD: Word Among Us, 2010.

Möhler, Johann Adam. *The Spirit of Celibacy*. Chicago/Mundelein: Hillenbrand, 2007; German orig. 1992.

O'Collins, Gerald, and Michael Keenan Jones, *Jesus Our Priest: A Christian Approach to the Priesthood of Christ*. Oxford: Oxford University Press, 2010.

O'Keefe, Mark. *In Persona Christi: Reflections on Priestly Identity and Holiness*. St. Meinrad, IN: St. Meinrad Abbey, 1998.

———. *The Ordination of a Priest: Reflections on the Priesthood in the Rite of Ordination*. St. Meinrad, IN: St. Meinrad Abbey, 1999.

Osborne, Kenan B. *Priesthood: A History of the Ordained Ministry in the Roman Catholic Church*. New York/Mahwah: Paulist Press, 1988.

Philibert, Paul J. *Stewards of God's Mysteries: Priestly Spirituality in a Changing Church*. Collegeville, MN: Liturgical Press, 2004.

Pope John Paul II. *Pastores Dabo Vobis*. I Will Give You Shepherds. Boston: Daughters of St. Paul, 1994.

Pope Paul VI. *Sacerdotalis Caelibatus*. Encyclical Letter on Priestly Celibacy. *AAS* 59 (1967): 657–97.

Ramsey, Michael. *The Christian Priest Today*. Rev. ed. London: SPCK, 1985, orig. 1972.

Rausch, Thomas P. *Priesthood Today: An Appraisal*. New York/Mahwah: Paulist, 1992.

Rossetti, Stephen J. *A Tragic Grace: The Catholic Church and Child Sexual Abuse*. Collegeville, MN: Liturgical Press, 1996.

———. *The Joy of the Priesthood*. Notre Dame, IN: Ave Maria, 2005.

———, ed. *Behold Your Mother: Priests Speak about Mary*. Notre Dame, IN: Ave Maria, 2007.

———. *Why Priests Are Happy: A Study of the Psychological and Spiritual Health of Priests*. Notre Dame, IN: Ave Maria, 2011.

Schuth, Katarina. *Priestly Ministry in Multiple Parishes*. Collegeville, MN: Liturgical Press, 2006.

Schwartz, Robert M. *Servant Leaders of the People of God: An Ecclesial Spirituality for American Priests*. New York/Mahwah: Paulist, 1989.

Secretariat for Priestly Life and Ministry. Priests for a New Millennium. Washington, DC: USCCB, 2000.

Smith, Karen Sue, ed. *Priesthood in the Modern World*. Franklin, WI: Sheed & Ward, 1999.

Sperry, Len. *Sex, Priestly Ministry, and the Church*. Collegeville, MN: Liturgical Press, 2003.

Toups, David L. *Reclaiming Our Priestly Character*. Omaha: Institute for Priestly Formation, 2008.

US bishops. The Basic Plan for the Ongoing Formation of Priests. Washington, DC: USCCB, 2001.

US bishops. Program of Priestly Formation. 5th ed. Washington, DC: USCCB, 2006.

Walsh, James, et al. *Grace Under Pressure: What Gives Life to American Priests*. Washington, DC: National Catholic Educational Association, 1995.

Wicks, Robert J., ed. *Handbook of Spirituality for Ministers*. New York/Mahwah: Paulist Press, 1995.

Wilson, George B. *Clericalism: The Death of the Priesthood*. Collegeville, MN: Liturgical Press, 2008.

Witherup, Ronald D., Lawrence B. Terrien, Michael Witczak, Paul G. McPartlan, and Kevin W. Irwin. *Ministerial Priesthood in the Third Millennium*. Collegeville, MN: Liturgical Press, 2009.

Wood, Susan K., ed. *Ordering the Baptismal Priesthood: Theologies of Lay and Ordained Ministry*. Collegeville, MN: Liturgical Press, 2003.

Index